A RICHER, BRIGHTER VISION FOR
AMERICAN HIGH SCHOOLS

In today's high schools, education is often reduced to a means of achieving financial security, leading to an overemphasis on quantifiable measures of performance. This approach encourages academically talented students to focus on test scores and rankings rather than intellectual enrichment and discourages students with nonacademic talents from pursuing them. *A Richer, Brighter Vision for American High Schools* advocates instead a unifying educational aim of producing better adults, which would encompass all aspects of students' lives: intellectual, physical, moral, spiritual, social, vocational, aesthetic, and civic. Nel Noddings offers suggestions to improve high schools by increasing collegiality among students and faculty, enriching curricula with interdisciplinary themes, renewing vocational education programs, addressing parenting and homemaking, and professionalizing the teaching force. This thought-provoking book will act as an important guide for teachers, teacher educators, administrators, and policy makers.

NEL NODDINGS is Lee L. Jacks Professor of Education, Emerita, at Stanford University. She is the author of nineteen books, including *Critical Lessons: What Our Schools Should Teach* (2006), *Peace Education: How We Come to Love and Hate War* (2011), and *Education and Democracy in the 21st Century* (2013).

A Richer, Brighter Vision for American High Schools

Nel Noddings
Stanford University

CAMBRIDGE
UNIVERSITY PRESS

32 Avenue of the Americas, New York, NY 10013-2473, USA

Cambridge University Press is part of the University of Cambridge.

It furthers the University's mission by disseminating knowledge in the pursuit of education, learning, and research at the highest international levels of excellence.

www.cambridge.org
Information on this title: www.cambridge.org/9781107427914

First published 2015

Printed in the United States of America

A catalog record for this publication is available from the British Library.

Library of Congress Cataloging in Publication Data
Noddings, Nel.
A richer, brighter vision for American high schools / Nel Noddings.
    pages cm
ISBN 978-1-107-07526-9 (Hardback) – ISBN 978-1-107-42791-4 (Paperback)   1. Education, Secondary–Aims and objectives–United States.   2. High schools–Curricula–United States.   3. Educational change–United States.   4. Holistic education–United States.   5. Vocational education–United States.   6. Teacher-student relationships–United States.   7. School improvement programs–United States.   I. Title.
LB1607.5.N64 2015
373.73–dc23   2014050303

ISBN 978–1–107–07526–9 Hardback
ISBN 978–1–107–42791–4 Paperback

Contents

Introduction

America needs a richer, brighter vision for its high schools. My primary concern is not the one we hear constantly today – that test scores are too low and that the achievement gap between rich and poor is widening and needs to be closed. I share the latter worry, but my main concern is broader: High schools today are not meeting the deep human needs of most of our students. Intellectually talented students are diverted from intellectual enrichment to a concentration on high test scores and top rankings; students with nonacademic talents are discouraged from developing those talents, and, forced into academic studies in the name of equality, they struggle to make sense of schooling that purports to offer a path to secure financial life. Students (and parents) are led to believe that the purpose of education is to get a well-paid job and achieve economic well-being. We seem to have forgotten that there is more to education than preparing to get ahead financially.

Educators once talked seriously about producing "better adults," about encouraging the development of all aspects of a complete life: moral, physical, social, vocational, aesthetic, intellectual, spiritual, and civic. We once considered optimal development in these aspects of life to be the *aims of education*.[1] Aims (as I use the word) are importantly different from goals and objectives, ends we expect to meet with some specificity. In contrast, we cannot specify exactly what outcomes our aims must produce – they will vary with intensity and breadth over the individuals with whom we work – but they guide all that we do. We do not rely on tests to prove that we are influencing moral and social development, but we refer to moral and social aims in explaining our choices for the whole range of content and pedagogical activity, and we watch for signs that our efforts are producing positive results. Will what we are teaching (and how we are teaching it) somehow contribute to the development of better

1

adults? How will we know if we are succeeding? We listen, watch, reflect, and live with the results of our decisions.

Some would object that "aims-talk" leads to interminable argument and distraction, but, in response, I argue that such talk keeps the intellectual door open to dialogue, reflection, analysis, collegiality, and creative planning. It *should* be interminable. We should never cease to ask the questions: Why are we doing this? How should we do it? What do we gain and what do we lose by doing it? Are we producing better adults?

I will posit the need for a unitary (or unifying) educational purpose: to produce better adults,[2] but I will caution readers at the outset that acceptance of this aim (or purpose) does *not* imply uniformity of those adults or of curricular content, school organization, or pedagogical methods. In what is suggested under this unitary purpose, there will be a wide space for variety and choice in all of these matters. Indeed, I will argue that commitment to this aim demands such openness to variety and choice. *Choice* will be a major topic throughout the book, but I will not emphasize or even endorse parental choice of schools. Properly guided student choice should be encouraged; it should displace – or at least greatly reduce – the habit of assigning students to programs and courses on the basis of test scores and grades. Teacher choice on content and method should be acknowledged as the hallmark of teacher professionalization. At present, there is far too much administrative coercion on both.

Accompanying that emphasis on choice will be emphases on collegiality and the use of interdisciplinary teams to make connections among the disciplines and to real life. All through the book, we will explore the "seven Cs": choice, critical thinking, caring, connections, continuity, collegiality, and creativity.

In the first five chapters, I will use a dialectical method of sorts, moving from a search for the meaning of a better adult to exploration of how the result might be achieved. As we make progress in the search, we will also encounter new problems to be tackled. Thus, interim results and conclusions will give rise to new explorations and analyses. By the time we reach Chapter 6, a critique of contemporary Common Core Standards, we should be ready to say something constructive on both the organizational content of our high schools and how to prepare teachers to work effectively in them.

Among the points to be discussed here are several that may be controversial. I will argue, for example, that we should expand our curricula to accommodate a variety of talents and interest; we should revitalize vocational education. Looking back on our educational history, we see that the

U.S. comprehensive high school led the world in providing secondary education to large numbers of children. The comprehensive high school introduced a variety of tracks designed, ostensibly, to provide secondary school education to students with varying talents and interests. The idea of tracks (or streams) is sound and consistent with democratic ideals. Clearly, however, we have to eliminate the evils of tracking as it was implemented in the twentieth century. We can do this by inviting well-informed students to *choose* their preferred programs instead of *assigning* them to tracks and by ensuring that every program offered is of the highest quality.

Not only must the curriculum be expanded by the addition of vocational programs. It should also be extended to include matters related to competence in personal and family life. Knowing how important effective parenting is to educational success, our refusal to teach something about parenting in our schools is irresponsible.

Although it may, on first hearing, seem paradoxical, I will suggest that we work enthusiastically to revive the spirit of the liberal arts. This does not mean prescribing a return to the classic great books or to any particular curriculum traditionally posited in the humanities. Rather, it means attending in a variety of ways and pervasively to the great existential questions about the meaning of life, truth, beauty, love, and goodness. In defense of this proposal, I will argue that it is unity of purpose, not uniformity of curriculum, to which we should be committed, and that argument will constitute the first chapter and establish the foundation for the following chapters advocating a variety of programs.

Another possibly controversial recommendation is that, if we are serious about encouraging critical thinking, we must say more about what we mean by "critical thinking," and we must find a way to introduce the study of critical topics such as parenting, poverty, peace, and religion into our regular studies; we must do this without resorting to indoctrination. One way to approach this area is to introduce themes that can be addressed in various ways across the disciplines. Instead of offering new courses on these topics, we would ask teachers in every subject to introduce material on the chosen themes. Every major subject should contribute something to our thinking on parenting, peace, poverty, and religion. The themes should be chosen by interdisciplinary teams. This arrangement is an example of another major topic – collegiality – that will be emphasized throughout the book.

Yet another controversial recommendation will come toward the end of the book, motivated by the preceding chapters. I will suggest that the education of teachers should proceed more like that of engineers; that is, four years of undergraduate teacher education should concentrate from the start in depth on education, on the school curriculum, and on teaching methods. It is ridiculous and embarrassing that we now so often assign middle school teachers to teach algebra when they admit that they do not know or understand the subject.[3] Many of our largest teacher training institutions do, of course, provide an undergraduate teaching major, but there is too little attention given to the high school curriculum in its collective entirety, and too much of it remains unconnected to the central project of teaching. Further, although these institutions produce most of our teachers, they suffer a lack of professional prestige. This is not a call to return to the teachers colleges of yesteryear, although we can learn much from that earlier movement and it should be reexamined appreciatively. There is a role for subject matter specialists, surely, but every teacher should know at least what every high school student is required to study. This means that every high school teacher should know the mathematics demanded of all students; the teaching of mathematics beyond that required level should be the domain of specialists.

What follows is a brief description of the chapters that support and fill out my main arguments: that unity of purpose can accommodate a variety of programs aimed at different vocational, personal, and civic ends and that teacher education must be designed to produce broadly educated teachers who are thoroughly in command of both their special subject and of the material that all students are required to learn.

Chapter 1, "Unity of Purpose": Theology once served as the unifying purpose of curricula in college and secondary schools.[4] With its loss, the liberal arts have suffered fragmentation, and the associated disciplines have become more highly specialized and separated from one another. Is there a way to redefine the unity of purpose and make the much needed connections? How should we describe it?

Chapter 2, "Vocational Programs": Fine vocational programs can be offered without sacrificing the unity of purpose. All students should experience a curriculum that includes the study of family, vocational, moral, and civic life. This can be done in a way that eliminates the evils of tracking as it was implemented in the twentieth century.

Chapter 3, "What Might Have Been: Women's Traditional Interests": In this chapter, I will ask readers to consider what the school curriculum might have looked like if women had been involved from the start. This exercise of imagination will then be applied to a set of recommendations on how to include much of this long-repressed material in today's programs of study without changing the basic structure of the curriculum.

Language arts, mathematics, science, and social studies will remain at the heart of the curriculum, but they can all be stretched to include much of the material described in our exploration.

Chapter 4, "A Better Adult: Continuing the Search": This chapter will concentrate mainly on moral education as a basic and universal element of the high school curriculum, but it will not neglect other features of what might be meant by the expression "better adult." I will argue that consideration of moral life – of the "goodness" emphasized in the liberal arts – should pervade the curriculum. A course in moral education is not sufficient. The chapter will set the stage for further development of the concept.

Chapter 5, "Parenting": Producing better adults implies producing people who will be more committed, more knowledgeable parents. We can teach much about parenting without adding specific "how to do it" courses that would be rejected on the grounds of overcrowding the curriculum, and we can do this without indoctrinating or moving too far in the direction of paternalism. We will ask what can be done in language arts, social studies, science, mathematics, and the arts.

Chapter 6, "The Common Core Standards": We will look critically at the Common Core. What should we endorse? What should we reject? What should be further explicated?

Chapter 7, "Critical Thinking": Critical thinking appears in the Common Core Standards and, indeed, shows up worldwide in statements of educational aims. Starting with a brief history of the topic, I will explore ways to encourage critical thinking in both our students and their teachers. Three ideas will be important: First, we should say more about what we mean by "critical thinking." Second, we should admit that we probably cannot teach critical thinking without open consideration of critical issues; this discussion will underscore the need to include material introduced in earlier chapters. Third, teachers should be capable of critical thinking, and they should be encouraged to use it collegially to direct their own work.

Chapter 8, "Collegiality, Caring, and Continuity": If teachers are to work effectively across disciplines under the guidance of a unified set of aims, they need opportunities to meet regularly for discussion on the connections between their disciplines and to life itself. This discussion should also include (and be inspired by) a dedication to the establishment of relations of care and trust. Teaching should not be defined as mere instruction.

Continuity will be discussed in some depth – continuity of place, curriculum, and people. Research has shown that continuity of faculty is a vital factor in teacher and student morale. Instead of fighting a losing battle to get rid of ineffective teachers, we might do better to work cooperatively to make them better.[5] One way to approach this (to be discussed more fully in Chapter 11 on teacher preparation) is to establish a rank of master teachers who will work collegially with both their contemporaries and novices.

Chapter 9, "The Curriculum and Its Setting": Schools should reflect the work and commitment of their communities. With the rising global concern for the natural environment, schools should give more attention to environmentalism in both their curriculum and physical structure. Students should be involved in planting and maintaining gardens, studying the ecology of their local environments. The emphasis on interconnectedness in nature should extend to an equal emphasis on interconnection in the curriculum. The obvious interdependence of people should be addressed in every subject, but social studies should serve as the integrating center of the high school curriculum. Extracurricular programs should also be thought of as integrating activities, activities that promote the development of citizens for participatory democracy. Perhaps these activities are best considered as part of an expanded curriculum – not "extra" or external to it.

Finally, we will consider the physical setting and structure of our school buildings and explore ways in which the schools might exemplify social and natural connections in their communities.

Chapter 10, "Planning, Enacting, Evaluating": This chapter will look at the practical tasks of teaching. Planning, I will argue, is not just a matter of preparing lessons; it is better construed as a continuing personal program of preparing the teacher. A fundamental commitment of professional teachers is to continue their own intellectual growth so that they can respond with "spontaneity" to a host of student questions as both teachers and students seek intellectual vitality. The section on planning will be followed by one on pedagogical methods and ways to expand student choice. The chapter concludes with a critical examination of problems in evaluating the work of both students and teachers. Serious consideration is given to how good teachers might evaluate their own work.

Chapter 11, "The Professional Preparation of Teachers": Perhaps the most controversial recommendation in this book is that preparation for teaching should be more like that for engineering; that is, four undergraduate years should be devoted to the school curriculum, history and philosophy of education, evolution of methods, and the social, personal, and political problems of education in a democratic society. I recognize that many of our "second-tier" public universities ostensibly maintain such programs, but they are too often perceived as second rate. They should be vigorously revised and developed. Their outstanding features should be recognized, publicized, and appreciated. We will look at the historic reasons for trying to move away from serious undergraduate preparation for teaching – trying to raise the academic appraisal of teaching as a profession – and explore an alternative that puts high value on teaching and teacher preparation from the start. A realistic plan for teacher advancement is also considered.

Chapter 12, "Reflecting on the Brighter Vision":This chapter will summarize the previous chapters and invite readers to think deeply about the problems identified.

Conclusion: Sometimes it is useful for readers to know where an author is headed so that they may prepare to agree, to argue against, to challenge, to anticipate great (perhaps insurmountable) difficulties, to suggest helpful revisions, or to decide not to read the thing at all. Readers should also keep in mind that, on many topics, instead of making definite recommendations, I urge them to think and engage in collegial discussion. This book is not a prescription for sweeping reforms that will involve semi-ignorant policy makers, throw teachers into confusion, make money for publishers, or tax students with yet more testing. Developing a richer, brighter vision will require many minds working together. In that spirit, here are some ideas to watch for.

High school education should recognize a unitary purpose: the development of better adults, "better" defined over the whole range of human attributes – moral, intellectual, physical, social, aesthetic, civic. Special attention should be given to moral thought and action throughout the curriculum. *Every* teacher is a moral educator.

Vocational education should be revitalized and expanded; it should be integrated with academic programs both physically on joint campuses and intellectually through a universal program in social studies.

Women's traditional interests should be included in the curriculum through the use of interdisciplinary themes – on, for example, homemaking, parenting, peace, and religion. These interests should be *everyone's* interests.

Much greater provision for choice (both teacher and student) should be provided.

The legacy or spirit (not the traditional curriculum) of the liberal arts should be preserved.

The centrality of relations of care and trust should be recognized in both planning and practice – especially in working with impoverished and academically weak students. A preparatory first year of high school should be provided, and continuity of teacher–student relationships should have high priority in the following years.

Teacher preparation at the undergraduate level should be revitalized and expanded across the disciplines, and provision for advancement within the teaching profession should be carefully defined and implemented. Teacher supervision should be conducted collegially by expert teachers in the higher rank.

We will start with an exploration of what might be meant by a "better adult."

1

Unity of Purpose

Many people today seem to believe that the main purpose – perhaps the only purpose – of getting an education is to make more money after graduating. Indeed, there is a move afoot to judge the worth of colleges by the salaries of their graduates. This move is motivated in part by unhappiness with the enormous increase in college tuition and the fear that graduates who have acquired large loan debts will be unable to repay them unless they can obtain well-paying jobs. One might say that making a lot of money provides a unity of purpose to aspiring graduates. But making money is not an *educational* purpose, and it is not what I am referring to when I argue for a unity of purpose.

Feelings run high on the matter of purpose. After an article appeared in the *New York Times* describing the rankings of colleges by graduates' salaries published in PayScale.com, two respondents wrote to praise the colleges from which they had graduated (Oberlin and Grinnell) for their low rankings on PayScale. The writers expressed pride on both the high academic rankings of their alma maters *and* their low rankings on PayScale. One quoted his former history teacher as saying, "Our graduates may not always do well, but they always do good."[1] One can admire the pride of these writers who have not given way to "money-grubbing" but still sympathize with the many students who have achieved neither financial security nor a sense of becoming somehow a better adult – one who "does good."

In this book, I concentrate on problems and debates about our high schools. However, disagreements over the purposes of higher education are closely related to those concerning secondary education, and a brief examination of the debate on higher education should be useful. If the purpose of higher education is economic gain, then – in the pursuit of equality – our society must try to prepare all students for college. I will argue that this move actually works against the equality it seeks, and it undermines both our democracy and the pursuit of genuine educational aims.

For centuries, the unifying purpose of higher education in the Western world was guided by theology. Andrew Delbanco puts it this way:

> In the early American college, since all studies were unified as one integrated study of the divine mind, boundaries between "fields" or "disciplines" did not exist. "There is not one truth in religion, another in mathematics, and a third in physics and in art," as one Harvard graduate (class of 1825) put the matter. "There is one truth, even as there is one God."[2]

In the last half of the nineteenth century, theology began to lose its grip as a unifying force on the university curriculum. Instead of a concentration on the divine mind and the relation of human beings to that mind, university studies expanded to include agriculture, engineering, and the professions. By the middle of the twentieth century, the very idea of the university was challenged. Referring to Clark Kerr, president of the University of California in the 1960s, Andrew Hacker and Claudia Dreifus write:

> In his view, the very word *university* was a relic of a fast-receding past. Its unitary prefix suggested a single focus, which was teaching, mainly of undergraduates, requiring little more than classrooms, a library, and some modest laboratories. All that had to change, Kerr asserted. . . So he coined a new idiom, *multiversity*: an institution willing to take on any assignment related to knowledge, no matter how remote the association.[3]

The clash between practical knowledge and the knowledge centered on the divine mind (intellectual knowledge) was already in full force in the early twentieth century. Robert Maynard Hutchins, president of the University of Chicago, echoed and promoted the medieval view of unified mind and truth. Drawing on the *Summa Theologica* (Thomas Aquinas), Hutchins wrote: "Education implies teaching. Teaching implies knowledge. Knowledge is truth. The truth is everywhere the same. Hence education should be everywhere the same."[4] Hutchins believed that the universities should not be in the business of professional training or any sort of vocational training. *Education* and *training*, he advised, are two different enterprises. His view is still embraced today by many critics of higher education, although few would endorse theology as a unifying purpose. Arguing for an end to vocational training at the undergraduate level, Hacker and Dreifus claim that it is "a huge mistake to squander years that could and should be devoted to enriching young minds."[5] I will invite readers to consider the possibility that enriching the mind need not be abandoned in vocational education.

While Hutchins argued that knowledge is that bit of truth we have acquired, John Dewey disagreed. In opposition, he argued that knowledge is bigger than truth; *knowledge* is the set of beliefs that guide investigation, and *truth* is the set of outcomes confirmed by that investigation. He also rejected a sharp distinction between intellectual knowledge and practical knowledge. When he spoke about vocational education at the high school level, however, he too worried that it often deprived students of intellectual enrichment and worked against social equality:

> Any scheme for vocational education which takes its point of departure from the industrial regime that now exists, is likely to assume and to perpetuate its divisions and weaknesses, and thus to become an instrument in accomplishing the feudal dogma of social predestination.[6]

But Dewey also saw the possibility for a richer vocational education, one "which does not subject youth to the demands and standards of the present system, but which utilizes its scientific and social factors to develop a courageous intelligence, and to make intelligence practical and executive."[7] From Dewey's perspective – and this will be important as we move along – the intellectual and practical are interactive, and one cannot judge the intellectual richness of a course or subject by looking at its title or even its content as listed. A course labeled "algebra" may or may not be intellectually rich. One labeled "wood shop" may not be intellectually poor. We have to see how the courses are implemented.

This might be a good spot at which to pause and notice that we have so far heard two very different objections to vocational education. One objection, largely based on the medieval/theological view of knowledge as preordained truth, universal and fixed, claims that such knowledge is captured in specific studies such as the traditional liberal arts; any form of "education" that deviates from this and concentrates on practical issues or skills is more accurately called "training" and should not be admitted to the university or to programs preparing students for the university. The second objection focuses on the way vocational education has been defined and implemented – that it has too often ignored the intellectual virtues and sharpened class differences. This second objection raises the possibility that vocational "training" can be redesigned as genuine education. Supporting this view, I will argue that genuine education requires a unity of purpose but not uniformity of content. It will be a major task in what follows to explore what that purpose might be. I will *not* argue for a restoration of theology as our unifying purpose.

Closely related to the debate over vocational education is one over the place of the liberal arts. The first objection to vocational education holds that genuine education is defined as a program in the liberal arts. Such a program *is* education, its advocates insist, and any deviation from it weakens the whole enterprise. From the second point of view, it is possible – even desirable – to advance the spirit of the liberal arts without insisting on the specific content traditionally associated with it.

DECLINE OF THE LIBERAL ARTS

Several factors have contributed to the century-long decline in the liberal arts. Increased interest in the practical arts and professions and the willingness of universities to support these new entities were major factors. But the acceptance of evolution and an increase in outspoken atheism and agnosticism also weakened theology as the unifying foundation for education. Hutchins recognized this and recommended that metaphysics should replace theology as a guide to first principles and the intellectual virtues.[8] Although I agree with Dewey against Hutchins on most matters, I believe that Hutchins's suggestion is worth exploring. If he meant to make the formal study of metaphysics the center of university education – or even the central interest of philosophy – that project is doomed. Metaphysics has been put aside as too abstruse, too separated from science, and several of its most important questions have been transferred to epistemology and ethics. If, however, we interpret him to mean that the great existential questions should be somehow embedded in all of our university studies – should, that is, provide a unity to the educational enterprise – that is well worth our consideration. There is no reason why the questions central to human life cannot be part of all programs of education, although they may take very different forms and suggest different emphases.

The "Great Books" program espoused by Hutchins and Mortimer Adler was designed to introduce students to universal questions concerning human life and knowledge through the study of great works in philosophy, history, literature, and science. Using metaphysics – the study of first principles – as a unifying theme, this program did not promote a sharp separation of disciplines, and, indeed, Hutchins strongly criticized the growing tendency of universities to encourage what he regarded as over-specialization. He noted that scholars, once intent on connecting studies to each other and to the great questions of human life, had become increasingly ignorant of these vital connections.

It is important to note here that both traditionalists (such as Hutchins) and pragmatic-progressives (such as Dewey) were concerned about the growth of specialization and the loss of connections. The traditionalists would restore connection by adhering to the pursuit of eternal truths and the study of universal human nature. The pragmatists and like-minded thinkers preferred a program that would address human problems directly in a spirit of observation, experimentation, and reflection. I will argue that it is possible to sympathize deeply with the questions asked by the traditionalists and yet agree with their critics that there is a better way to approach these questions.

The tendency to specialization in the late 1800s and early 1900s caused disruption both inside and outside the liberal arts. Unity of purpose was lost, and philosophy, history, literature, mathematics, and sciences became more and more highly specialized and separated from each other. Hutchins accepted the inevitability of specialization but still argued for a common base of knowledge: "If professors and students had a common stock of fundamental ideas, it might be possible for those in physiology to communicate with those in physics, and even law and divinity might begin to find it worthwhile to associate with one another."[9] Hutchins advocated a form of common general education to precede all specialties, and this basic education would be uniform in content and aimed at the development of intellectual virtues. Note that we might agree with him on the need to develop intellectual virtues and yet deny the wisdom of insisting on a uniform, traditional content. Is it not possible to encourage the development of intellectual virtues in a class on carpentry or cooking or anatomy? Further, is it not possible to make the desired connections across disciplines through planned collegiality as we move forward in our own specialties? On making these connections today, Edward O. Wilson argues:

There is, in my opinion, an inevitability to the unity of knowledge. It reflects real life.

The trajectory of world events suggests that educated people should be far better able than before to address the great issues courageously and analytically by undertaking a traverse of disciplines. We are into the age of synthesis. . .[10]

We need not go all the way to consilience with Wilson, but we should enthusiastically embrace a "traverse of disciplines."

Besides the loss of connections induced by specialization, the liberal arts suffered another internal blow. The content in each subject became an end in itself. Works chosen from classic literature, for example, became required educational goals instead of guides to a better life. Commenting on the "swamp of books," E. M. Forster wrote: "No disrespect to these great names. The fault is ours, not theirs. They mean us to use them for sign-posts, and they are not to blame if, in our weakness, we mistake the sign-post for the destination."[11]

Acquaintance with the titles, names, and special words contained in the content of each required specialty became a mark of the educated class, and belonging to that class was, on one level, taken for granted (one was born into it) and on another level desperately misunderstood and longed for. Leonard Bast in *Howards End* and Jude Fawley in Hardy's *Jude the Obscure* are memorable examples of the intellectual longing of those not born to it and the snobbery that glorified a difference that would keep them out forever. As readers, we sympathize with Leonard and Jude as they suffer minor agonies in trying to decide whether to use certain names and words in conversation because they are not sure of the proper pronunciation. They have seen these words in print but have not heard them in conversation. It might rightly be taken as great democratic progress that, as the twentieth century progressed, higher education and secondary preparation for it became open to a much larger number of students. But what besides "moving up" was the purpose of this education for those who sought it?

Because the unity of purpose has faded and all but disappeared, it should not be surprising that so many now ask what liberal education is good for. What does one gain from it? Certainly, one does not learn much about making or repairing things or even about performing everyday tasks. Matthew Crawford quotes the director of the California Agricultural Teachers' Association as saying, "We have a generation of students that can answer questions on standardized tests, know factoids, but they can't do anything."[12] Of course not! Liberal education was designed primarily for people who would not have "to do" anything. They would hire others to do whatever manual work was required. But that implies that the liberally educated would either be born into wealthy families or would obtain lucrative work on graduation. Hence the current and growing worry about the salaries that graduates may expect. Why else would one spend four years and a small fortune of borrowed money on a liberal education? At the beginning of this chapter, I mentioned letters to the *New York Times* suggesting that "to do good" might be more important than "to do well," but clearly it is hard to maintain this attitude in the face of great debt. And it is even harder if this attitude is not somehow inspired by the education offered. Again we see the importance of a revitalized discussion on unity of purpose.

The discussion so far should not be taken to suggest that opening higher education and college preparation to many students has been a mistake. Neither will I argue that academic studies should concentrate on the liberal arts as traditionally conceived and that many students simply cannot do this sort of work.[13] Nor will I argue for a unifying purpose that can be easily specified in detail. Rather, I will argue for something like the "better adult" mentioned by Jerome Bruner in *The Process of Education*.[14] This will be an invitation to the ongoing dialogue about what we might mean by a "better adult" and what aims we will posit to serve this purpose. Although there will be a unity of overall purpose in this plan, there will be a multiplicity of aims guided by it. Indeed, the unity of purpose will *necessitate* a multiplicity of aims.

Although I will not argue that it is a mistake to make college and college preparation more widely available, I will argue that alternative forms of post-secondary education should be more generously supported and recommended. The United States led the way toward this goal in establishing the comprehensive high school. The idea was indeed wonderful, and we can be justly proud that the United States led the world in promoting high school education for all. But despite the world-leading achievement, something went badly wrong in our implementation of the comprehensive high school. It is worth spending some time to consider the merits and demerits of the comprehensive high school.

THE COMPREHENSIVE HIGH SCHOOL

The philosophical (and ideological) dispute over what constitutes *education* has been continuous, and it has at times become acute. In the decades from 1890 to 1910, for example, it became heated. The economic base of U.S. society was shifting from agriculture to industry, and it was believed that schooling must also change. The skills required for industrial workers would surely be different and more demanding than those required for farm workers. (We should note, as a preview of sorts, that a similar problem faces us now as we move rapidly from an industrial/manufacturing economy to one of information/service.) It was widely agreed that schools must change accordingly; in particular, it was argued that more children should go to high school. But what should they learn there? Should their education be designed on the model of the classical academy then in existence or should it provide for the vocational training required by the rapidly growing industrial complex?

In 1892, the National Education Association appointed the Committee of Ten, chaired by Charles W. Eliot, president of Harvard, to address these questions. The committee recommended that high school education should be made available to many more children, and the recommended program for the expanded public school system should replicate, with some judicious changes, that of the existing academies. The argument given for this recommendation would, as already noted, be repeated some years later by Hutchins, who declared that "education should be everywhere the same."[15] (Another brief look ahead: The same argument is popular today – that all children should have the same pre-college education in the name of equality – this time to prepare them all for college. This, I will argue, is a monumental mistake.)

Although the plan endorsed by Eliot and the Committee of Ten recommended several programs, they were all variations of a college preparatory curriculum. Critics – foremost among them the psychologist G. Stanley Hall – spoke against these recommendations. Herbert Kliebard notes that Hall expressed three major objections to the committee's proposal. The first was the claim that many children would not succeed in a college preparatory program. Kliebard remarks, "The school population, presumably, was so variable as to native endowment that a common curriculum was simply unworkable."[16] (Note again that a similar argument is alive today over the capacities of students to manage college work.) Reasonable people might well agree with this argument and yet deeply regret the sort of language that sometimes accompanied it – talk of incapables, probable destinies, and mental defectives. What of the wonderful variety of much-needed talents and interests that mark fully human lives?

In his second objection, Hall voiced an opinion siding with that of John Dewey's opponents, namely, that it is false that any subject can be intellectually rich (or impoverished) depending on how it is taught. Hall criticized Dewey's claim as an unwarranted attack on intellectual content. As we will see, this argument, too, would have a long life; it is still lively today. I will side enthusiastically with Dewey on this. Indeed, much of this book will be a defense of the claim that intellectual matters can be addressed in many forms of human activity. Hall's final objection was directed at the claim that preparation for life and preparation for college are essentially the same. This claim is also with us today. It needs closer examination, and we will return to it. But it is Hall's first objection that carried most weight. People today who disagree with Hall are likely to use the slogan "All children can learn!" but we need to inquire closely as to what this might mean.

Those who advocated several programs (or tracks) for the new high schools won the day, and even Eliot reversed his position, arguing, "There is no such thing among men as equality of nature, of capacity for training, or of intellectual power."[17] Probably inspired by his own introduction of electives at Harvard, Eliot saw possibilities in the expansion of courses and programs for high schools. The resulting comprehensive, or differentiated, high school introduced a whole new era in schooling. In 1910, fewer than 10 percent of U.S. children completed high school; by mid-century, about 60 percent graduated, and by 1970, the graduation rate topped 75 percent. The United States led the world in advancing secondary education.

The debate continued, however, and is with us even today. Traditionalists believed that the comprehensive high school had abandoned the true purpose of education: development of the intellect. In the 1950s, Arthur Bestor protested that "it is *not* the job of the school to meet the common and the specific individual needs of youth."[18] Bestor and many other critics believed that the home, community, school, and church all had distinct roles to play in the upbringing of children, and the special role of the school was to concentrate on knowledge and intellectual development.

This ongoing debate has several facets. One view, already discussed, is that all students should receive the same academic education, one that concentrates on intellectual content. A second view, increasingly discussed today, holds that although the classic liberal arts education is indeed the best, not all students are capable of handling it. Charles Murray, for example, says right out:

> If all children were put on a mathematics track that took them through calculus, and then were given a test of calculus problems, the resulting scores would not look like a bell curve. For a large proportion of children, the scores would not be merely low. They would be zero.[19]

There is some evidence to back Murray's contention. We often hear current cases of Advanced Placement (AP) calculus classes in which not one student has passed the AP test. Is the fault poor teaching? Is it the faulty preparation that preceded the calculus class? Or are some students just not cut out for this kind of work? Murray's stand angers many people. It seems antidemocratic and likely to support – even to aggravate – class and race differences. We should pause for a bit to introduce a significant point that will be addressed repeatedly in this book. Although we should keep in mind the ideological affiliations of writers and speakers, we should listen to their arguments and try to follow their logic. We should not pre-judge their conclusions. An attitude of open-mindedness will be continually advised. Too often, opposing sides – for example, liberals and conservatives – agree on a loosely defined problem such as poverty and then proceed to do ideological battle over exactly how to define the problem and its causes. Meanwhile, the problem persists, and its victims continue to suffer. It would be far better for the two sides to engage in genuine dialogue under a generally agreed-on purpose: *to make things better* for all involved. Instead of fighting over who has best defined the problem, all involved would agree to listen, to try several (even competing) approaches, and to work together in a campaign to solve the problem.

At the end of *Real Education*, extolling the importance for all children to find "something they love doing and learn how to do it well," Murray concludes:

> Educational success needs to be redefined accordingly. The goal of education is to bring children into adulthood having discovered things they enjoy doing and doing them at the outermost limits of their potential. The goal applies equally to every child, across the entire range of every ability. There are no first-class and second-class ways to enjoy the exercise of our realized capacities. It is a quintessentially *human* satisfaction, and its universality can connect us all. Opening the door to that satisfaction is what real education does.[20]

Murray tells us nothing, however, about the sort of real education that would accomplish this end for those whose talents are not academic, nor does he prod us to think how we might increase our society's respect for those whose talents differ, nor again why this is important for our democracy. His primary interest is in "real education" for the gifted. If we reject the view advanced by Hutchins, Mortimer Adler, and E. D. Hirsch that all children should receive the same education as too confining, too concentrated on specific content rather than intellectual processes (even though the alleged aim is intellectual development), and if Murray's view leaves us uneasy (we do not want to be accused of elitism), perhaps we should return enthusiastically to the comprehensive high school.

The comprehensive high school has been promoted as a democratic ideal. In opposition to traditionalists who insisted that democracy demands the same education for all, advocates of the comprehensive high school argued that democracy implies respectful recognition of differing talents and interests. In the mid-twentieth century, James B. Conant strongly defended the comprehensive high school as an example of "our devotion to the ideals of equality of opportunity and equality of status."[21] In his defense of the comprehensive high school, Conant made a point to which I will return in later chapters. He pointed out that, in contrast to the European custom of providing separate academic and vocational schools, the U.S. comprehensive school brought all students together on one campus where they are encouraged to work cooperatively in extracurricular activities, athletics, and student government. This is an important point, one that deserves further consideration.

The idea of tracks or different programs for students with different abilities or interests seems to be a sound one. I have defended it in recent work,[22] and I will extend that defense here. However, we cannot defend the idea enthusiastically without suggesting ways to remedy its reprehensible effects in implementation. Using the notion of "probable destinies," educators *assigned* students to tracks; students were rarely given a choice. This in itself might be considered antidemocratic. Further, the tracks were hierarchically perceived with the college preparatory track at the top, an assortment of vocational tracks far lower, and a "general" track at the very bottom. Even if choice were available, why would students willingly choose a clearly lower track? To make the comprehensive high school democratically respectable, two related faults must be corrected: First, students must be allowed, with guidance, to choose their tracks, and, second, every course in every track must be rightly judged as part of a "real education."

A BETTER ADULT: SOME PRELIMINARY THOUGHTS

Suppose we suggest as a unifying purpose for education: to produce better adults. What might we mean by this? Bruner suggested it as a criterion by which we should judge the content of curriculum: "We might ask, as a criterion for any subject taught in primary school, whether, when fully developed, it is worth an adult's knowing, and whether having known it as a child makes a person a better adult."[23] In this paragraph, Bruner was defending the idea of the spiral curriculum, a plan to introduce important concepts early in developmentally appropriate form and return to those concepts continually, deepening them, throughout the years of schooling:

> If the hypothesis with which this section was introduced is true – that any subject can be taught to any child in some honest form – then it would follow that a curriculum ought to be built around the great issues, principles, and values that a society deems worthy of the continual concern of its members.[24]

Even if we hold a doubt about Bruner's claim that any subject can be taught to any child in some honest form, we can still endorse his conclusion that the curriculum should be built around a society's great issues, principles, and values. I would go a bit further and say that the whole structure of education should be so planned. There is more to schooling than the curriculum. Everything we do in schools may work for or against making better adults.

Critics may protest immediately that such a statement of purpose is too vague. How will we describe a better adult? We have to say much more about this, of course, but the vagueness will not be entirely removed. Indeed, we might regard it as a virtue, one that invites intellectual and practical exploration. It may be a mistake to seek a unifying theme or purpose that is specified in detail. Isaiah Berlin warned against the belief that there is a final solution to this kind of search:

> This is the belief that somewhere, in the past or in the future, in divine revelation or in the mind of an individual thinker, in the pronouncements of history or science, or in the simple heart of an uncorrupted good man, there is a final solution.[25]

In addition, Berlin advised, we may not be able to promote or secure all of our values at any one time; we may occasionally have to sacrifice one in order to promote another. In what follows, I will say a great deal about what constitutes a better adult, but, taking Berlin's advice seriously, the description will be left open for continual discussion. I should point out, however, that under Bruner's conclusion we are not free to define "better adult" in ways that might be politically or morally objectionable. We must keep in mind the principles and values we deem worthy and be prepared both to defend them and to reflect on them. After all, a noble type or best adult has been described by fascists, communists, and religious fanatics.[26] We must, however, say more about what is meant by the "issues, principles, and values" cherished by our society. Bruner was surely right to make a close connection between the student/child and the better adult we hope to produce. Too often educators have either ignored the child, concentrating on a preordained model of adult life, or focused on the child almost as though he or she were a different species. It seems logical to consider both the whole child and the whole adult as we devise our educational plans.

We were offered a promising start in this direction in 1918 with the *Cardinal Principles of Secondary Education.*[27] This influential report listed seven aims for secondary education: health, command of the fundamental processes, worthy home-membership, vocation, citizenship, worthy use of leisure, and ethical character. Because the report said little about traditional subject matter, it was attacked as anti-intellectual. It was also criticized for asking too much of the schools. Arthur Bestor, as noted above, criticized work that tried to advance the Cardinal Principles as both vague and wrong-headed, arguing that it is not the job of the school to meet all of the needs of students; much of this work, he said, should be done by parents. The school should concentrate on learning and development of the intellect.[28] This is an example of the bureaucratic style of thinking that must be reevaluated. The work of raising children to be better adults cannot be divided up neatly and assigned task by task to schools, parents, churches, or communities. Every group or institution involved with the welfare of children must contribute in an appropriate way to the whole child – not to one feature of child life. When we look at the constellation of agencies and agents involved in producing better adults, we should expect each to respond to the question: What can we contribute to the accomplishment of each of the aims identified under the unifying purpose?

Let us consider how the conversation might unfold. If we use the aims listed in the Cardinal Principles as a starting point, we might ask whether we should add to them. (Certainly, none of them should be dropped.) Perhaps we should add "intellectual development" as suggested by traditionalists, although we would not make this the only or principal aim. Perhaps also we should add an aim directed at religious (or spiritual) life. The usual response to such a suggestion is that this task is one for religious institutions and parents; it is not the job of the school. But in the approach we are taking here, the high school should contribute something to religious/spiritual education. It should not indoctrinate; it should inform and encourage critical thinking. Planning for this contribution should not require adding a course; that approach to curriculum reform will almost certainly fail. Each subject in the standard curriculum must make a contribution. Let us consider briefly, for illustrative purposes, using religion as a common theme.

What might be done in English class? We can make suggestions that arise from a way of thinking about holistic forms of education without making a highly specified list of content. What I offer is meant to be illustrative. Certainly, students should have an opportunity to read Bible stories during their high school years. Both believers and unbelievers should approve the study of the Bible as literature.[29] As the stories are read, the teacher can help students to understand that it is not insulting or antireligious to refer to many of these stories as myths. Myths are not mere fictions; they are meant to embody deep truths, although those truths are not facts and may be contested.

English teachers might also have their students read the chapter on animal pain in C. S. Lewis's *The Problem of Pain*, and a discussion could follow on the nature of God's goodness.[30] Why would a good God allow animals to suffer pain? Why would he have created a world in which its creatures must eat one another to survive? A reading from Lewis should be attractive to literature teachers, who will remind students that Lewis also wrote *The Chronicles of Narnia* and the *Space Trilogy*. Further, concern about animal pain makes a connection to current work on animal life in environmental studies. A main idea of our curricular exploration is to make connections among the disciplines and to life itself.

An objection might be raised here – and in many other parts of this book – that public school teachers cannot possibly engage in such discussions. Metaphysical or existential questions related to religion are simply out of bounds. If that is so, we should drop the current hypocritical intention to teach critical thinking. We cannot teach critical thinking without addressing critical issues. But we must be open-minded, fair, and sensitive in doing this.

Social studies (or history) teachers might discuss the religious views of the nation's founders. In doing this, students might be surprised to hear that several early presidents and their colleagues were deists or even atheists. Was the United States founded on Christian principles? George Washington said that it was not. That does not mean that its founding principles are incompatible with Christianity, merely that Christianity was not their source. Here is an opportunity to make students familiar with a new vocabulary: deism, atheism, secularism, and agnosticism (which entered the vocabulary later in the nineteenth century). At other points in the study of U.S. history, teachers might want to mention when "In God We Trust" first appeared on U.S. coins and what the nation was suffering when this was done. Similarly, what was happening in the world when "under God" was added to the Pledge of Allegiance?

In science classes, the history of debates over evolution should be discussed as well as the theory. It is an exciting history. Who was Bishop Wilberforce? What did he say that so insulted Thomas Huxley? And why was Huxley called "Darwin's bulldog"? What is the "watch-maker" argument, and how do evolutionists respond to it?

All of these discussions would be greatly enhanced by regular seminar-like meetings of teachers from the various disciplines. Andrew Delbanco has described how useful such meetings have been for teachers at Columbia University who work together in the Core Curriculum.[31] Not only is the Core Curriculum invigorated but each teacher's work in his or her own discipline is enhanced – a great benefit of intellectual collegiality. At the high school level, this sort of collegiality would revitalize the whole curriculum and bring meaning to what students are required to learn. I will say much more about this in later chapters.

What might be done in mathematics classes? Mathematicians have long argued over the source of mathematics. Is mathematics discovered or invented? Most of the material on this question is too difficult for high school students, but, if Bruner is right, we should be able to introduce the topic in some useful and interesting way. It was not unusual in the days when theology served as the unifying theme of academic studies for mathematicians to believe that mathematics existed, as Mary Somerville put it, in "that sublimely omniscient Mind from eternity."[32] It could be especially powerful to use this quotation from Somerville (1780–1872), a distinguished self-taught scholar who – because she was a woman – was excluded from the academic circles of her day. David Noble describes the way she was treated:

> Her book was used as a required text in a university in which she could not teach nor have her daughters study. Her bronze likeness was placed in the Royal Society's Great Hall, from which she herself was barred. . . Mary Somerville was a staunch advocate of women's rights and especially, of higher education for women. Hers was the first signature on the parliamentary petition drawn up in 1868 by John Stuart Mill to demand voting rights for women. . .[33]

A "digression" such as this in math class has much to contribute to both the cultural knowledge cherished by traditionalists and the connections we are trying to advance here.

Somerville was not alone, of course, in locating the roots of mathematics in the mind of God. Even today, although few mention God, many mathematicians believe that mathematics is "out there" to be *discovered*. Others believe it is *invented*. The history of these opposing views is fascinating, but for present purposes it may be enough to recognize that some mathematicians have been ardent believers and some atheists.[34] An account of the beliefs of the great mathematicians Joseph-Louis Lagrange and Pierre-Simon Laplace is illustrative. Laplace had given a copy of his book on the nature of the solar system to Napoleon:

> Thinking to get a rise out of Laplace, Napoleon took him to task for an apparent oversight. "You have written this huge book on the system of the world without once mentioning the author of the universe." "Sire," Laplace retorted, "I had no need of that *hypothesis*." When Napoleon repeated this to Lagrange, the latter remarked, "Ah, but that is a fine hypothesis. *It explains so many things*."[35]

Many would argue against Lagrange that the God hypothesis explains things too easily and retards investigation. Sometimes, the belief that mathematics is discovered in the search to understand the mind of God has led to a mistaken acceptance of axiomatic concepts as absolute truths or a stubborn unwillingness to accept promising inventions as well grounded.[36]

The past few pages were not intended as prescriptive content; they were provided as an illustrative example of the rich potential in teaching themes across the disciplines under the unifying educational purpose of producing better adults. In them, we considered just one theme selected under that purpose. The conversation contributes to cultural knowledge and critical thinking. It also illustrates the potential power of faculty collegiality. Many more such examples will appear in succeeding chapters.

In the next chapter, attention will be focused on another of the aims we have listed: preparation for a vocation. On finding a vocation, John Dewey said:

> To find out what one is fitted to do and to secure an opportunity to do it is the key to happiness. Nothing is more tragic than failure to discover one's true business in life, or to find that one has drifted or been forced by circumstances into an uncongenial calling.[37]

The discussion of vocational choice will serve as an important prelude to further analysis of what might be meant by a "better adult."

2

Vocational Programs

In our search for what should be meant by a "better adult," we will have to look at least briefly at every major facet of adult life. That search will be assisted by a preliminary look at the difference in talents and interests relevant to vocational life (in this chapter) and at major differences in gender interests (in Chapter 3). By starting this way – with an emphasis on differences and variety – we should avoid the mistake of describing a better adult in specific, idealized terms.

Preparing for a vocation is one of the seven aims posited by the Cardinal Principles, and it is at the top of today's popular list of educational/financial aims. In this chapter, we will look first at the question of whether all students should be prepared for college and what reasonable alternatives might be suggested. Then, assuming we agree to expand vocational educational at the secondary level, we will explore ways in which that education can be intellectually enriched. As we move along in this exploration, we will encounter political and social issues; these, too, are controversial, but they must be addressed. Finally, we will consider how our middle schools can contribute to the success of vocational programs in high school.

EVERYONE TO COLLEGE?

At least two of our recent presidents have explicitly endorsed the idea that all of our young people should attend college, and many in the general population seem to agree. I have already mentioned some critics who disagree with this recommendation, claiming that some (perhaps many) students are not capable of rigorous college work. Either we admit fewer students, they advise, or we sacrifice the quality of our college courses. Whether or not we agree with this argument, we must acknowledge that interests and talents vary, and I will argue that the job of the school is to help students locate and develop those interests and talents. The wrong question has been asked repeatedly. The educational question is not whether all students can do rigorous academic work, but, rather: What *can* each student do, and what should the schools do to prepare him or her to succeed at it? One is more likely to do well at something one loves than at something one is forced into in the name of equality.

Suppose a young man has mediocre academic skills but is exceptionally talented in mechanical work. Should he be encouraged to go to college and engage in typical academic studies toward a bachelor's degree? Or should he be encouraged to make the very best of his talents? Charles Murray, whose view on education for the gifted was considered in Chapter 1, makes the interesting point that the young man should look at the *range* of salaries in the line of mechanical work that interests him. It is true that the average college graduate makes a higher salary than an average worker who does not obtain a degree, but how does the salary of the average holder of a bachelor's degree compare with that of someone at the top of the mechanical line the young man is considering? He might well do better financially in mechanical work, and he would be doing work he loves.[1] This is a powerful argument, and its spirit was endorsed also by John Gardner in his work on excellence:

> We must learn to honor excellence in every socially accepted human activity, however humble the activity, and to scorn shoddiness, however exalted the activity. An excellent plumber is infinitely more valuable than an incompetent philosopher. The society that scorns excellence in plumbing because plumbing is a humble activity and tolerates shoddiness in philosophy because it is an exalted activity will have neither good plumbing nor good philosophy. Neither its pipes nor its theories will hold water.[2]

There are valuable lessons here for both potential vocational students who are trying to make a wise decision and for academic students who should learn to respect the full range of talents in their fellow citizens. It is for this reason, too, that the comprehensive high school is to be preferred over separate academic and vocational schools. Ideally, the comprehensive high school is a microcosm of democracy that encourages joint participation across programs not only in student government but in the arts and community service. We will return to this theme in Chapter 9 on the physical and social climate of schools.

Before returning to discussion of the comprehensive high school, more should be said about Murray's advice on looking beyond average salaries.

Clearly, it is good advice for those young people who have identified their own strengths and interests. But many young people are more or less in the middle on most scales. They may have no outstanding talents, no burning interests. Contrary to Murray's judgment on who should go to college, their middling academic ability may be sufficient to get them through to a degree, and they should probably be encouraged to try, keeping in mind that a real interest may arise during the college years. Better still would be a more vigorous attempt to provide an interesting array of high school programs. Schools must provide an adequate education not only for the gifted – whether that gift is intellectual or practical – but also for the majority who may or may not find a highly satisfying vocation.

Possibly the most egregious fault in the twentieth-century implementation of the comprehensive high school was the practice of *assigning* students to tracks according to their "probable destinies" in adult life. Choice is the very essence of democracy, and yet students were denied the choice of their high school program. One could argue, of course, that teenagers are not competent to make a choice that will profoundly affect their adult lives, and I am not suggesting that they should make such a choice without careful guidance. However, decisions should not be determined solely by tests and grades, by social or economic class, by peer pressure, and certainly not by whim. Young citizens should be assisted in making a judicious choice, and they should be reminded that a choice made today is not necessarily made for a lifetime.

Another great fault in the implementation of tracks was a failure to provide high-quality courses in the nonacademic programs. I have never come across a persuasive argument for the "general" track in our schools. Some of the vocational and commercial courses have been excellent, but the courses offered under the "general" label have been rightly condemned as dumping grounds. There needs to be a clear commitment: Every course offered by our schools should be excellent. With guidance, students should be able to choose their programs with pride.

We should also consider another issue that is alive and well today: Is there a single form of education that can prepare students equally well for college and for work? Recall Hall's response that such a claim is simply false. On this, we may agree with Hall (I do), although there are certainly essential elements that should appear in all programs of education. At the level of purpose – to produce better adults – we have universal guidance. At the level of individual courses within different programs, content may differ substantially. Even here, however, what we might call collateral or supplemental content directed at general aims (aesthetic, moral, civic, etc.)

should appear in all courses. Quite reasonably, we should be able to claim that courses with very different basic content should nevertheless contribute something to all facets of a full human life. But a college preparatory program does not prepare one for a skilled job in a machine shop, and manual training is not adequate preparation for courses in the liberal arts. In general, preparation for a vocation is not in itself synonymous with preparation for life, nor does education confined to the liberal arts constitute such preparation. Under our unifying theme, every facet of education that is directed mainly at one subsidiary aim (e.g., vocation, worthy home membership) must also contribute what it can to the other aims. The unifying theme does not imply uniform content.

It may be possible, however, to make vocational courses more compatible with post-secondary education. We should consider closer collaboration between high school vocational courses and those in related fields at community colleges. Just as students in the academic program have access to Advanced Placement courses, so might vocational students save a year of schooling by enrolling in a strong high school program closely connected to one at the community college and thereby be encouraged to continue their studies beyond high school. And, of course, once at the community college, students may become aware of further possibilities. The important element in such an arrangement is the promise of further education and the motivation that can provide for success at the high school level. This arrangement would eliminate the stigma so often associated with high school vocational programs as "terminal."[3] Like their academic counterparts, good vocational programs would also lead to further education.

Both college preparatory and vocational programs must consider ways in which they can promote the full range of aims. The response of many critics to this proposal has long been that it is not the job of the schools to provide education for home life, leisure time, spiritual life, social life, and so on. A far better response to this challenge is to ask what the schools *can* reasonably do in each area without taking full responsibility, and every school subject should be studied for possibilities. Is there *any* school subject, for example, that has nothing whatever to contribute to successful parenting?

The main objection to this recommendation is that a focus on such material is "anti-intellectual," and that criticism has been made again and again against proposals such as the Cardinal Principles. It has also been made against vocational education itself, but clearly vocational education can be both intellectually challenging and useful. Perhaps, however, we should explicitly add intellectual aims to our list of principles and aims.

Our unifying purpose surely includes intellectual development, but that is not our sole aim and not necessarily our main one. Nevertheless, to avoid the familiar charge of anti-intellectualism, let us add it.

INTELLECTUAL AND PRACTICAL KNOWLEDGE

There are several meanings and connotations attached to the words *intellect* and *intellectual*. Which should we endorse in our educational planning? On one, we can easily agree that "intellectual" activity requires the active involvement of the mind, of thinking. That eliminates activity that can be done physically in machine-like repetition, with little or no thinking. Relatively few tasks today can be done so mechanically, and no educational program would purport to prepare students for such work. Still, it is important for students – future citizens – to understand that some such work must be done and to consider how those who do it should be recompensed. All students should become acquainted with one or more utopian works that address this problem. How is it handled, for example, in Edward Bellamy's *Looking Backward*, a utopian novel admired by John Dewey?[4] Should we try to find a way to share the meanest, dirtiest, least cognitively demanding jobs so that they do not fall entirely on one segment of the population? Should people who now perform this work be paid more – a reasonable compensation for doing work most of us would abhor?

In traditional thought, intellectual knowledge is often defined as knowledge that is worthwhile in itself; it is sharply differentiated from the practical, which is motivated from the outset by its use. A college education, Robert Maynard Hutchins asserted, should be directed at intellectual knowledge and the intellectual virtues.[5] All practical training should take place elsewhere. But the distinction between intellectual knowledge and practical knowledge is not easy to specify, and it may even disappear when we pay careful attention to the knower. For example, one person may read a utopian novel as an end in itself; another may seek it out and study it carefully to find a way to cure one of society's ills. As mentioned earlier, even the acclaimed literary classics have an end beyond themselves: to help us understand, or at least think about, the great existential questions. When we admit this, we see that other, lesser works might also contribute to human understanding. We might reasonably use themes as the starting point for the selection of content.

For present purposes, we might define *intellectual knowledge* as knowledge that has no immediate application in practice and *practical knowledge* as knowledge acquired and applied for use in practical activities such as making, repairing, selling, transporting, and curing. Both forms of knowledge should be included in vocational education, but – as in all forms of teaching – decisions will have to be made on how far to press the acquisition of intellectual knowledge. The decision depends not only on the interests of students but in large part on the repertoire and personality of the teacher. Ideally, teachers should have an impressive store of knowledge that connects the disciplines to each other and to the present and future life of students. The material thus shared should inspire students to investigate further.

A better move might be to avoid the intellectual/practical dichotomy in favor of an emphasis on the *cognitive*. If we set aside the drudge work mentioned above, both intellectual work and practical work usually require thinking, and this point should be emphasized in the planning and enactment of all programs of study. This emphasis is made vivid in the work of Mike Rose, who has written so powerfully about the cognitive dimension of physical work.[6] "Intellectual" work can deteriorate to mindless memorization and recitation; "practical" work can also become mindless and slipshod. The use of "cognitive" is also consonant with the current emphasis on critical thinking, about which more will be said in Chapter 7. Still, the distinction is not empty, and we should consider ways to include the intellectual material – introduced for its own merit – into vocational as well as academic programs. I have already mentioned one such possibility: reading and discussing various utopian novels.

Let us consider some other possibilities. Vocational students should have an opportunity to read literature related to labor and its history. Ken Koziol and W. Norton Grubb suggest several fine examples: *The Jungle, The Grapes of Wrath, Babbitt, Good as Gold,* and many others.[7] In addition to fiction, students should read something about the history of work and biographical accounts of working-class intellectuals and supporters. English and social studies teachers can work together in sharing the stories of Rosa Parks, Pete Seeger, Fannie Lou Hamer, Eleanor Roosevelt, Paulo Freire, and Myles Horton.[8]

Both vocational and academic students should become aware of recent analyses purporting to show that the working class has been led to think, vote, and work against itself. Thomas Frank castigates conservatives who have recruited working-class people to a false conservatism:

> Over the last three decades they have smashed the welfare state, reduced the tax burden on corporations and the wealthy, and generally

facilitated the country's return to a nineteenth-century pattern of wealth distribution. Thus the primary contradiction of the backlash: it is a working-class movement that has done incalculable, historic harm to working-class people.[9]

Should Frank's analysis be presented as unquestionable truth? Of course not. In sharing and discussing such views, teachers try to encourage the development of intellectual virtues: listening to all reasonable sides, questioning, evaluating, reflecting on one's own views and why they are held. Again, if we are serious about cultivating critical thinking, we must find ways in which to address critical issues. In Chapter 9, I will suggest that four years of social studies should form the base of a common curriculum for both academic and vocational programs. It is in these classes, carefully composed of students from both groups, that problematic political and social issues should be openly, analytically discussed. The dramatic differences of views between social classes that now appear so regularly may disappear as our future citizens study and discuss these issues together. Again, we will say more on this in Chapter 7, on critical thinking.

Aesthetic appreciation should also be listed among the intellectual and practical virtues. Usually, when we speak of aesthetic appreciation, we have in mind the fine arts and music, and we should certainly encourage such appreciation. But we should also consider what Matthew Crawford refers to as "stochastic arts":

> Because the stochastic arts diagnose and fix things that are variable, complex, and not of our own making, and therefore not fully knowable, they require a certain disposition toward the thing you are trying to fix. This disposition is at once cognitive and moral.

> Getting it right demands that you be *attentive* in the way of a conversation rather than *assertive* in the way of a demonstration.[10]

When I read this, I thought immediately of teaching as a stochastic art. It certainly requires attention to those we teach. Teachers are trying to produce better adults, but they cannot *create* those better individuals, and they must continually revise what they are doing in response to what they see and hear from their students. One who fixes or repairs things must deal with the objects as they are presented to him/her. Similarly, teachers must deal with the students who appear in their classes. Such occupations require a sensitivity to both beauty and weakness. They imply possible failure, sometimes enormous (and unpredictable) effort, and faith that things can be made better, not perfect.

For present purposes, aesthetic appreciation in the vocational arts should lead to a sense of wonder at the multitude of contrivances already invented and to a deep commitment to preserve and protect them. It should encourage thrift and discourage waste. Before we carelessly throw something away, we might more often ask whether it can be fixed. There is a deep aesthetic reward in restoring an object or mechanical device to working condition. Closely related to aesthetic sensitivity is personal (or group) pride in a job well done, and this too should be encouraged.

Collegiality plays an important part in promoting both intellectual and practical knowledge. Typically, teachers of academic mathematics know little about the practical applications of math in the shop or industrial workplace. I can remember how surprised I was, as a high school math teacher, to learn from former students who went on to engineering schools, that measurement denominations could be included in equations. How convenient to cancel inches and feet right in the equation rather than painstakingly removing such designations before setting up the equation! Cooperation between academic and vocational teachers is described in another of the chapters of Grubb's volumes on vocational education.[11] This collegiality is both intellectual and practical. It increases the intellectual knowledge of the teachers, and it facilitates their practical work in instruction.

POLITICAL AND SOCIAL ISSUES

We might approach the problem of revitalizing vocational education with a bit of justified cynicism. Without question, there are knowledgeable and ethically motivated people who want to eliminate tracking and give all students an opportunity to prepare for college.[12] However, there may also be some who endorse a common curriculum because academic education in its most rudimentary form is far less expensive than excellent, up-to-date vocational education.[13] We should not conclude that the present campaign to prepare everyone for college is motivated by a commitment to increase equality. It may very well work, if unintentionally, against the very equality it purports to endorse.

Here we must pause to distinguish two different meanings of *tracking*. In the one used so far in the discussion of vocational education, tracking refers to the provision of different programs such as academic (preparation for college) and vocational (preparation for work). Sometimes this sort of tracking is called "streaming," and it can be done within a school, as it is in a comprehensive high school, or it can be done in separate schools, as it is often done in Europe. I have argued in favor of such programs if they are well planned and well staffed, and if students are allowed to *choose* their program with intelligent guidance.

Another form of tracking refers to ability grouping within particular subjects. For example, most ninth-grade students are now required to take Algebra 1, but their classes differ dramatically from gifted or honors to classes that barely resemble algebra. Students who complete these courses may find themselves forced to take remedial algebra (even pre-algebra) if they go to college. Some studies have shown that students assigned to lower ability-grouped classes within a school experience some loss to their self-concept in the subject.[14] One reason suggested for this loss is that students assigned to a lower ability group within a school program think of themselves and their entire group as inferior to those in higher ability classes. In contrast, those located in a distinct "stream" have a different reference group and, apparently, do not suffer a significant loss of self-esteem. It is an interesting conjecture, but we should also consider the possibility that many of those students grouped within a school are suffering an even greater and largely unconscious loss of general self-esteem because *their real talents and interests have been ignored*. They have been designated as academic math students and found deficient. They have been given little or no opportunity to compare themselves to others with whom they share interests and abilities.

The "streaming" form of tracking – condemned by so many critics – may in fact offer the most generous protection from the perceived evils of ability-group tracking. It implies, of course, that we give far more attention to the intellectual/practical content of courses offered. We might, for example, offer excellent courses in industrial/commercial mathematics that would of necessity contain some algebra, geometry, and statistics without the mathematical formality that superficially pervades the usual courses. I say "superficially" because much of what appears in our standard math courses is formal only on the surface; much of it is meaningless for large numbers of students and easily forgotten. To establish courses appropriate to vocational programs requires collegial cooperation among academic and vocational teachers, local employers, and those who have some knowledge of industrial and commercial needs beyond the local level. Where are our students likely to find work? How do we inform the business community about the skills our students offer?

Among the most important social issues in schooling – and perhaps especially in vocational education – is the development of standard oral language. There have been periods in the social history of the United States when social critics and educators have urged the populace to accept not only the continued use of original languages in ethnic communities (a recommendation with which I agree) but also the use of characteristically nonstandard language in English-speaking communities. This is a tricky business.

Again, as in the discussion of tracking, we face two problems, not just one. It is unquestionably right, as a moral and educational practice, to respect the full range of native languages and the people who speak them. But educators must face the fact that we are all judged by the quality of our oral language. Possibly no other human trait is so easily and pervasively used to establish social class, and yet, while cramming volumes of useless facts into our students, we allow significant numbers of them to graduate from high school with poor oral language skills. Ruby Payne identifies standard language with a *formal register* and nonstandard language with a *casual register*, and notes that the difference between the two marks a most significant distinction in social class.[15] One may disagree with some of her description of the two registers, but one can hardly disagree with the importance of the difference and what it conveys. Schools, of course, use formal register. Payne comments on the need for poor (impoverished) students to learn the use of formal register, pointing out that they do not acquire this language in their home and community relationships: "Therefore, when we ask students to move from casual to formal register, we almost need to direct-teach it. Natural acquisition of formal register would require a significant relationship."[16]

The real problem now arises with full force. I am concerned here only with the use of standard oral language, not the full range of Payne's "formal register." We *do* direct-teach standard language, but by itself this direct instruction does not work. Effective teaching requires the establishment of a relationship. Instead of using the lack of relationships as an excuse for the failure to acquire standard English and that failure as a reason to direct-teach it, we might think more seriously about ways to build genuine relationships between teachers and students and between students of different linguistic and economic communities.[17] Relationships are fundamental in education. Scott Nearing, himself a graduate of Central Manual Training High School in Philadelphia and later of the Wharton School (University of Pennsylvania), taught in several schools, including the Philadelphia School for Social Work. Of that teaching experience, he wrote: "With several hundred new students each year it is difficult to establish and maintain personal relations, which are an essential feature of all good teaching. However, I always tried to know students personally, as well as in class ... such contacts are time-consuming but vital."[18] Nearing, as a university teacher, could meet with his students in the evening in a social setting, but the option is not usually available to high school teachers. We should think instead about continuity – keeping teachers and students together for more than one year so that relations of care, trust, and open dialogue can be established.

Teachers are more than instructors. If we believe that the only function of teachers is to instruct, it would make sense to do that work through technology, using the most effective programs and model instructors. But a *teacher* serves as an intellectual model, as a sympathetic advisor, as a moral guide, as a companion in social conversation. This theme – that teachers are more than instructors – will pervade the discussion throughout this book. Good teachers, like parents, build supportive relationships with their students. In one of his novels, Alexander McCall Smith notes a conversation between a parent and a teacher, both deeply concerned about the future of children with whom they live: "The teacher fiddled with a piece of paper: Looking after thirty children meant that you gave thirty hostages to fortune. A parent's heart may be broken once, maybe twice or thrice; as a teacher your heart could be broken thirty times."[19]

Every teacher has a responsibility to help students acquire standard English. Constant, gentle correction should be accompanied by continual invitations to speak, not simply to listen. Just as conversation is fundamental in the informal education provided at home, so it should be in schools – in classes, school government, social activities, and extracurricular activities of all sorts. Such universal emphasis on standard language does not imply scorn for either native languages or the charming variations in intonation that characterize regional dialects. By the high school years, students might engage in enjoyable episodes of code-switching that demonstrate not only the beauty of dialect but also how some things are more effectively conveyed in dialect than in formal English. Note, however, that one cannot engage in code-switching if one does not know both languages. Note also that one can do well in this society with just one of the languages, the highly favored standard English.

The issue of learning standard English is especially important for African-American students. This is a central active issue in both vocational and academic education. John Baugh has pointed out clearly and convincingly that "many educators (and politicians) underestimate the significance of linguistic barriers that impede academic progress among students for whom Standard American English is not native."[20] His advice underscores the concern I am expressing here: "Let us acknowledge the importance of respecting our students' home language while at the same time motivating them to employ professional linguistic norms to their economic benefit."[21] It is important, however, that we work on both the teaching of Standard English and the respect that should be shown to nonstandard speakers. While I was rereading this paragraph, the dreadful killing of an unarmed black man and its aftermath in protests arose in Ferguson, Missouri. In one confrontation, a white man shouted at a black man, "Why don't you learn English?" As educators, we should want to ask this man why he does not learn to respect his fellow citizens. We have to work steadily on both projects.

Before leaving this topic, it is important to assure readers that I am not arguing against the maintenance of native languages. On the contrary, research has convincingly shown that continued use of a rich native language together with growing competence in English enhances educational experience. As Sonia Nieto has pointed out, "In the United States, attitudes about languages and language varieties other than the mainstream language have oscillated between grudging acceptance and outright hostility."[22] The effective use of more than one language should be celebrated, not denied. I am arguing against impoverished language, that is, linguistic practice that employs a small, nonstandard vocabulary. James Comer cites a study showing that "a group of children from nonmainstream families were exposed to 30 million fewer words than the children of college professors" by three years of age.[23] It is this sort of language deprivation together with the lack of standard English that should be remedied, and several suggestions for doing this appear in the next section and in following chapters.

THE ROLE OF MIDDLE SCHOOLS

Middle school might be the ideal place to introduce students to the vocational possibilities they should consider. I am not suggesting that students should make a definitive decision about their future vocational lives at this stage; they are too young for such a decision. The idea is to make them aware of possibilities. Some years ago, in a discussion with Detroit teachers, I was told that many of their students had never known anyone who held down a full-time job. How can we expect children to believe that what they are learning in school will someday help them to make a living when they have no first-hand knowledge of vocational life and what it might entail? Too often we design each level of schooling as preparation for the next with little or no attention to the whole enterprise and its connection to life itself.

In the past – and often still today – the middle school years have been used as part of the great sorting project. These are the years when school authorities have decided who is and who is not academically fit for college preparation. At the other extreme, in righteous indignation at past sorting practices, educators and policy makers today simply push everyone into academic courses, ignoring the fact that many children have no real sense of why these required courses might be useful. The message seems to be that one must go to college or be nothing.

Middle school should be a wonderful period of exploration. Every middle school should have kitchens, shops, gardens, pets in well-housed spaces, and art and music studios, where students can work together in a broad set of activities. In each of these areas, professional workers should be invited regularly to talk with students about their work. If possible, the professional workers invited to speak should have command of standard language. At least, we should have regular discussions with our students about the judgments that are so often made on the basis of oral language. In one of Ruth Rendell's wonderful mystery novels, two characters discuss how easy it is, usually, to distinguish "middle-class mums from the working-class ones" by appearance. They comment on the fact that their cleaning lady, quite slim and elegant, is an exception. "You'd have taken her for a doctor's wife." "Until she opened her mouth," responded her companion.[24] Everyone is aware of the judgments we make on the basis of language, and yet educators insist on trying to change the judgment instead of removing the difference on which it is based. As pointed out above, we should work on both. Once again, the theme of collegiality arises. Teachers and workers from a variety of vocational fields should meet regularly to discuss how they can cooperate to encourage standard oral language.

In addition to a generous introduction to a variety of occupations, students should also be introduced to rigorous academic possibilities. Should all students be forced in high school to take formal courses in algebra, geometry, and calculus? No. But in middle school, they should be required – risk-free – to explore the core concepts of academic mathematics. By "risk-free" I mean no grades or high-stakes testing. This is to be an interval of exploration, loaded with both challenges and opportunities for the development of native talent. Will this arrangement, in effect, reinstitute the sorting process to which we rightly object? It will certainly help students to discover what they might be good at and thus, in a healthy way, lead to self-sorting by interests and talents. The aim is to help students make wise choices at each stage in their school careers. It is also to advance the democratic education of our students. In a true democracy, all forms of honest work are respected, and *choice* is cherished. To become wise choice-makers, children must be guided at every opportunity to make age-appropriate decisions.

The decisions we are considering here are not once-and-forever decisions. It should be possible for students to change programs midstream. Must we insist that high school be completed in four years? Some interesting experiments are now underway with six-year vocational high schools. More such experimentation should be encouraged. There must be some limit, of course, but if a student decides after two years in a vocational program that she really wants to prepare for college, she should be allowed to do that in the high school setting, and there should be close coordination with a community college if a joint program can be arranged. As mentioned earlier, a high school vocational program leading to one at the community college level should be both useful and attractive in encouraging further education.

I want to say just a bit more about the centrality and power of choice in democratic education. As a high school math teacher years ago, I allowed students to join my honors geometry class regardless of previous grades if they wanted to do so and understood that the workload would be quite heavy. I can remember only one student who chose to do so; she had a tough time, but she succeeded. Allowing a well-informed choice removes the stigma of authoritarian evaluation, ranking, and assignment to an "upper" or "lower" course. It also puts a heavy responsibility on the student who chooses, and that can be in itself a profoundly educational experience. No student needs to say, "I didn't qualify for that," but simply, "I didn't choose to do that."

A middle school committed to preparation for democratic life might also use some of the practices recommended by Kohlberg's Just Community Schools.[25] A school need not institute the program as a whole or even slavishly copy particular features, but it might usefully employ the practices of class meetings, of regular discussion on moral/social issues, of establishing student reference groups (or partnerships) to support one another in abiding by school rules. Instead of establishing zero-tolerance *rules* and harsh punishments, such schools work toward zero-tolerance *attitudes* aimed at the inclusion of all students in the school community. In employing these practices, the school again recognizes the importance of getting students to participate in dialogue and decision making.

The ideas discussed here are not new. Many of them – and others worth further investigation – were promoted more than three decades ago by John Lounsbury and Gordon Vars in their seminal work on middle school education.[26] Indeed, as Lounsbury and Vars point out, the basic orientation they recommend can be found in the much earlier work of John Dewey and the progressive experimental schools reported in the Eight-Year Study.[27] But despite the enthusiasm of many educators for dramatic changes, the middle schools have actually regressed; they aim today almost entirely at preparation for high school, defined as college preparation, and that means a heavy concentration on instruction and testing. Dewey spoke eloquently against the popular view of education as primarily preparation for some future event or way of life. That we are all, always, in some way preparing for the future Dewey did not deny, but it is the present that "offers so many wonderful opportunities and proffers such invitations to adventure."[28] This is true for all of us, but especially for children. Deploring the tendency to define education entirely as preparation, Dewey wrote: "It is impossible to overestimate the loss which results from the deflection of attention from the strategic point to a comparatively unproductive point. It fails most just where it thinks it is succeeding – in getting a preparation for the future."[29]

When we adopt as a unifying purpose the intention to produce better adults, our attention is focused on individual students, what interests them, what they are capable of doing, how they interact with others, and how they can be encouraged to build community. We do not lay down one detailed description of a better adult and try to squeeze every individual into that mold. If it turns out that we cannot revitalize the middle school as a time of exploration, we must still try to broaden what we offer in our high schools. The invitation to explore must be extended.

In this chapter, I have concentrated on careful and appreciative attention to individual differences as a prelude to describing a better adult. In the next chapter, we will look at gender differences. Where might women put emphasis in their description of a better adult?

3

What Might Have Been: Women's Traditional Interests

What might the school curriculum have looked like if women had been involved in its planning from the start? Women are not all alike, of course, and it would be a mistake to suppose that they could be represented by a single, universal mind. Indeed, to build on that supposition would be to repeat the error made by so many men in the past. However, it is undeniable that women lived for centuries under the expectation that they would spend their lives maintaining a family and household. In the "best" homes and families, girls learned *at home* how to manage this challenging work. But how should these "best" homes be described? Just as we must continually deepen our exploration of what should be meant by a "better adult," we must similarly examine the nature of "best homes." If we can discover some powerful possibilities, it would make sense to include this information in the school curriculum.

There is a great emphasis today on the connection between poverty and education, and it is often assumed that schools could be more effective if something were done to alleviate poverty. This is almost certainly true. However, it should be worthwhile to explore the idea that educating for better home life might contribute not only to a reduction in poverty but to the greater effectiveness of schools in teaching the standard curriculum. The single most important factor in determining children's success in school is almost certainly the quality of their parenting, and yet we teach little or nothing in our schools about parenting. A whole chapter (Chapter 5) will be devoted to this topic. What else about home life should appear in the school curriculum?

HOUSEKEEPING

It is not unusual for thoughtful critics to poke a bit of fun at neatness. Witold Rybczynski, for example, writes: "Hominess is not neatness. Otherwise everyone would live in replicas of the kinds of sterile and impersonal homes that appear in interior-design and architectural magazines."[1] He goes on to describe the condition of his own study and writing desk: "covered three-deep with a jumble of half-opened books, encyclopedias, dictionaries, magazines, sheets of paper, and newspaper clippings." He follows this with a long paragraph listing the "many personal mementos, photographs and objects" that fill his study.[2] But notice that he *has* a study in which to pile up his treasures.

Contrast Rybczynski's account of somewhat messy but productivehominess with Andrea Elliott's description of a family – mother, step-father, and eight young children – living for three years in a city-run shelter for the homeless.[3] They are all crammed into one large room with no privacy dividers. They must share bathroom facilities with other residents; the bathrooms are filthy and at night so dangerous that the family keeps a pot in a corner of their room for nighttime emergencies. Clothes and other belongings are heaped in corners and under beds. Obviously, there is no available place for the kids to do homework or for the parents to keep accounts in order. Where would one keep a jumble of half-opened books or any books at all?

The longing for order pervades human experience. Norman Crowe notes: "Historically the idea of our constant search for order in both the man-made world and nature runs counter to the empiricist views, most convincingly argued by John Locke, that our minds are *tabulae rasae* to be filled with sense impressions and cultural information."[4] Crowe's point is that humans are so constituted that we seek order, but, just as important, we need it. We could not seek order in science, beauty in art, rational expression in philosophy without some order in our daily lives. The order provided by a place set aside for study, for example, frees us from the compulsive pursuit of order in everyday things. The unfortunate residents in the city-run shelter described by Elliott are never free of an ineffective flailing about for order.

We get a sense of what women might have wanted in the school curriculum by studying what they produced when they were finally able to put their thoughts into writing. Without rejecting the important tasks of homemaking, they set out to make those tasks more manageable. Gail Collins quotes Jane Addams as saying that "women could not fulfill the two functions of profession and homemaking until modern invention had made a new type of housekeeping practicable."[5] One cannot pursue order in the wider physical and political world until one has achieved or been given order in one's immediate living space. While maintaining an open-door policy at Hull-House, which certainly contributed to an atmosphere of constant change, Addams also insisted on the provision of places and moments for contemplation.[6] Her dedication to increasing respect for women's traditional work is captured in her admiration for "bread-givers," the name given to Saxon ladies who gave bread to their household workers. I will return to the work of Addams in a later discussion of peace, critical thinking, and religion. Her thoughts on all of these topics reveal an exquisite sense of intellectual and practical balance.

Powerful women writers before and after Addams took up the dual task of increasing respect for women's work and removing much of its drudgery. In the mid-nineteenth century, Catherine Beecher produced *A Treatise on Domestic Economy*, a book designed both to honor women's traditional work as housekeepers and also to make that work more efficient. Gail Collins remarks on Beecher's work:

> [S]he fought all her life to elevate women's position by raising the stature of housework.

> She argued that the wives who were charged with educating the nation's children . . . had to be prepared for the job – preferably in an excellent boarding school that taught philosophy, chemistry, astronomy, botany, geology, mineralogy, and moral philosophy in the afternoon and washing, sewing, and cooking in the morning.[7]

Beecher was interested not only in the daily tasks of housekeeping but also in the practical aspects of home design. Unlike most male architects, who often totally neglected the role of women's work in homes, Beecher gave practical attention to sanitation, ventilation, and the placement of stoves, closets, shelves, and work surfaces. With her sister, Harriet Beecher Stowe, she designed a small, affordable model house that "managed to provide space for eight persons in less than twelve hundred square feet, not ignoring generous closets and storage space."[8] She was indeed ahead of her time.

In the early twentieth century, several women contributed to the growing interest in an efficiency engineering movement by applying those ideas to domestic engineering. Christine Frederick, Mary Pattison, and Lillian Gilbreth studied, conducted, and wrote about efficiency experiments on kitchen and other housekeeping tasks. Commenting on the contributions of these remarkable women, Rybczynski writes: "Anyone who works comfortably at the kitchen counter, or takes dishes out of a dishwasher and places them in a convenient overhead shelf, or dusts the house in an hour, not a day, owes something to the domestic engineers."[9]

Today's students may be especially fascinated by the story of Lillian Gilbreth – told in the film *Cheaper by the Dozen* – who worked with her husband, Frank, as an industrial engineer. She raised twelve children, wrote books on household efficiency, and took over much of Frank's work when he died. Her story makes vividly clear the dual purpose of women's active involvement in improving the efficiency of housework: to promote genuine respect for that work and to reduce the drudgery associated with it.

From an educational perspective, it is interesting to note that the efficiency movement has been more successful in its second objective – removing drudgery – than in its first. Household work is still often shunned and poorly paid. For many women, the hard-won efficiencies have meant freedom to engage in work outside the home; men helping out with domestic tasks rarely have an appreciative understanding of what that work contributes to family peace, order, and companionship.

It is clear that if women had been involved in designing the school curriculum from the beginning, some material on housekeeping would have been included. Would that material have aimed at the deeper meaning embedded in the idea of housekeeping, or would it have been a sort of "how to do it" curriculum? Might it have dealt with the larger search for order and the contribution made by good housekeeping? It is impossible to say. Some home economics courses – for girls – did appear in the curriculum for a while, but they remained unconnected to the universal search for order.[10] For that matter, however, the same criticism can be fairly directed at the whole curriculum – heavy emphasis on knowing-that, a bit of knowing-how, almost nothing on knowing-why or the sort of knowing-about that piques curiosity, and a further search for the other forms of knowing.

Can such inclusion be accomplished today? A main point of this book is that, while exploring possibilities, we have to accept realities. Almost certainly, the basic structure of the high school curriculum will not change. Indeed, if the last few decades are predictive of the future, the curriculum will become more deeply and fully mired in academic standards and their measurement by tests. We can, however, recommend that each discipline be carefully examined for what it might contribute to the topic at hand, housekeeping. Obviously, material such as that mentioned in the last few pages should be included in the historical accounts provided in social studies courses, but that could easily deteriorate into another set of facts to be memorized. As we consider possibilities for each discipline, we see a prominent role for disciplinary specialists, but that role is not the traditional one of defining their subject more deeply and narrowly. On the contrary, the challenge is to stretch the discipline and to show how it can be connected to other disciplines and to the real-life subject at hand.

As a philosopher, I would like students to read a bit of Gaston Bachelard's *Poetics of Space*. The house, or dwelling place, is central to human life. Bachelard writes: "The house shelters daydreaming, the house protects the dreamer, the house allows one to dream in peace..."[11] How might the children living in cramped city shelters respond to this? Bachelard goes on: "In the life of a man, the house thrusts aside contingencies, its councils of continuity are unceasing. Without it, man would be a dispersed being. It maintains him through the storms of the heavens and through those of life... It is the human being's first world..."[12]

But philosophy is rarely offered at the high school level, and even if it were, it would be unusual to suggest Bachelard as an introductory author. However, we have another audience to consider: the teachers of our high school students. These people should read and discuss material on the central importance of the house in human life. What makes a house into a home? How does order in the home contribute to the search for order in the wider world? How are the lives of children affected by the sort of conditions described by Elliott? Bachelard writes about the lasting effects of childhood homes: "In how many tales of childhood – if tales of childhood were sincere – we should be told of a child that, lacking a room, went and sulked in his corner! But over and beyond our memories, the house we were born in is physically inscribed in us. It is a group of organic habits."[13] If Bachelard is right on this, we should be very worried about the organic habits inscribed by life in miserable public shelters. Can teachers do anything to encourage a healthier, more orderly set of organic habits?

Bachelard relates all of this to daydreams and poetry. At this point, we must ask how the material we share with teachers can be used in high school classrooms. We need specialists, teachers who are experts in their subjects, to advise us. What can be suggested by English teachers? Science teachers? Art and music teachers?

As a former high school math teacher, I can offer a few suggestions on what might be done with this subject. Quite a lot can be done with consumer mathematics, and it should be pointed out that the household engineers already mentioned had something to say on the topic of household finance.[14] My own preference would be to suggest some ideas on the concept of order. Not only is the concept of order fundamental in mathematics, but its study requires an atmosphere characterized by order. Students need a quiet, orderly place to work. It is useful, too, to encourage them to study their own habits and preferences with respect to time, place, posture, food, drink, and whatever else promotes their effectiveness in study. I might read aloud for them excerpts from Jacque Hadamard's *Psychology of Invention in the Mathematical Field*[15] and encourage them to think about what influence the order in one's daily life might have on mastery of order in various fields of study. Hadamard was interested in different approaches to mathematical thinking, but he also asked questions about daily working habits such as a preference for morning or evening, before or after exercise, and the effects of diet. Here is a sample of his questions: "Does one work better standing, seated or lying down; at the blackboard or on paper; to what extent is one disturbed by outside noises; can one pursue a problem while walking or in a train; how do stimulants or sedatives (tobacco, coffee, alcohol, etc.) affect the quality and quantity of one's work?"[16]

In addition to encouraging students to think about their own work spaces and habits, some may want to follow up by reading Hadamard, and then E. T. Bell's *Men of Mathematics*, and – who knows? – perhaps even Paul Hoffman's *The Man Who Loved Only Numbers*. Or, inspired by Hadamard's discussion of Mozart's creativity, others may want to explore ideas on order in music, art, science, and literature. Perhaps a few might try Douglas Hofstadter's *Gödel, Escher, Bach: An Eternal Golden Braid*. How many of today's math teachers could direct such reading? This will be a central concern in Chapter 11, on teacher preparation.

More generally, in our attempts to introduce topics related to housekeeping, is there any possibility that we could change the configuration of our schools to allow time for work in kitchens and household shops? We find accounts of such arrangements in work on holistic education,[17] and I will say more about the possibilities in Chapter 9, on the physical design of schools. It is unlikely, however, that any such accommodations will be made in our high schools, and even where shops and kitchens are provided, they will rarely be used for the general education of all students. Education for home life is simply not a high priority in American education. Paradoxically, we know that many children do poorly in the subjects that are offered, in part, at least, because they are deprived of the resources derived from the material we refuse to teach.

Whatever we decide – if educators and policy makers can even be induced to think about it – we should avoid succumbing to "how to do it" approaches on the one hand and complete neglect of all the study of homemaking as a dull duty to be shared by both men and women. It can be a wonderful theme in itself for interdisciplinary study or it can be a substantial part of a larger theme on order. Beneath the tedium and hard labor of housekeeping lies its undeniable support for happy home life and for the universal search for order. How can we sustain this without glorifying the subordination of housekeeping to all other occupations?

The writing of Virginia Woolf captures the ambivalence experienced by women in the last century or so. Mrs. Ramsay, the beautiful mother/ homemaker in Woolf's *To the Lighthouse*, became an icon of virtue to many readers and a symbol of female negation to others.[18] If Woolf has portrayed Mrs. Ramsay as almost a goddess of home and hearth, she paints a very different picture of women's subordination and deprivation in *A Room of One's Own* where she describes the semi-fictional writer Mary Carmichael, struggling against all odds to write. Woolf sympathizes: "Give her another hundred years ... give her a room of her own and five hundred a year, let her speak her mind and leave out half that she now puts in, and she will write a better book one of these days."[19]

What shows up vividly in Woolf's work is the basic thesis that educators should find a way to acknowledge and develop: that an orderly home life stripped of drudgery is the foundation for creativity in the wider world. There is no need to sanctify the homemaker as one who must make enormous sacrifices, but there is a need to recognize the sanctity of the well-ordered house.

Ideally, we would have a home-like kitchen and home shop in each of our high schools, and we would have occasional lessons in each of these. Without offering detailed how-to-do-it courses in housekeeping, we would acknowledge the importance of these tasks. More important, we would ask our disciplinary specialists to suggest material in their own subject matter to contribute to the theme of homemaking in order to establish connections between the disciplines and everyday life.[20] As we think about how to do this, we should remember that the order of an orderly house is not fascistic order aimed at the support of domination; rather, it is order that provides peace in the household and freedom for its residents to engage in chosen activities in both house and larger world. *Peace* is another topic that many women would like to see more deeply explored in our schools.

PEACE

The connection between a safe and stable home life and community and world peace has been noted by many female writers. Virginia Woolf, for example, in responding to a man's request for ideas on how to prevent war, starts her response by suggesting that they both look at the same photograph from war-torn Spain. "For now at last we are looking at the same picture: we are seeing with you the same dead bodies, the same ruined houses."[21] She notes that she and her correspondent may even use the same words to describe what they see. "War, you say, is an abomination; a barbarity; war must be stopped at whatever cost. And we echo your words."[22] But at the end of her response, Woolf sadly remarks on the enormous difference between the lives of educated men and those of their wives and daughters. For Woolf and many other women, the figure of a uniformed man – replete with weapons, medals, and military posture – arises like a ghostly monster from the photograph of dead bodies and ruins, and that image produces very different emotions:

> For it suggests a connection and for us [the daughters of educated men] a very important connection. It suggests that the public and the private worlds are inseparably connected; that the tyrannies and servilities of the one are the tyrannies and servilities of the other... It suggests that we cannot dissociate ourselves from that figure but are ourselves that figure...[23]

Woolf concludes, not at all optimistically, that women can best help men prevent war "not by repeating your words and following your methods but by finding new words and creating new methods."[24] Notice, however, that she recognizes women's complicity in the perpetuation of war – the military figure is "ourselves." If, for example, we use the traditional male language of equality and freedom to remove tyrannies and servilities, we might well free women from the subordination and drudgery of house-keeping; we might achieve for women equality in the public world. But, at the same time, we might well undermine Woolf's project to eliminate war. Today, for example, some women clamor for the right to participate in military combat. It is this sort of perversion that Woolf feared. She wants us to think of and speak of "peace," not just the prevention of war. High school students should at least be made aware of the differences in thinking and speaking that Woolf points out. However, we will leave open for continuing analysis whether the image of the heroic warrior should figure at all in our search for a better adult.

Woolf is not alone. The domestic engineers discussed in the previous section also wanted to emphasize the connection between order and stability in the home and peace in the wider world. Jane Addams, too, pressed for the deeper meaning of home and house that we have been addressing here:

> Like other social feminists, she infused domesticity with a wider moral and social meaning, finding in it a way to serve others and to enact

citizenship. Social feminism stressed the importance of women's ties to the wellsprings of tradition and extolled the centrality of family and children in women's lives; but the domestic arena was seen as a springboard into wider civic life rather than an inhibition to matters civic.[25]

In the quest for peace, Woolf sought a new language and new practices that included abstinence from the entire masculine/military tradition. Addams, more mildly, recommended patient and open dialogue with opponents. I will say more about Addams's generous approach to those with whom she differed in a later discussion of critical thinking. Although Woolf's views seem entirely justified given the horrors of the age in which she lived, we shudder at the depth of her despair. With Addams, we hope to find the courage to persist in dialogue and to reflect on our own views.

More recently, Sara Ruddick has provided us with a view that connects the quest for peace with maternal thinking. She describes the best maternal practice as encompassing "four ideals of nonviolence – renunciation, resistance, reconciliation, and peacekeeping."[26] Like Addams and contemporary care theorists, Ruddick strives for reconciliation as well as nonviolent resistance and firm renunciation of violence. The four ideals serve as a structure for maternal order and global peace.

What can schools do to promote the ideals of peace? This question will be explored from several angles in the chapters that follow. It is not an easy task. We know from past experience that the traditional language and patriotic practices so deplored by Woolf are enormously powerful. One can say a bit about pacifism and nonviolence when there is no war in progress, but once war is under way, any such talk is severely castigated. Woolf knew this, and Addams suffered public criticism when she spoke out against World War I; pacifists in general have often been accused of cowardice and even treason.[27]

We, like Addams, have to keep trying. Years ago when I was teaching a calculus class, the topic of radioactive decay came up, and a student made several remarks about the atomic bombings of Hiroshima and Nagasaki. It was morally wrong, he said, to kill so many civilians. The class went silent briefly, and then I quietly asked, "How many is it all right to kill?" We did not pursue it, but I hope the question nagged at them.

We must find a way to introduce such questions and the material that peace advocates have promoted, but we have to use methods that avoid indoctrination. On this, I agree with Addams, who was always ready to listen – to seek reconciliation – even when she felt strongly about an issue. Her expressed sympathy, even admiration, for the uneducated farmers (with whom she disagreed) who appeared at the Scopes evolution trial is characteristic. She demonstrated a dedication to both reform and reconciliation.[28] American educators, however, have not always rejected indoctrination. For many years, it was acceptable to indoctrinate the basic ideas of Christianity. Now, having rejected that indoctrination, some critics claim that the schools have turned 180 degrees and are now waging a war against Christmas and Christians. We have not found a rational, generous, Addams-type approach to talking about a controversial topic without authoritatively endorsing one side or the other. In the mid-twentieth century, George Counts, in a dedicated effort to promote social justice, actually advocated indoctrination in that cause.[29] He argued that we should get over our aversion to imposition and indoctrination when our cause is well justified. With Addams and Dewey, I think that to do so would be a great mistake – a betrayal of the very idea of education.

We can teach about controversial topics – giving all sides their due by presenting their cases accurately – and even confess our own position without insisting that students adopt it. Teachers, as I pointed out in the previous chapter, are not simply instructors. Rather, they should be models of intellectual practice. As such, they can endorse a view and still insist on a fair hearing for the opposition. Both the evidence and the argument may change in the future. Isaiah Berlin put it this way:

> Principles are not less sacred because their duration cannot be guaranteed. Indeed, the very desire for guarantees that our values are eternal and secure in some objective heaven is perhaps only a craving for the certainties of childhood or the absolute values of our primitive past. "To realize the relative validity of one's convictions ... and yet stand for them unflinchingly, is what distinguishes a civilized man from a barbarian." To demand more than this is perhaps a deep and incurable metaphysical need; but to allow it to determine one's practice is a symptom of an equally deep, more dangerous, moral and political immaturity.[30]

The line quoted by Berlin above is, I think, from Joseph Schumpeter. Students might find it interesting to check on this.

We have so far considered two huge topics of central importance to women's lives and thinking, but there is another on which, it can be argued, women should have spoken out strongly. Even those who have spoken out courageously on homemaking, slavery, voting, and pacifism have been reluctant to speak out on male-dominated religious practice. We turn to that topic next.

RELIGION

It was hard work (and still is hard work) for social feminists to elevate the stature of housekeeping while, simultaneously, trying to promote opportunities for women in the public world, and it has always been hard for women to oppose war and violence. To say anything in opposition to established religion was to invite rebellion among one's own supporters. Elizabeth Cady Stanton dismayed her colleagues in the work for women's franchise by speaking openly in favor of changes in the dogma of institutional religion. At her eightieth birthday celebration in New York (1895), her speech included these words:

> Nothing that has ever emanated from the brain of man is too sacred to be revised and corrected. Our National Constitution has been amended fifteen times, our English system of jurisprudence has been essentially modified in the interest of woman to keep pace with advancing civilization. And now the time has come to amend and modify the canon laws, prayer-books, liturgies and Bible... Woman's imperative duty at this hour is to demand a thorough revision of creeds and codes, Scriptures and constitutions.[31]

Her audience, it was noted, was "restive." Her colleagues were understandably afraid that her criticism of traditional religion would impede their campaign for women's voting rights, but Stanton did not give way. Shortly after the birthday celebration, the first volume of her *Woman's Bible* was published, and Stanton reveled in the anger of clergy but suffered from the alienation of her feminist colleagues. Might we ask students today – as part of the new emphasis on doing research – to find out and report what Stanton wrote that so enraged the clergy? Almost certainly, even today, teachers would be sharply criticized if they *introduced* paragraphs from Stanton's work. Requiring students to read material that claims to destroy the foundation of Christian theology would likely be forbidden. But perhaps students can find it and be encouraged to discuss it rationally.

And what role has religion played in the conduct of science? It is often thought that science and religion have always been in opposition. (We think here of Darwin and Bishop Wilberforce, of Galileo and the Church.) But the development of a male clerical culture and a culture of Western science that virtually excluded women worked together to produce a "world without women."[32] How did this develop, and were there episodes in history when women had more influence? How, for example, did scientists react to the increase of intellectual interest among women in the late nineteenth and early twentieth centuries? Are there potential setbacks that we should be aware of today?

Topics in religion are difficult to handle in schools. In part, the difficulty arises from centuries of schooling in which indoctrination was not only accepted but prescribed. In the initial discussion on unity of purpose, I noted that education was for many years unified by theology. For American public schools, that day is over. Yet the topics – religion itself and its connection to other areas of life – remain of vital importance. Exploring possibilities, we should keep in mind several points stressed throughout this book: choice of curriculum topics through themes, connecting the disciplines, teachers as intellectual models, and the importance of teaching as raising awareness, not simply inculcating facts and skills.

We teach *about* certain topics in order to make students aware of them, to provide the motivation for active study and investigation. I have often advocated such an approach. The teacher makes a comment, shares a story, asks a rhetorical question, or provides a list of topics from which students may choose for further study. Here we are concerned with the relation between women and religion, a huge topic. But we can approach it as we did housekeeping and peace. What have prominent female writers said about the topic? What should be included in the school curriculum and how?

In discussing the women's suffrage movement, for example, we might encourage students to explore some related topics in depth. I have already mentioned Elizabeth Cady Stanton and her *Woman's Bible*. Some students might want to learn more about women's objections to various characters and ideas in the Bible. English teachers might suggest that students read Pearl Buck's biography of her mother, *The Exile*. Reflecting on the harm done to her mother, Carie, by the religious tradition in which her father (Carie's husband) served as a preacher, Buck writes: "Since those days when I saw all her nature dimmed I have hated Saint Paul with all my heart and so must all true women hate him, I think, because of what he has done in the past to women like Carie, proud, free-born women, yet damned by their very womanhood."[33]

But not all women hate St. Paul, and not all are eager to replace the military and religious order so feared by Woolf and Stanton with the home-order described by Beecher and Gilbreth or with Ruddick's maternal thinking exercised at the global level. I would still argue that students should hear the criticisms voiced against the ideas and practices of traditional, male-dominated religions. Becoming aware of these criticisms, reflecting on them, is surely part of learning to think critically. But this material should be balanced with views that accept and find comfort in the traditional order. When topics in peace education are discussed, for example, the work of Dorothy Day will be mentioned, and at that time teachers might make students aware of her religious dedication and refer them to her biographical story.[34] Similarly, when we discuss Simone Weil's powerful essay on the *Iliad*, we might say a bit about her religious beliefs and direct interested students to her writing in that area.[35]

If a school is intellectually liberal enough to offer a course in the history of religion, it will be easy to list supplementary readings and topics, and certainly "women and religion" should be one of those topics. If no such course is likely to be offered, an interdisciplinary faculty group might suggest themes to be considered in each subject, for example, women and serpents, goddess religions, witches and the witch craze, women's intellectual life and religion, Christian socialism, women and evil, the legacy of Adam and Eve, and religious myths. Regular meetings of such faculty groups will promote the intellectual growth of teachers and help to ensure that individual faculty members are not engaging in indoctrination or overzealous promotion of controversial views.

Not all of these topics will be addressed by every discipline, and the topics may well change from year to year. Further, they should be exempt from testing. Students will not be required to repeat what Pearl Buck said about St. Paul, what Stanton said about revision of the Bible, or what Merlin Stone wrote about the Serpent Goddess.[36] The tasks undertaken by students within each topic will be judged on a basis suitable for that task: thoroughness of research, quality of the report, balance in treating controversies, and connection to other parts of the curriculum.

There are several obvious difficulties in launching such a program. First, we live in an intellectually impoverished era of American education. Too many of us have come to believe that everything to be taught and learned must be specified and tested. We need to criticize this movement more strongly and effectively. Some things should, of course, be tested, but many of the most important goals of education should be subjected to more powerful methods of evaluation, and we will discuss this in some depth in Chapter 10. In the meantime, instead of worrying that the material discussed in this chapter will distract teachers from the contents of the standard, to-be-tested curriculum, we should worry that the present concentration on standardization and testing is distracting us from the real enterprise of education.

The second great difficulty is that most American secondary school teachers are not prepared to do this work. The faculty groups mentioned above will contribute to continuous teacher growth, but – even to get started – far better teacher preparation will be required. I noted this problem more than twenty years ago:

> Most teachers today are not prepared to conduct the kinds of exploration I have described. But they could be. High school teachers should be what we once called "renaissance people"; that is, at an appropriate level, they should know a great deal about most of the subjects taught in secondary schools and, in addition, should be acquainted with a vast volume of connected material. This sort of breadth could be achieved if the undergraduate preparation of teachers was frankly aimed at preparing teachers.[37]

We will return to this important topic in Chapter 11. By "preparing teachers" I mean preparing them intellectually in a breadth of subject matter, not only in pedagogy.

In this chapter and the preceding one, the focus has been on the variety of educational needs that arise when we consider the host of differences in talents and interests between individuals, genders, and people with varying religious and philosophical allegiances. Special attention was given to the idea of *order* – the forms of order that nurture full life at both the individual and public levels and the forms of order that support domination and a diminishment of life for many. This exploration should provide a broad background for further analysis of what we might mean by a "better adult." It certainly suggests that all of the aspects of human life should be examined in our search for that better adult, but it also warns that some features are contentious.

4

A Better Adult: Continuing the Search

I have suggested that producing a better adult might serve as a unifying purpose for education. What should we mean by a "better adult"? So far, we have looked at two aspects of human life to explore as we consider what makes people "better": vocation and homemaking. What follows in this chapter should be construed not as a prescription but, rather, as an invitation to think, reflect, and engage in a continuing dialogue – a never-ending, vibrant examination of what we mean by a "better adult" and by "education."

It is important to remember that we are *not* seeking to construct one saintly ideal that will serve as a model of that better adult. In Chapters 2 and 3, on vocational education and women's interests, respectively, the variety of human interests and talents was emphasized, and that variety should continue to influence our search for a way to describe better adults. What may properly be thought of as universal is the whole range of categories that constitute human life and that we seek to enhance through education: moral, physical, emotional, intellectual, aesthetic, social, home/family, vocational, civic, and spiritual. In this chapter, we continue the search by examining three areas of education that contribute substantially to the development of better adults: command of the fundamental processes, education for citizenship, and moral education.

COMMAND OF THE FUNDAMENTAL PROCESSES

In today's postindustrial society, it is obvious that command of some basic knowledge and skills is essential. For many years, the fundamental processes were known as the 3Rs, and these were the skills to be addressed in elementary schooling. Today we would have to add certain technological skills, and I have suggested also that we should add oral language, or "speaking." As pointed out earlier, inability to speak grammatical English can be a handicap comparable to the inability to read a newspaper or to manipulate the numbers involved in daily life. An acceptable level of oral language should certainly be regarded as one of the fundamental processes.

It is generally supposed that the command of fundamental processes is to be achieved in elementary school. When it is not, the deficiency should be remedied at the middle school. But this book is about high schools, and we cannot deny that some children – probably a substantial number – reach high school with glaring deficiencies in all of the fundamental processes. Indeed, some even enter college with those deficiencies. We should be committed to doing something about this widespread failure. But what should we do?

When obvious academic deficiencies are discovered at the level of college admission, our attitudes and recommendations vary. Some argue that many of today's college applicants should not be going to college at all, and I have already agreed that vocational programs should be expanded. Others direct their criticism – even outrage – at the high schools that produce deficient graduates. These critics may or may not suggest remedies beyond "holding teachers accountable." Still others grit their teeth and support colleges in offering a host of remedial courses. Which path should we take?

Consistent with a main point of this book, I think we should listen to advocates of all these positions. Certainly, many students who now insist on enrolling in college would do better to seek vocational preparation elsewhere, and our society should make it a major objective to provide such preparation. However, we should also support our colleges in providing remedial courses in situations where the aspirations of students are compatible with latent abilities and when the deficiencies are demonstrably connected to the goals sought in a program of study.

Of primary concern here is the second reaction to deficiencies in our high school graduates. To the degree that high schools are at fault and should be accountable, what should be done? It is not reasonable to simply blame teachers or to institute more and more testing. And it is ludicrous to suppose that the deficiencies will be somehow removed by establishing higher standards. If we have not figured out how to help students meet the present standards, how will we push them to meet even higher ones? Students should not begin legitimate high school studies with major deficiencies in the fundamental processes. I am not suggesting that we simply redirect our outrage from the high schools to the lower schools. I do think that most of the deficiencies could be and should be eliminated at the middle school level, but we have to face reality. At present, many children enter high school without command of the fundamental processes. We cannot refuse them admission as a college might.

We have to engage in remedial work. In doing so, I think we must also avoid a well-intentioned mistake that seems to infect everything we do in today's education: to insist that everyone can do whatever the school offers in the same length of time and at pretty much the same level of proficiency. With this seemingly generous attitude ("All children can learn!"), we avoid ability-grouping and any overt recognition of the enormous differences in student aptitudes over a wide range of activities. Instead, we might generously, lovingly, help students to understand their own strengths and weaknesses and work realistically with them. Lots of smart people are no good at math. Lots of academically bright people are hopeless at mechanical tasks. There are people who cannot carry a tune, and people who cannot draw. (On the latter, the great mathematician Henri Poincaré might have been rejected for admission at the Polytechnique because he had a score of *zero* on the entrance exam in drawing, and a zero on any of the exams meant disqualification! Fortunately, an enlightened admissions group looked beyond his artistic failings and recognized his extraordinary mathematical talent.[1]) The objective in education should be not to make everyone competent in everything that is offered, but to help students identify and develop their special talents.

But there are fundamental processes at which all students must be at least minimally competent. In addition to the original 3Rs, basic technological skills, and speaking, we should add an understanding of the processes of schooling, of what schools offer and how they operate. It is odd, and very worrisome, that so many high school students know little about what they might learn in high school and how they might advance their education after graduation. Much of this ignorance can be traced to the rapid growth of large high schools in the last half of the twentieth century. Whereas the schools were once integral parts of relatively small communities, they are now large organizations often at some distance from the places where students live. Some of the ignorance, however, is the result of twentieth-century faith in bureaucratic methods and a lack of relational guidance. By "bureaucratic methods" I mean methods guided by the notion that every problem can be assigned to one agency or department and we need only identify the appropriate agency correctly. Other, related groups or agencies do not interfere with the first group's tasks; they, too, do their properly designated tasks. We have hired guidance counselors in our schools who, with far too many students to counsel, are supposed to handle the process of guiding students through high school and on to postsecondary schooling. "Guidance" has become a specialty, and it does not work well for many students. The students who handle this fundamental process best have the support and knowledgeable guidance of parents and teachers who have taken a special interest in them. This is not a criticism of guidance counselors but of the system in which they are forced to work. It would be better if, in addition to the technical operations of helping students with transitions from one level to the next, guidance counselors worked more closely with teachers, helping them to provide the personal and academic advice so needed and valued by students.

The remedial work required in moving from middle school to high school is both essential and badly needed. It might take several forms, and decisions on time, space, and money will have to be made locally. Some schools might provide a full year of remedial/preparatory work. Some might find one or two periods each day sufficient. I would advise against trying to do the remedial work within regular classes because the deficiencies to be remedied are often too large, and it is simply too much for teachers to handle. We are rightly concerned about the stigma of separating students into ability groups, but that does not mean that all separations must be avoided. By providing the suggested preparatory year we avoid the much greater stigma of retention in middle school or, perhaps even worse, likely retention in ninth grade. The school drop-out rate for ninth graders has been notoriously high. A built-in preparatory year should encourage students to continue their studies. Further, the suggested separation is not drastic; prep students would join their peers in physical education, the arts, extracurricular activities, and a universal social studies course that will be described in some detail in Chapter 9.

Consider what the preparatory year might look like. A continuing relationship among the remedial students should be established consisting of no more than twelve students and a teacher who can teach the basic math, reading, speaking, and tech skills. These teachers will act as parents/teachers for the students in their groups. The relationship should continue throughout the group's high school years with, perhaps, weekly meetings after the initial, preparatory year.

There should be a continuing emphasis on discussion, on learning the language of what Payne refers to as the "formal register." Students should be encouraged to ask questions about all of the fundamental processes – especially those of the school – and they should also be allowed to comment on their own progress: what helps them, what discourages them, and what they would like to learn. All of the subject matter might be enriched by the thematic and connective material discussed throughout this book. Remedial work should not be "nose to the grindstone" drill. Instead, there could be games, stories, and projects – all sorts of projects across the disciplines. If the schools were indeed at fault in the earlier years, this preparatory year might be thought of as compensatory – an educational apology of sorts.

Assessments should be nonpunitive and used formatively, and teachers and students should be encouraged to assess their progress informally. An important factor in the improvement of learning is an increasing ability to assess one's own mastery, and certainly a vital skill for teachers is competence in making judgments about students' progress. Occasionally, standardized tests might be used as confirmation of what good teachers and well-informed students already know, and, of course, the results should be used to support the continued development of the preparatory year.

In addressing the fundamental processes, as in pursuing the other aims listed, we are guided by those larger aims that pervade all we do under the unifying purpose of producing better adults. When a social or moral problem arises, it should be addressed. Students should be encouraged to talk regularly about what they owe to each other, to their school, to their communities. When an opportunity arises to deepen the intellectual exploration of a topic, it should be pursued with enthusiasm. Teachers should watch for and embrace opportunities to discuss matters associated with the aesthetic and spiritual.

Social life in high school is closely related to the civic life of our better adults, and guidance in school life should be regarded as significant preparation for life in adult communities. There is more to education than learning the material in a curriculum, and the preparatory/remedial year should reflect the breadth and depth of our commitment to education as both life itself and preparation for a full future life.

CIVIC AND SOCIAL LIFE

Probably everyone agrees that a good citizen is one feature of the better adult we seek to produce, but there has long been some contention over what constitutes a good citizen. Of particular concern to educators are questions about the nature and extent of knowledge required of good citizens. Every now and then (increasingly often, it seems), polls or surveys reveal an astonishing ignorance among adult Americans about the history and governmental structure of their country. With each such revelation, critics assail the schools for failing to teach essential facts. But the sad truth is that schools *do* teach most of the material over which critics lament. It is taught, "learned," and soon forgotten – very like grammatical oral language is "forgotten" by those whose home culture does not embrace it. For some reason, this material holds little meaning for many students.

One possible reason that much school material seems meaningless to many students is that they feel it has nothing to do with their present or future lives. They are not participants in the events and activities described. The same evaluation can be made of many of our social programs outside schools. Consider the example mentioned earlier – that of a large family living in a shabby, crowded city shelter for the homeless. In that case, the problems were certainly not meaningless for the homeless. They were suffering the problems directly, but they were left out of the process of seeking solutions. Those in authority deplore the conditions and demand that they be improved. They "care about" the victims, but they find it difficult to move from this "caring about" to the "caring for" required for effective change.

Caring-about, or concern, is commendable at the policy level. In all large organizations, genuine concern aimed at positive change begins at an authoritative policy level. Agitation, expressions of discontent, and protests may trigger the needed concern, but the process of actual change begins at the policy level. The challenge, then, is to move from caring-about to practical caring-for where such care is needed. But caring-for is a person-to-person activity, and it requires the establishment of caring relations on site. Schools, like other organizations, often try to accomplish changes at the level of caring-about. Those in authority, even with the best intentions, make decisions based on the assumed needs of their clients or students and fail to establish the relations in which *expressed* needs can be heard, negotiated, and acted on. Those in need of care are left out of deliberations on what is to be done.

The residents of the city shelter, for example, should have been involved in setting priorities for improvement, and they could have been invited to help themselves by appointing committees to patrol the hallways and bathrooms and, perhaps, to paint and clean some of the rooms. Without their active participation, the lines of authority remain firm, and those in need are merely recipients of "care" that does not feel like care. This way of operating, familiar at local, national, and global levels, consolidates the lines of power. To promote genuine democracy, there must be near-universal participation.

Democratic participation should not require participants to give up their group identification. As Kenneth Howe has argued, they should not be put in the position "of either giving up who they are or forgoing full membership in the democratic public and the other goods that go with it."[2] Students should not have to give up or hide their race, sexual orientation, or cultural background. Participatory democracy *is* democracy. I have argued that all students in our schools should have command of grammatical oral English, and I stand by this. But that requirement does not imply that students should give up a native language or entirely abandon a cultural or regional dialect. The habit of participation should be encouraged in schools, and the mistakes often made in social programs where decisions are made at the policy level – the level of caring-about – should be avoided.

Today most decisions in schools are made by policy makers and administrators. Over and over again, we hear policies and practices instituted and defended because "we care about the kids." But in many cases, neither those in daily contact with the kids nor the kids themselves are in any way involved in the decisions. It should not surprise us that, in many places where authorities claim to care, students often declare that "nobody cares." I will say more about what this implies for social studies education a bit later.

Consider now an example of what a concern for participatory democracy means for the conduct of social life in our high schools. Bullying has been recognized and condemned at almost every level of schooling, but the measures instituted to control it have usually been authoritarian and punitive. School people have at last become aware of the harm done by zero-tolerance rules, and more thoughtful responses are being considered. The problem is not one that will yield to harsh, authoritarian rules and punishments. Students must be involved. Regular class meetings at which problems are discussed openly should be helpful. The point of such meetings is not to identify and castigate bullies but to explore why people engage in bullying, why so many of us adopt the stance of bystanders, and what we can do to care for both victims and perpetrators.

Two things are clear at this stage. First, if we want to produce adults who know something about the history and governmental structure of their country, we must find a way to make this material meaningful. Second, if we are serious about relieving social injustice, we must move effectively from caring-about at the policy level to caring-for on-site. Caring-for by its very nature is relational; both carer and cared-for are necessarily involved. This means that, without blaming victims for their plight, we must find a way to include them in both the plans for improvement and their implementation.

To make school studies meaningful, we might employ two approaches already suggested: building the curriculum on themes and establishing interdisciplinary committees to bring the themes alive. In Chapter 2, on vocational education, I suggested the labor movement as a theme that might arouse considerable interest among vocational students. In the discussion of women's issues, I mentioned the treatment of women in religion as a powerful theme that appears in all of the disciplines. The study of both of these themes should avoid indoctrination and contribute substantially to the development of critical thinking. Candidates for interdisciplinary themes are numerous, for example, sanitation, racism, political corruption, advertising, transportation, museums, music, food, water, wild life, entertainment, sports, crime, manners, competition.

In Chapter 7, on critical thinking, we will return to a discussion of the central importance of a meaningful program in social studies. My concern in this chapter is with the many students who seem to learn little or nothing from the courses we now offer. They seem to believe that the material they are required to learn has nothing to do with their own lives. As Thomas Frank – mentioned in Chapter 2 – has argued, people who go through school feeling left out are easy targets for demagogues who endorse their belief that intellectualism and critical thinking will destroy – not improve – their way of life. Frank quotes Barbara Ehrenreich on the failure of dialogue between working-class and middle-class populations:

> From above come commands, diagnoses, instructions, judgments, definitions – even, through the media, suggestions as to how to think, feel, spend money, relax. Ideas seldom flow "upward" to the middle class, because there are simply no structures to channel the upward flow of thought from class to class.[3]

A main point of this brief section on civic life is that the two-way dialogue between classes should begin in school.

There is one area of civic study that has long influenced working-class and lower-middle-class students, and that is patriotism. As history and social studies have been taught, emphasis has often been on American exceptionalism, war heroes, and patriotic devotion. Thus it is not surprising that military enlistments after high school graduation come heavily from the very group of students who have felt left out in much of the formal discussion in school. The military offers an opportunity to belong in ways lauded by their study of history. This underscores the worries expressed by Virginia Woolf and reminds us that school should be a place where dialogue and democratic participation are regularly practiced. They are central to the development of better adults.

Certainly, in seeking to produce better adults, we should ensure that our students have command of the fundamental processes, and we should want them not only to be knowledgeable about their nation's history and system of government but to be active participants in it. But increased knowledge does not guarantee a better adult in the moral sense, and when we speak of a "better adult," the moral aspect is what we usually have in mind.

MORAL GROWTH AND UNDERSTANDING

The better adult we seek is not a "bionic man," but we should certainly be interested in the physical well-being of our students. I will engage this discussion in the next chapter, on parenting and homemaking. Here, let us consider what is generally regarded as the most essential feature of good (or better) people: their moral thinking and conduct.

Volumes have been written on moral philosophy and what it means to live and act morally. Some of that work is highly technical; I will not address it here, and I will not make a distinction between *moral* and *ethical* unless it is essential to do so. We all (at least most of us) have a cultural/intuitive idea of what it means to be a morally good person, and that will be a good starting point.

To begin with, it is clear that academic knowledge does not necessarily make people more moral. Germany had one of the most highly educated populations in the mid-twentieth century, and yet many of its citizens supported Nazism. We could argue that many of these citizens were from the working class, suffering from depression and deluded by ideas they were unprepared to criticize – people very similar to those described by Frank. But oppressed and poorly informed workers were not the only supporters of Hitler and Nazism. Of the fifteen officials at the Wannsee Conference – at which the program for the extermination of Jews was planned – eight held doctorates. More generally, support for Nazism was dismayingly high among professionals in medicine, law, and university teaching. In U.S. society today, we find corruption among highly educated financial officers, business executives, and Wall Street leaders. Knowledge alone does not guarantee morality. It is merely the form taken by various immoral acts that varies across educational and economic lines. Business executives are unlikely to hold up banks or burglarize houses, but their corrupt acts are no less immoral. Thus, as educators we cannot equate more years of schooling with a higher degree of moral responsibility. We have to look at the content and quality of that education.

What can we do to produce better, more moral, adults? The question has been with us at least since the days of the ancient Greeks. Even Socrates could not decide on a definitive answer. On the one hand, he was quite sure that virtue cannot be taught; on the other, he believed that teaching must contribute *something* to the production of moral adults. Thus, we should start this exploration with both humility and hope.

For centuries the primary approach to moral education was what we call today character education. The idea is to identify the moral virtues and find a way (despite Socrates' reservations) to inculcate them. Astute readers will identify a major difficulty immediately. Not only is the process of inculcation itself fraught with problems, but – at a more basic level – who will decide what the virtues are and how they should be described? The process of defining and describing virtues occurs at the cultural level, and cultures, like individuals, can go wrong; that is, they can endorse practices as virtues and later condemn those very practices. Further, cultural groups within a larger culture may emphasize different virtues.

From the perspective of care ethics, there is another, major difficulty with the virtues approach and that is its concentration on the individual. We may all agree, for example, that honesty is a virtue, but if an act of honesty harms an innocent other, is that act virtuous? There are absolutists who insist that the virtue of honesty is paramount regardless of the consequences. Sissela Bok discusses several prominent thinkers who advocated an absolute prohibition against lying. Immanuel Kant, for example, wrote, "By a lie a man throws away and, as it were, annihilates his dignity as a man."[4] Kant would not lie even to distract a murderer from his victim. The main consequence considered by absolutists such as Kant, John Wesley, and St. Augustine is the taint inflicted on the liar's character and person. But should we give no thought to the consequences of our honesty on others? All sorts of hurtful comments are made in the name of honesty – "I'm just being honest" – when a small "white lie" would have protected the one at whom the comment was directed and contributed to the maintenance of caring relations. Bok, for example, points out that some Jewish texts allow exceptions to the rule against telling lies – "especially those told to preserve the peace of the household."[5] At what cost to virtue do we pursue peace?

Clearly, a discussion of lying and truth-telling is a theme worth developing with high school students. When is a "white lie" justified? Can we go too far with such lies? With this theme, we are teaching *about* virtue, encouraging critical thinking about the whole idea. We are not engaged in a direct attempt to inculcate the virtue of honesty and build it into the character of our students, although – with the reservation expressed above – we would welcome this outcome.

The virtues approach – character education – uses one method compatible with the thematic approach advocated in this book. It employs stories, poems, and biographical accounts. It should not be dismissed as a "bag of virtues" approach (as Kohlberg called it), but it does give rise to some substantial concerns. Not only is there a problem of defining and describing the virtues to be taught, but there is an even larger problem that might be phrased as a question: When is a "virtue" not a virtue?

We looked briefly at the virtue of honesty and quickly located some ambiguity in it. Now consider another example, the very first virtue named in a widely used book published in 1909 by the Character Development League: *obedience*. The writer gives this definition: "Obedience is to do what those in authority over us tell us to do."[6] This first lesson in virtue was meant for young children, but nowhere in the entire book was there even a hint that something might go wrong if one simply obeys those in authority. In addition to obedience to parents and school authorities, obedience to duty was stressed, and military examples were given. As inspiration, lines from Tennyson were quoted: "Theirs not to make reply/Theirs not to question why/Theirs but to do and die." Why should children too young for serious critical thinking be exposed to such lines as "inspiration"? Comparable examples of lessons in character education can be found in school material through at least the first half of the twentieth century. Surely, even if the students are not encouraged to exercise critical thinking, teachers should be encouraged to do so. At some point in their school days, students should be urged to think deeply on this "virtue." When should we obey and why? Can we find historical examples where obedience was used as an excuse for the most disgusting, immoral behavior?

Character educators today do not advocate unconditional inculcation of obedience or any other virtue (although some programs come perilously close), but the dangers illustrated in the example above are inherent in the approach. Keep in mind that most character education is done at the elementary school level where it is difficult to examine each virtue critically for its downside.[7] To avoid the dangers arising in methods that involve inculcation, critical thinking must be developed and exercised, and this must be done at the high school level. Moral education should be part of education at every level. At the high school level, it is time to exercise critical thinking, and I will devote all of Chapter 7 to that concept.

Instead of concentrating on a critique of the moral virtues associated with good character, some character educators now put an emphasis on "performance character," a "mastery orientation": "It consists of those qualities – including but not limited to diligence, perseverance, a strong work ethic, a positive attitude, ingenuity, and self-discipline – needed to realize one's potential for excellence in any performance environment, such as academics, extracurricular activities, the workplace, and through-out life."[8] While we should not discourage the development of a mastery orientation in our students, we should remember that an interest in mastery is realistically preceded by an in interest in *something* that requires or invites mastery. It is not simply a matter of helping (or requiring) all students to master the material we impose on them; rather, it is our obligation as moral educators to help students find and choose topics and occupations to which they will give their best. A "mastery orientation" defined entirely by authorities holds dangers similar to the old "obedience" orientation.

Today, after centuries of trying the virtue approach (character educa-tion), many of us agree with Socrates that virtues cannot be taught effectively. However, we can learn a great deal by studying, analyzing, and discussing the virtues. Every virtue extolled in literature, religion, or social/political life should be examined for its historical roots in group affiliations. Consider *courage*, for example. Although "courage" has several connotations, it has long been associated with manliness (the Greek word for courage *means* manliness) and thus with the military.[9] Without deny-ing the courage of many soldiers, we should acknowledge the courage of those who refuse to bear arms. Literature presents many opportunities for students to consider both sides: the poetry of World War I, Erich Maria Remarque's *All Quiet on the Western Front*, and stories about the white feathers forced on young men who were not in uniform during World War I. And we should draw attention to the frightening spectral, military image Virginia Woolf saw rising from the ashes of a Spanish town. Courage associated only with males and the military is not an unadulterated virtue.

Just as young men have sometimes joined the military to prove their courage by association, people often claim the assumed virtues of other groups to which they belong. This is not an altogether bad phenomenon, but it needs thoughtful study. For example, is it virtuous to claim proudly, "My country right or wrong"? Is it somehow more virtuous to be a Christian than an atheist? Why do most people believe that an atheist could not possibly be elected as president of the United States? Students need to understand that most people want to belong, to feel part of a group that provides identity and purpose in life. They need also to understand that this longing to feel a part of something valuable (and virtuous) can lead to intolerance and even violence. Our longing to belong sometimes encourages opposition to people perceived as members of less worthy groups. Eric Hoffer reminds us: "Unity and self-sacrifice, of themselves, even when fostered by the most noble means, produce a facility for hating. Even when men league themselves mightily together to promote tolerance and peace on earth, they are likely to be violently intolerant toward those not of a like mind."[10] The dilemmas of virtues might be discussed over a broad range of themes, such as religion, patriotism, loyalty, obedience, duty, and peace.

In general, when we think of a morally better person, we envision someone who "does good." A good person, we believe, stands in opposition to an evil one, thought of as doing wrong or harm. Again, as we saw in the discussion of virtue, we will encounter ambiguities in the concept of evil and a need for critical thinking. (Critical thinking will itself present some ambiguities; certainly, it does not guarantee a moral motive or outcome.) But let us consider what we might discover about our "better adult" through a brief exploration of evil.

Evil may be named in three forms: natural, moral, and cultural/social.[11] Each is called "evil" because of the harm and suffering caused. Natural evil – earthquakes, floods, storms – can cause enormous damage and pain, but there is not usually a human agent responsible for its occurrence. The reaction of good people to those suffering from a natural disaster is to help, to relieve the suffering and contribute to the restoration of damaged communities.

Moral evil may be defined as harm or hurt inflicted by a human agent. The harmful act may be done deliberately or carelessly through negligence. In both cases, the agent has committed a violation of morality; he or she is morally culpable. There is a third case that must be considered. Sometimes an act is committed for personal gain with no consideration of the likely effects on others. There is no intent to cause pain, but the agent of the act is indifferent to the likely outcome. Moral indifference often appears in the financial world, and it is encountered in almost every field where competition governs activities. We hope to control moral evil by raising and educating good people, but we perhaps give too little attention to the harm done by indifference. We should note that this is a potential weakness in the current "mastery" movement.

Character education concentrates on the inculcation of virtues. Kantian/Kohlbergian education emphasizes moral reasoning. Education guided by care ethics encourages moral sensitivity to what others are going through and to a caring response. It is interesting and important to note that our intuitive sense of what constitutes a moral person has not changed dramatically over time. Certainly, there have been changes in beliefs about sin and personal behavior, and differences still appear in religious practices, but – at bottom – most of us think of a good person as one who will not hurt others and will act to relieve suffering.

The third form of evil, cultural evil, is the one that invites the most controversy: "Human beings frequently participate in the practices of their culture without reflective evaluation ... cultural evils have a way of embedding themselves in the tissue of society. They resist elimination and instead undergo transformation; sometimes the transformation is merely cosmetic and sometimes it is moderately significant, but the evils remain potent."[12]

Americans today live in an age when some of the worst elements of racism have been eliminated, but there remain vestiges that come alive periodically and pose a continual threat. Similarly, although the full citizenship of women is acknowledged, a strong economic prejudice is still directed at women's traditional work. And in this time of growing economic inequality, there is a widespread tendency to blame the poor for their own misfortune. There is a pervasive attitude that posits the successful, white male as the image of the better adult to be emulated. If we are serious about eliminating, or at least reducing, cultural evil, we must recognize the varieties of excellence that should be included in our vision of a better adult.

At the global level, many Americans are fond of the notion of American exceptionalism. The attitude is so strong that some of us even declare our country to be best in areas – such as medical services – where we are demonstrably weak or mediocre. The attitude is strongly associated with patriotism. We need not reject our commitment to patriotism, but we should examine it critically. Attempts to do so have not often been well received, but, then again, critics of American policy – for example, during the Vietnam War – have also failed to listen critically to their opponents. Stories of returning veterans being spat upon and accused of murder remind us that the longing for global justice is not likely to be satisfied simply by outrage, especially if that outrage is directed at people who did not intend to do evil and have their own stories to tell.

Difficult problems arise whenever the schools become involved in arguing against cultural/social evil construed as social injustice. Some forms of social injustice have been condemned by religion, and in the days when school studies were openly guided by religion, it was relatively easy for the schools to encourage students to unite in their opposition to dictatorship, threats to personal liberty, infractions of the Ten Commandments, and the assumed evil of atheism. As Andrew Delbanco has argued, Americans (but not only Americans) have a history of locating evil outside ourselves. We seem to need Satan or some devil on whom to blame the evils around us.[13] With the demise of Satan, we have had to find new devils. Through the second half of the twentieth century, Communism served that purpose; it ruled over the "evil empire." Now "socialism" is regarded by many as both a national and international devil of sorts. Most Americans seem to have forgotten that there was once a respectable Socialist party in this country. Educators might remember that John Dewey voted for Socialist candidates several times and hoped that a democratic socialist party would gain a firm footing in America.

Delbanco asks us to remember that there are two ways of looking at evil: as something or someone out there or as something caused by a deprivation in our own love or fellow feeling. He comments that "the former way – evil as the other – is, at least at first, psychically rewarding. The latter way – evil as privation – is much more difficult to grasp. But it offers something that the devil himself could never have intended: the miraculous paradox of demanding the best of ourselves."[14]

Now, I hope, we can see the connection between looking at evil and searching for ways to educate toward better adults. We must encourage not only critical thinking but reflection. The better adults we seek will be able use critical thinking not only on social practices in the wider world, but also on their own lives and practices.

In Chapter 1, I noted the loss of theology as a unifying influence on the curriculum, but I did not recommend that it be restored. I suggested, instead, that we engage in a continuing conversation on how to produce better adults and on what we mean by a "better adult." Similarly, in this chapter, I have suggested that we should stop concentrating on the devils outside us and turn our attention to our own weaknesses. The capacity for moral reflection is part of what we seek in a better adult. It is very hard, however, for schools to encourage moral reflection on the ideas and practices of our own groups. It is difficult to reflect critically on the principles espoused by the group to which we belong or aspire to belong. Suppose, for example, that our religious group condemns homosexuality or abortion. What might move us to consider opposing views? It is quite remarkable that we Americans have made considerable progress in overcoming several forms of intolerance. But even when there is general agreement that something should be done about a problem – say, poverty – there is strong disagreement on *what* should be done. This in itself is not necessarily a moral problem. But one arises when the whole approach to the problem deteriorates to a battle over who is right rather than on what should be done. Positions harden and a search for devils may displace a cooperative search for solutions. Further, either or both sides may – in their earnest partisanship – engage in indoctrination instead of critical thinking.

In the period between World War I and World War II, there was a strong effort to emphasize social justice in the new school social studies program. Theology was being displaced as the unifying guide to education. Socialism was an active political source. Even formal religion was giving more attention to justice in movements such as the Social Gospel. Surely, there was much to applaud in this awakening of critical reflection on public life and practice. But there was also the worrisome feature mentioned above. Advocates of social justice were sometimes willing to use the authority of schools to press their political views on social justice. George Counts, for example, spoke out against a "liberal-minded upper middle class who send their children to the progressive schools." He gave an admirable description of this "class" but then castigated it for having no deep convictions and being "rather insensitive to the accepted forms of social injustice. . ."[15] Counts urged the schools to build a new social order. To do this, he said, the new education must "emancipate itself from the influence of this class, face squarely and courageously every social issue, come to grips with life in all its stark reality, establish an organic relation with the community, develop a realistic and comprehensive theory of welfare, fashion a compelling and challenging vision of human destiny, and become less frightened than it is today at the bogies of *imposition* and *indoctrination*."[16]

Many of us would endorse his vision of a new social order but draw back from his willingness to indoctrinate the views we share. To achieve and maintain "an organic relation with the community," we must find a way to include all reasonable members of the community and to encourage all to develop a critical-reflective attitude in tackling political/social problems cooperatively.

Consider another problem widely discussed today in educational circles: the achievement gap across socio-economic classes. Some argue that the underlying problem, the likely cause, is poverty. Others argue that the cause is a breakdown in family structure and abandonment of the traditional work ethic. In their zeal to win the argument, too many well-intentioned people on both sides do little or nothing about the problem and concentrate instead on proving the other side wrong. But suppose both sides are at least partly right. What might we then do? Similarly, when the achievement gap across races is discussed, arguments arise over the basic cause of the gap between black and white students. Is the main cause a failure to provide adequate instruction and support for black children? Is segregation the main cause? Supposing that segregation is the main cause, we tried to desegregate schools only to find ourselves up against an increase in residential segregation and enormous increases in transportation costs. We also gave too little attention to possible psychological injury to black children. Do they need the presence of white children in order to learn?[17] We should certainly work on segregation as a social problem, but we should help children to seek success with pride wherever we find them.

Let us review what we have explored so far. We have a unifying purpose: to produce better adults. In Chapter 2, we considered the variety of occupations in which people can exhibit excellence and emphasized the need to respect this variety and to reject the notion that there is one ideal or template that describes the better adult. In Chapter 3, we applied this thinking to matters of gender and noted that homemaking, an occupation traditionally filled by women, should be more widely and deeply appreciated. We noted also that the better adult woman might well be significantly different from the better adult man. This, again, affirms a rejection of the idea that we should define and pursue some single ideal that all people should emulate. In Chapter 3, it was acknowledged that the command of certain fundamental processes is necessary for all adults. But it was reaffirmed that the variety of human interests and talents should be respected and that civic/social improvement depends on the participation of both those giving help and those receiving it. Finally, it was suggested that a morally better adult is one who offers help where it is needed, who avoids the deliberate or careless infliction of harm and suffering, who has the capacity to use critical thinking and reflection on both personal and public affairs, and who is committed to using that thinking for moral purposes.

Now we can direct this thinking to one of the tasks central to human life: parenting. How should our better adult approach this task? And how can the schools help?

5

Parenting

It is widely recognized that the quality of parenting is important in determining a student's success in school. Indeed, it may be the single most important factor in promoting that success. Yet while we insist – in the name of equal opportunity – that all students must study algebra, we stubbornly refuse to teach parenting in our high schools. Admittedly, there are difficulties in making such a move. Some critics insist that instruction on parenting belongs in the home (another example of the bureaucratic thinking that pervades public life). Others argue that only some students require this instruction, and their identification would be another example of blaming the victim, of singling out kids who are already economically disadvantaged. Still others would dismiss the very idea as anti-intellectual and demand to know what important subject matter would be displaced to make room in the school day for a course on parenting.

I am not recommending that we add a course on parenting to an already full academic program, and I certainly do not advocate singling out those students who, we suspect, are especially in need of such instruction. Rather, in the spirit of what has preceded this chapter, I suggest that we recognize the supreme importance of parenting in human life and ask how each subject already in the curriculum can contribute to the development of better parents. In addressing themes related to parenting, I do not suggest that we teach how to feed and bathe infants, change diapers, and establish regular visits to the pediatrician. These things are important for new parents, of course, and classes should be available for teenage mothers and others who need immediate help. But I am talking here about the deeper meanings of parenting and homemaking that we discussed in Chapter 4. It is a matter of connecting school subjects with the central aspects of human life, of bringing real meaning to the school curriculum. The major topic is parenting, and the questions for an interdisciplinary team are these: What themes can our individual subjects generate on parenting, and how can we connect their contributions to each other? Within the major topic, I will suggest several themes that figure prominently in the practice of good parenting: conversation, health, growth, and acceptability.

CONVERSATION

The importance of conversation – of talking with and listening to – has already been mentioned, and an enormous vocabulary gap between the young children in privileged families and those in impoverished families has been recognized. There are at least three ways to address this problem, and we should probably do something along the lines of all three. First, the problem must be recognized, and schools must support the building of relationships in which students can participate actively in the language of schooling – the "formal register" that is learned primarily through linguistic relationships. Second, schools should do more to inform parents about the importance of conversation in building vocabulary. Third, schools should encourage subject matter teachers to introduce material relevant to child development and early education. All three approaches emphasize the need to make connections.

In her impressive and enormously useful study of children's language in homes and schools, Shirley Brice Heath advises that "unless the boundaries between classrooms and communities can be broken, and the flow of cultural patterns between them encouraged, the schools will continue to legitimate and reproduce communities of townspeople who control and limit the potential progress of other communities and who themselves remain untouched by other values and ways of life."[1] Among the differences noted by Heath is one that we will focus on here. Parents in some subcultures talk *with* their children; they have regular conversations. In other subcultures, parents – who obviously also love their children – talk *at* them – direct, scold, compliment – but do not engage them in conversation.

Without ridiculing the language children bring from their communities into the classroom, teachers have to find ways to help them master the language of formal education. This is best done through the establishment of relationships in which conversation plays a major role. At the high school level, there should be many opportunities to encourage discussion and collaborative activities. In the remedial groups advocated earlier, discussion plays a central part in both academic and social education. Indeed, a primary purpose of these groups is to help students understand the fundamental processes of high school education, and one fundamental process is, of course, to master the language of schooling. In all classes, however – not just in those for the remedial group – there should be an emphasis on discussion. Discussion and critical dialogue are central purposes for the universal social studies courses recommended earlier. In these carefully composed classes, students from all programs and socio-economic backgrounds meet together to study and discuss salient social-political issues. All students should emerge from these courses better informed and more sensitive to the concerns of their fellow citizens, and those still struggling with the formal language of schooling should become more competent.

Teachers might encourage family conversation by asking students to consult their parents and family members on various themes chosen for study, for example, advertising, recreation, or favorite meals. Occasionally, instead of assigning written homework, teachers could ask students to interview their parents and share the results in classroom discussion. The reports should be voluntary; students should not be forced to share what their parents say; no grades should be attached to the assignment; and great care should be taken to assign themes that are not likely to arouse controversy or embarrassment. The idea is to encourage conversation in homes and between home and school communities. Students and teachers might find it quite fascinating to ask parents: What was your favorite (or most hated) school subject? Why? Schools might also send occasional letters or short pamphlets home advising parents to "Talk with Your Kids" and providing some suggestions on possible topics. The aims here are dual: to increase conversation in the home and to break down the barriers between language communities.

Now the question arises: Who will make this assignment? Will it be made in math or English class? Or will it, like so many other "extraneous" topics, be handed over to social studies? The answer will require imagination and collaborative exploration, and the decision will depend on both the nature of the theme and the ingenuity of the faculty. If the theme is "your most hated subject," perhaps math teachers will volunteer because, surely, that subject probably heads the list of most hated.

A third way to increase conversation among relevant groups is to include material connected to parenting in all subjects of the curriculum. This is a challenging task for the interdisciplinary teams that should meet regularly to choose themes that will connect the subjects and make them more meaningful. A possible interview topic might center on food. What is your favorite family dish? Can you share a recipe? This is a popular method of cultural exchange, and it can invite both intercultural and interdisciplinary discussion. Further, it should promote the idea that meal-time is an ideal time for family conversation.

Family mealtime may be something of a rarity for today's children. The topic of food is so central to human life that our faculty committee might well decide to do a collaborative unit on food. What do we talk about over meals? And where in the curriculum might we talk about mealtime talk? Certainly, there must be stories and poems that include references to food, table-talk, and manners. The English/literature expert on the interdisciplinary committee can direct us here. Math and science teachers can work together to produce lessons that discuss calories and how to count them, the varieties of fresh foods and their costs, and the contributions of various vitamins and minerals to our health. Art teachers can introduce students to the wonderful world of still-lifes depicting foods. And social studies teachers can plan a series of lessons on the food of classical Greece or eating habits in the Middle Ages.[2] In each of these discussions, students should be encouraged to share what they learn with their parents.

An interdisciplinary unit on food and mealtime conversation could be stimulating and broadly educational. However, although we might ask students to contribute recipes and share information about cultural customs, we should probably not ask them to report on their own family's mealtime habits. One can imagine all sorts of disclosures that might embarrass both students and parents. Our human-life objective in planning a cooperative unit around food is to promote the development of better adults, better parents, not to highlight differences in existing family practices.

Another activity that invites parent–child conversation is reading together. In reading together – sitting side-by-side, pausing to look at pictures, and talking about what is happening in the story – parents learn something about their children's interests, fears, and growing abilities. The children gain in vocabulary and in a sense of security. This is an area I would recommend as an addition to the regular curriculum. Surely, one semester of English could be devoted to the literature of childhood. For some teenagers, this would be their first exposure to that literature; for others, it would be a delightful opportunity to revisit loved stories. For both, however, it should be a well-planned unit of study that includes not only the literature itself but psychological arguments for and against various forms of children's literature. What arguments have been made in favor of fairy tales? What warnings have been issued against some of them?[3]

It is not only English teachers who can contribute to the uses of children's literature. Such literature can also promote growth and interest in mathematics and science. Some years ago, I was introduced to Japanese children's literature. Reading Kenji Miyazawa's stories, I was astonished to find some mathematics in almost every one of them. No wonder Japanese children were doing better than American children in arithmetic! In one of the stories, a medical doctor conducts a diagnostic session on a weary army general who has just returned from an over-long deployment. Students should have pencils and paper ready:

DOCTOR: What does one hundred and one hundred make?
GENERAL: One hundred and eighty.
DOCTOR: And two hundred and two hundred?
GENERAL: Let's see. Three hundred and sixty, if I'm not mistaken.
DOCTOR: Just one more, then. What's ten times two?
GENERAL: Eighteen, of course.[4]

On the basis of this diagnosis, the doctor decides that the general is a bit off – "about ten percent, in fact." The doctor treats his patient medically, and then repeats his diagnostic questions. Now the general responds accurately! After reading this story, discussion might follow on what the students have learned about math and science through their own reading of stories. What stories or poems (or songs) might they suggest?

Still another source of material for the education of future parents is the history of childhood. Looking back at the topics discussed in Chapter 3, on women's interests, we are reminded of the male-dominated topics that have long been emphasized in school studies. War is a prominent topic, and some school-book histories are organized in time periods defined from war to war. The history of agriculture and industry is usually mentioned. Nations, political leaders, markets, economic ups and downs in world economy, and disputes over resources are popular topics. But little appears on the history of food or the history of childhood, yet food and children are essential to human life, and there are beautiful, accessible histories of both.[5]

In this section, I have concentrated on topics that invite conversation between parents and children and between various subcultures and that of our schools. In addition, the study of childhood literature and the history of childhood should persuade students that schools regard preparation for parenthood as serious educational work – every bit as important as preparation for an occupation and for citizenship.

HEALTH

Parents and educators have always been concerned with the health of children, and "health" was listed as one of the seven great aims of education in the Cardinal Principles. Sara Ruddick named "preservative love" as the first great maternal interest.[6] There is also a psychological reason for discussing health under parenting. It may be more effective to invite teenagers to think about how they might talk to their future children about, say, sex and drugs than to preach at them about their own behavior. I am reminded here of a story that came from a school in southern California some years ago. A group of near-delinquent teenage boys was recruited to serve as big brothers to children who were not doing well in their elementary school work. One day a big brother heard himself advising a little boy that he must listen to his teacher and do his homework. He caught himself up, somewhat dumbfounded. "What am I saying?" he asked himself. He answered himself by starting to do his own homework. Teaching directed at future parenting may well have positive effects on the current lives of teenagers.

Our guiding question continues to center on what each discipline or school subject can contribute to important life themes. Traditionally, topics related to health have been assigned to physical education classes and, more recently, to special short courses on sex. To bring more meaning to this topic and so many others, we must show how the major school subjects connect to life and to each other. Again, the suggestions offered here are meant to be not a prescription but, rather, an invitation to think more deeply on the topics under discussion.

When we consider what might be addressed in science classes, we should give some attention to popular science. Most high school science classes today consist of introductory courses in sharply separated branches of science – biology, physics, and chemistry – and many students drop science from their programs after completing the minimum requirement. The courses are regarded as too difficult for many students, but "popular science" is scorned as not "real science" by many educators. On this last, universities bear a major responsibility for encouraging this judgment and continually questioning the rigor of high school courses; the greater the "rigor," the more highly a course is valued by offices of college admissions. Any course that does not conform to the pattern of pre-college rigor is automatically downgraded. Yet most highly educated nonscientists in our society depend heavily on nontechnical reports of scientific work – that is, on popular science that comes to us from reliable sources. (The identification of reliable sources is another theme for the universal social studies courses.)

Besides the unfair advantage granted to courses that satisfy college-defined rigor, there is another pernicious effect. If all college-bound students take the rigorous courses, we can assume that those submitting to courses in popular science must be somehow deficient, and it follows that the courses too must be deficient. Just as courses in the "general" high school curriculum have been of disgracefully poor quality, any course deemed lower in rigor becomes even less respectable over time. It is thought that these courses can be taught by anyone, and neither teachers nor students are held to high standards. Such courses are meant for students who cannot or will not measure up. This attitude has undermined the noble vision of the comprehensive high school, and it must change. Under a new vision of the high school, every course should be interesting, useful, challenging, and directed at the problems of real life.

If we are going to maintain the traditional program of high school studies, all students should study science for four years, but that does not mean that all students should study the standard college preparatory courses in biology, chemistry, and physics. Rather, it means that all students should have access to courses that emphasize physical health, child development, mental health, and community responsibility for the welfare of its citizens. Under the current movement toward standards involving critical thinking, reading, and writing, well-designed courses in popular science could contribute substantially to college preparation without providing technical preparation for specialized courses in any one of the sciences.

The design of such courses would necessarily involve teachers from most, if not all, of the disciplines. How should we design lessons to help students read semi-technical articles in the life sciences? How should we judge their written reports? Is it important for them to know something about the history of sanitation and disease? Of childbirth and contraception? Of child development? Is there fine literature that says something about these matters? (Perhaps: J. G. Farrell, *The Siege of Krishnapur*; Albert Camus, *The Plague*; Pearl Buck, *The Exile*; Charles Dickens, *Hard Times* or *Bleak House*.) Are there classic nonfiction works on the topics? (Perhaps: Benjamin Spock, *On Parenting*; Adrienne Rich, *Of Woman Born*; Erik Erikson, *Childhood and Society*.) The selection of such works requires cooperative discussion among representatives from all of the fields involved. The notion that "critical reading" can somehow be taught without the careful, regular examination and discussion of critical issues is absurd. The same can be said about critical thinking; such thinking necessarily involves critical issues that arouse it.

In this section, we have been concentrating on health education and its connection to parenting, and I have suggested that appropriate treatment of the topic might involve expansion and revision of the high school science curriculum. The details of such work should properly be left to science educators working in collaboration with experts from other fields. Before leaving the topic, however, we should consider another reason for undertaking this expansion. Many biology teachers confess that, without further preparation, they could not possibly teach high school physics or chemistry. Something is wrong here. We expect students to absorb the elements of three sciences, but they are taught by people who know only one. Both the courses offered and the preparation of teachers must be critically reappraised. We will return to this problem in Chapter 11.

PROMOTING GROWTH

A second great maternal (parental) interest identified by Ruddick is "fostering growth." Good parents want their children to be successful in school and in life. Any consideration of how to achieve this involves some attention to the concept of order introduced in Chapter 3. How should parents interpret order? For years there has been a running argument between parent-centered and child-centered approaches to order – indeed, to parenting in general. Certainly, an authoritarian, parent-centered approach can produce order in a household, but it can also lead to a lack of creativity and independent thinking in children. On the opposite side, a child-centered approach can lead to household chaos and somewhat fearful uncertainty in children.[7] Today we often see a strange combination of these two contrasting orientations, one that is extreme in itself. So-called helicopter parents hover over their children constantly – scheduling their play and work, evaluating their homework, prescribing everything from playthings to playmates.[8] In one sense, this hovering is child-centered: The child occupies the center of parent attention. In another sense, it is parent-centered: The parent exercises complete (if somewhat gentle, even mushy) control over the child's life.

It is probably best to avoid all of these extremes, and the position taken in this book is thoroughly relational. Through regular conversation, genuine dialogue, both parent and child contribute to the establishment and maintenance of order. Children learn to make wise choices when parents allow them to exercise age-appropriate choices, help them to reflect on those choices, and plan more prudently for the future.

The approach in school should also be two-pronged. The curriculum should include parenting-related themes connected to each of the subjects, and the teacher–student relationship should, within reason, model a good parent–child relation. Practically, it is obvious that teachers will not take financial responsibility for their students, supervise their medical care, take them on outings, or supervise their religious training. However, they should model a mode of conversation and engagement that lies at the heart of caring relations. They should listen and respond to expressed needs, provide generous guidance, and promote the general growth of the students in their classes. It takes time to develop relations of care and trust, and I will return to this topic in Chapter 8, on continuity.[9]

Under present high school conditions, teachers rarely have enough time with students to get to know them. Increasingly, teachers are encouraged to rely on test data even to evaluate their students on the outcomes stated in the curriculum standards. What sort of "teaching" requires a standardized test to inform teachers on what their students have learned? Good teachers know from regular interaction and dialogue whether or not their students have learned the material taught. The test merely confirms the teacher's evaluation and adds formal impartiality to the result. Elliot Eisner warned us more than thirty years ago that we were headed in the wrong direction with the emphasis on measurement; objecting to the growing tendency to reduce everything to numbers, he said: "It's better to talk about subjects rather than students, better to refer to treatment than to teaching, better to measure than to judge, better to deal with output than with results... Cool, dispassionate objectivity has resulted in sterile, mechanistic language devoid of the playfulness and artistry that are so essential to teaching and learning."[10]

But in any case, there is more to promoting growth than helping students to learn the basic material prescribed in the curriculum. What does the student want to learn? What is he or she afraid of? What student interests or talents are ignored in the curriculum? Can any of these interests be recognized and promoted within the teacher's subject matter expertise? A mathematics teacher might, for example, allow students to choose projects relating math to music, literature, biography, art, religion, war, or gambling. If the results of such a project count for as much as a major test, students who experience math-test anxiety may breathe a sigh of relief. And students often react with increased energy on the day-to-day assignments of teachers who have recognized and applauded their interests. Teachers are not simply purveyors of information; their task – like that of parents – is to foster the growth of their students. Like good parents, good teachers protect without hovering, encourage limited risks, endorse careful choices, applaud success, commiserate with failure, inspire trust, and point the way to better adulthood. In later years, as parents, students may remember one or more of their teachers as models of the finest parenting.

SHAPING AN ACCEPTABLE CHILD

The third great maternal interest identified by Ruddick is shaping an acceptable child: "Many mothers find that the central challenge of mothering lies in training a child to be the kind of person whom others accept and whom the mothers themselves can actively appreciate."[11] This comment raises several important questions: To whom should the child be acceptable? What do we mean by "acceptable"? And how should we describe this training or shaping?

Parents usually start training for acceptability with daily manners defined by the family: "Say thank you to Grandma." "Say please if you want a cookie." "Don't pick your nose." "Don't talk with your mouth full." Little by little, in an orderly household, children acquire the veneer of their elders. With loving guidance, the outer layer of manners is supported by a solid concern for the well-being of those around them, but it takes time, patience, and dialogue to build this foundation. Good parents listen to the expressed needs of their children, but they also help their children to hear and respond to the needs of others. This requires the development of a capacity to feel with and to feel for others.

In today's psychological literature, this capacity is often referred to as *empathy*. Martin Hoffman, for example, writes: "The key requirement of an empathic response according to my definition is the involvement of psychological processes that make a person have feelings that are more congruent with another's situation than with his own."[12] The feeling should, of course, be followed by an appropriate response. One weakness, noted by a number of critics, is that empathy aroused may have a short life; it may just fade away. This often results in the bystander syndrome. A bystander might experience a brief arousal of feeling-with or feeling-for but, for a variety of reasons, decide not to intervene. Perhaps the feeling itself evaporates, perhaps a stronger feeling (e.g., fear) displaces it, or perhaps self-doubt pushes it aside.

Readers should also be aware that definitions of empathy vary widely even within fields such as neuroscience.[13] Some emphasize the cognitive aspect of empathy (as did its original definition in aesthetics); some emphasize the affective aspect; and some give equal attention to both aspects. For present purposes, to avoid confusion, I will use "feeling with" and "feeling for."

Hoffman discusses a useful technique he calls "induction" by which parents can encourage children to notice when they have hurt someone and, aware of their role in causing pain, to begin to develop a sensitivity to the feelings of the injured party. The parent might ask the perpetrator how he or she would feel if treated that way. A better question, however, is aimed directly at the victim's feelings: "How do you think Bobby felt when you said that?" Putting the question this way emphasizes receptive attention, the sort of attention that is ready to receive what the other is feeling. It asks, through words or body language, Simone Weil's question: "What are you going through?"[14] And the questioner stands ready to listen.[15]

Good parents – the better adults we are seeking – want their children not only to avoid causing pain but to notice and respond to the needs of others. This is an important topic of concern at every level of human life: in homes, friendships, schools, local communities, and the global community.[16] Interest in empathy has spread to every level, but, in addition to definitional confusion, there is the problem of how to sustain empathy. In a review of recent literature on empathy in the public arena, Paul Bloom noted that empathy can be narrow-minded, aroused by graphic accounts, and short lived.[17] Some of his criticism can be traced to the confusion of definition already noted – for example, his claim that empathy is noncognitive and devoid of reason. Obviously, empathy need not be, and was not originally, confined to feeling. However, the feeling aroused by faraway disasters, the accidents of strangers, and the unhappy living conditions of people on the other side of town (aroused temporarily by graphic images) is generally short lived and cannot be depended on to have lasting effects. Topics in the whole range of concern for others are properly included in the school curriculum, but here we are mainly concerned with what parents and teachers can do to encourage a sustained attitude of feeling with others in daily life.

The basic idea is to build relations of care and trust. The child should *want* to behave in ways that please the child's parents. Punishment is rarely useful in encouraging this attitude. One needs only to read George Orwell's account of the misery of his school days to be convinced that corporal punishment should be abolished. Describing the loneliness and helplessness of his school days, he wrote: "[T]his was the great abiding lesson of my boyhood: that I was in a world where it was *not possible* for me to be good... Life was more terrible, and I was more wicked, than I had imagined."[18] Things turned out all right for Orwell eventually, but for a lifetime, he remained ambivalent about his treatment in school. No present-day reader could be unmoved by the childhood misery he described.

Why do so many of us even today believe that strict rules and penalties will ensure the safety and good behavior of our students? Too often, such treatment induces fear and hatred of authority, possibly increasing the likelihood that "unacceptable" behavior will continue. School people – who should have known better at the outset – are now actively opposing zero-tolerance rules and their rigid penalties because they are ineffective. What we should encourage is zero-tolerance attitudes, and these are developed not by rules and penalties but by the exercise of genuine feeling for others. Class meetings to discuss social problems, establishment of partnerships to reinforce school regulations, and opportunities to work as helpers with younger students are all ways to encourage sensitivity to the needs and feelings of others.

As we take on the challenging task of shaping "acceptable" children, we must consider a fundamentally important question: To whom should the child be acceptable? One would hope that every group to whom the child should be acceptable is itself morally acceptable. This observation puts a tremendous responsibility on parents and teachers. Parents recognize the responsibility when they watch carefully over their children's friends and associates. Schools have been slow to explore and employ methods that might open the doors to friendship across the lines of acceptability. Various forms of group work across the disciplines might help to reduce the chains of loyalty that sometimes trap youngsters in groups that impede their social and academic progress. Continuous attention should be given to developing relations of care and trust between teachers and students and among students.[19] It is especially important for at-risk students to feel accepted among students who already have a place in the school community.

All of this is easier said than done. In the earlier discussion of teaching standard English, it was noted that care must be taken to treat speakers of nonstandard English with respect, and it was emphasized that people should not have to give up membership in a cultural subgroup in order to achieve acceptability in another, perhaps more powerful, group. These worries should be kept in mind as teachers work to bring students together to widen their spheres of acceptability. To accomplish this widening of community, teachers must know their students as persons. I will return to this topic in a later discussion of continuity. It is certainly easier for a teacher to intervene in matters of student relationships if the teacher has the opportunity to work with students for two or three years rather than the typical, and very limiting, one year.

There is another important matter to keep in mind as we explore the business of shaping acceptable children. Parents are quite naturally concerned first and foremost with the acceptability of their own children, and they often react with unease if the children are found in "bad company." Connections between their child and the bad company must be severed or at least reduced. For teachers, however, the "bad company" is composed of individual children who need care and guidance. Teachers have a responsibility to foster acceptability in all of their students. One of the most powerful ways to do this is to identify what is already good in a troubled student and build on this goodness. Martin Buber refers to this process as one of confirmation.[20] Instead of accusing and punishing, teachers practicing confirmation try to build on the offender's good points; they assume the best possible motive consonant with reality:

> Confirmation is not a ritual act that can be performed for any person by any other person.
>
> It requires a relation. Carers have to understand their cared-fors well enough to know what they are trying to accomplish. Attributing the best possible motive consonant with reality requires knowledge of that reality. We cannot just pull a motive out of thin air. When we identify a motive and use it in confirmation, the cared-for should recognize it as his or her own: "That *is* what I was trying to do!" It is wonderfully reassuring to realize that another sees the better self that often struggles for recognition beneath our lesser acts and poorer selves.[21]

There are also serious political topics that should be included in the curriculum when we aim to foster acceptability. We discussed earlier the emphasis once placed on obedience to authority in moral education and education for citizenship. Where in the curriculum do we address critical reflection on authority and the documents that are purported to represent our moral values on national and international relations? How does it happen that whole nations sometimes go wrong? When studying World War II, for example, students could be asked to think about how they might have reacted if they had been subjected to the sort of education inflicted on German youth during the reign of Nazism. It is too easy for those of us who have never undergone such indoctrination toward blind obedience and racial hatred to suppose that we would staunchly hold to our moral values no matter what our teachers and political leaders urged upon us. Possibly no theme is more important in social education than a critical examination of our political beliefs, and this is a theme to which all of the school subjects can contribute.

In an essay addressing problems of forgiveness, revenge, and moral justification, in discussion of Nazism and the Holocaust, Friedrich Torberg remarks on the difference between those who opposed Hitler's hate campaign and those who did nothing to speak out or act against it: "It is in this intact morality . . . that we are superior to the others and to those who held their peace about the murders when they were committed and are still holding their peace today."[22] But what does it mean to have an "intact morality," and how is this intactness preserved?[23] Because I was a young teenager during World War II and adored my teachers, I have wondered again and again what I might have believed and accepted if my teachers – backed by our government – had espoused some form of fascism or totalitarianism. How, even today, might students react to the celebration of a "noble type" expressed in the following quotation?

> This will to sacrifice in staking his personal labor and, if necessary, his own life for others, is most powerfully developed in the [___]. He is greatest, not in his mental capacity *per se*, but in the extent to which he is ready to put all his abilities at the service of the community. With him the instinct of self-preservation has reached the most noble form, because he willingly subjects his own ego to the life of the community and, if the hour should require it, he also sacrifices it.[24]

The empty blank in the quotation above was filled in as "Aryan" by Adolf Hitler. Suppose we put "American patriot" in the brackets. Who would reject the sentiment?

There is more than a hint of "moral luck" in our possession of an intact morality. Where and when we were born and how we were educated have enormous influence on our moral thinking. Pause for a moment, then, and think about our responsibility as educators in maintaining a world in which it is possible for our students to be good and to retain, as adult citizens, an intact morality.

Some parents today believe that they are being asked to do too much of the job once allocated almost exclusively to the schools – supervision of homework, major preparation for college, provision for all sorts of extracurricular educational activities. I agree with them. And in this chapter, I have argued the opposite side – that the schools should be more involved in promoting the activities and interests associated with parenting. A program supporting parenting in schools has two main parts:

teaching about parenting through the use of interdisciplinary themes and teachers' modeling of the best parental practices, especially through the establishment of relations of care and trust and the continuous line of conversation/dialogue that characterizes such relations. Schools, I have argued, share responsibility in preserving the health of students, fostering their growth in a variety of individual talents and interests, and helping to guide them toward moral acceptability in a range of morally acceptable social groups. Overall, schools share with good parents the responsibility to preserve and improve a social/political world in which acceptability is under continual moral scrutiny – a world in which one can be morally proud to be acceptable.

6

The Common Core Standards

In the first five chapters of this book, I have tried to make some sense of what might be meant by a "better adult" and how our schools might promote the development of that adult. On the basis of that exploration, I have made some general suggestions and a few definite recommendations. First, in our search for a "better adult," we do not seek one, carefully detailed, ideal toward which we will educate every child. The production of better adults gives us a unity of purpose, but it does not imply uniformity of curriculum, pedagogy, or outcomes. In trying to develop better adults, we are directed to consider every important facet or aspect of human life and to renew our respect for the full range of human talents across those aspects and within them. With this understanding, I have recommended the following for our high schools.

- Vocational education should be expanded and enriched. That expansion should be accompanied by the establishment of a four-year social studies program that includes students from all of the school's programs and socio-economic groups.
- Deeply meaningful material on homemaking and parenting should be included in the curriculum.
- Teachers from each discipline should work together in interdisciplinary teams to select themes that connect the disciplines to each other and to life itself. The great existential themes associated with the traditional liberal arts should be among the themes included in both academic and vocational programs.
- A first-year preparation period should be provided for students who are not academically ready to move from middle school to high school. Teachers selected for this year's work should model the best parenting practices and provide not just remedial work but a rich,

stimulating environment that will – in a sense – make up for the previous years of possible deprivation.

• Good schools, like good parents, should give far more attention to the social and moral development of students and, in general, to the sort of society they are promoting – one that will help its citizens to develop and retain an intact morality.

Now perhaps we are ready to ask how the current reform movement – the Common Core Standards – might contribute to or impede this vision. I should acknowledge at the outset that there is a temptation to give way to the oppositional tendencies that I have been warning us to avoid. There is so much misleading language, so many conflicting interests, so much monetary waste – especially in testing – that thoughtful educators could be forgiven for shouting their dissent and taking to the picket lines. But let us take a calm look at the movement and consider how we might work together. We will look first at the language of the Common Core, then at its attempt to promote intellectual meaning in the curriculum, and, finally, at its emphasis on modeling and order.

THE LANGUAGE OF THE COMMON CORE

In recent news articles, debate over the Common Core has been described in political terms, as one more battle between left and right – the left supporting government involvement in school reform and the right opposing that involvement. This, I will argue, is a bad mistake that may lead otherwise intelligent liberals to support a movement that is badly flawed. What we need is rational, critical thinking that explores two basic questions about the Common Core: What is it? And why should we adopt it?

First, what is it? The Common Core is defined as a set of standards for mathematics and English language arts. There was an attempt also to establish standards for history (social studies), but that fell apart under political attack in the mid-1990s.[1] I will say more about that in Chapter 7, on critical thinking. Paradoxically, political debate may help to salvage the math and English standards by encouraging the left to support them just because the right opposes them. But let us put politics aside for the moment and *think*. What are these proposed standards? The "standards" are not standards in the usual sense; standards are usually thought of as established measures of acceptability in a product or performance. In contrast, the standards of the Common Core are more like lists of contents and skills to be taught by teachers and learned by students. In the standards for high school mathematics, for example, lists of topics are provided for the usual domains of mathematics: number and quantity, statistics, algebra, functions, geometry, and modeling; in addition, eight "mathematical practices" are prescribed for the entire set. Still it is insisted that the standards do not dictate a curriculum. The main reason for this contradictory language is the longstanding opposition to federal control of schools and curriculum. The federal government is still forbidden by law to prescribe a curriculum.[2] Groups working on core standards are careful, therefore, to refer to them as "national" standards, not "federal" standards, and most insist that – contrary to the obvious fact that topics for instruction are listed in considerable detail – they are not prescribing curriculum.

A careful examination of the high school math standards leads us to ask why it was thought that this list of subjects and topics was necessary.[3] The subjects required for academic mathematics have long been almost universally established in our high schools, and the near-standardization of their content has been ensured by college admissions requirements, the oversight of professional groups such as the National Council of Teachers of Mathematics, tests such as the SAT and ACT, and the textbook industry. It is true that some high schools in America do not offer the full range of recommended courses in academic mathematics. Given that shortcoming, it would be logical to suggest as a standard that all high schools make the usual array of academic courses available. But that "standard" has long been recognized if not met.

In response, then, to the question of what is the Common Core, we have to admit that – even on this basic question – we do not agree. Many, probably most teachers would say that it is a new curriculum. A close look at the math content, however, casts doubt on the contention that it is new. (We will look at the English language arts in a bit.) The topics in secondary math are not new; almost all of them (except computer methods and applications) were in place during the years of the New Math. As an example of misunderstanding on the newness of the Common Core material, consider a comment from Frederick Hess on a prescribed benchmark for algebra: ". . . all students should be able to 'determine the 126th term of the arithmetic sequence whose third term is 5 and seventh term is 29.' Knowledge at this level is well above anything we've previously expected our schools to teach or expected all students to master."[4] This comment astonished me because the sample problem really is easy (if one remembers the relevant formula; even if one forgets the formula, it is easy to reconstruct), and the topic was part of the algebra program in the 1960s.

In that earlier time, arithmetic sequences, geometric sequences, and the binomial expansion were already part of the curriculum.

What prompted the largely irrelevant movement to establish core knowledge (standards) in academic mathematics? Apparently, critics were worried about the standing of American students on math tests given worldwide. In Goals 2000 (adopted by Congress in 1994), it was stated, "By the year 2000, United States students will be first in the world in mathematics and science achievement."[5] This did not happen, and critics became increasingly alarmed about the seemingly mediocre achievement of American students. Reformers suggested strongly that standards must be raised, that math courses should be "more rigorous."

Thoughtful readers might want to interrupt here to inquire why raising the bar (if that is what we are doing) would help to raise achievement when, on the available evidence, we seem unable to meet the current, lower, standards. Why should we expect students to do better if we make the work harder? And what about the needs of students who might prefer vocational rather than academic courses? The response to this question has been that a solid program of study based on the standards should be adequate preparation for either college or work. This claim, as we have seen, has been both popular and highly contested in educational literature since the early 1900s.[6] I have argued strongly against that claim throughout this book. Unity of purpose does *not* require uniformity of curriculum or pedagogy and may even work against the democratic ideals we want to promote.

Perhaps we should take a closer look at the new standards. The topics and tasks – other than computerized content and methods – are not new. The emphasis on understanding and being able to explain the internal workings of mathematical operations sounds new, but it is largely a renewal of the concentration on meaning as described by William Brownell in the mid-twentieth century and by the New Math a bit later. This emphasis may well lead to lower test scores and a general expression of discontent among both teachers and students of mathematics. I confess to ambivalence on this. On the one hand, I believe math teachers should share the theoretical foundations of mathematical operations with students and encourage interested students to delve more deeply into these matters. On the other hand, I am not at all sure that we should expect all students to engage in such studies, and I would certainly not demand that a mastery of theoretical underpinnings be demonstrated on a standardized test. Demanding such mastery by all students is sure to enliven opposition to the whole movement. It may be wiser to include these deep understandings as extra, added attractions for the highly motivated.

We should recognize also that many teachers do not have the mathematical competence to teach foundational aspects of their subject. This lack of competence was recognized during the era of the New Math, and a major program was launched to increase the mathematical knowledge of math teachers. The National Science Foundation sponsored an ambitious program of full-year fellowships culminating in master's degrees for highly qualified math teachers. These fellowships paid the teachers' tuition and provided a stipend for the year of study. There is nothing comparable today. Instead there is a proliferation of commercially endorsed short courses and publications aimed at preparing teachers to work with the new standards. I will return to a discussion of teacher preparation in Chapter 11, but for now we might consider asking what might be done to improve math education with the teachers we have. One possibility – almost never even mentioned – is to abandon the present requirement that all students take two or three years of academic mathematics and seriously consider a math sequence roughly similar to the one in "popular science" suggested in Chapter 5.

Perhaps, however, we may find something useful – if not new – in the eight standards for "mathematical practices." The first, I confess, made me chuckle: Students are to "make sense of problems and persevere in solving them." This has long been the hope of math teachers, but we have not as yet figured out a way to get most students to try it. Indeed, the fear and hatred of word problems, so endemic to the learning of mathematics, were vividly captured in a Far Side cartoon by Gary Larson titled "Hell's Library," depicting library shelves, monitored by a smiling devil, stacked entirely with "story problems."[7] I am not suggesting that we discard this aim but, rather, that we recognize how long it has been embraced and how little success we have had in achieving it. Making sense of problems is part of a larger aim not only of learning math but of finding meaning in all of education. Let us consider, then, the possibility that the Common Core has something to contribute to the search for meaning.

Before concentrating on that important issue, let us briefly explore the standards for English language arts.[8] These are stated as skills and understandings in several areas: reading, writing, speaking, and listening. Again, as in the math standards, there is nothing new in the basic categories. The standards simply state what students will do as a result of instruction in each category; for example, in reading informational texts, students in grades 11 and 12 will "analyze a complex set of ideas or sequence of events and explain how specific individuals, ideas, or events interact and develop over the course of the text."[9] There is little guidance, however, on the contextual knowledge students will need to accomplish this task in various areas, and – as in the math standards – there is no mention of the themes suggested so far in this book. Standards for literacy in history/social studies, science, and technical subjects are listed, but they are almost the same from subject to subject, and no attempt is made to connect them to each other or to the aspects of real life that we have been discussing. Proficiency in standard English is listed as a standard, but we are given no reason to suppose that such proficiency will be attained before it is required in any reasonable attempt to meet the other, more rigorous, standards. It is just repeated again and again at every level from grade 3 on. Let us return now to the search for meaning.

THE QUEST FOR MEANING

Emphasis on teaching for meaning in mathematics was prominently endorsed in the mid-twentieth century by William Brownell. At the time Brownell was writing, there was actually some outspoken opposition to the very notion of teaching for structural or foundational meaning in arithmetic. Such opposition sounds incredible to us today. Of course we should teach for meaning! But those who expressed opposition were not advocating that meaning in the sense of applications and daily use should be discarded. They were worried that emphasis on *internal* meaning in mathematics would simply make math too hard for many students. A more appropriate emphasis would concentrate on rapid and correct computation and its relevant applications. Brownell argued that meaningful arithmetic would encourage the use of practices now endorsed by Common Core Standards. Today we want students to make sense of problems, use mathematical tools strategically, attend to precision, and model with mathematics. Brownell argued along the same lines and claimed that understanding – achieving meaning – would safeguard students "from answers that are mathematically absurd."[10] Well, maybe, but knowledge of the real, practical world might be even more effective in avoiding absurdity.

It is possible to go too far in the emphasis on internal meaning. Indeed, we did just that during the era of the New Math. Some readers may recall that even in the early grades the difference between "number" and "numeral" was emphasized and that in geometry we were told not to say, "Angle A equals sixty degrees" but, more precisely, "The measure of Angle

A is sixty degrees." But there were also positive advances in the movement – introduction of the basic language of sets and emphasis on com-
mutative, associative, and distributive properties. The internal, relational
meanings of mathematics are vitally important, but we have to observe and
be continually reflective on the effects of teaching them. For students who
will make mathematics a major study, such meaning is essential; for some
others, it may indeed help to avoid absurdity. But for most, it will almost
certainly prove too difficult. We may now be repeating some of the
pedagogical errors of the New Math.

Another source of meaning – one I have been recommending throughout this book – is the whole domain of interdisciplinary themes connected
to existential questions. The Common Core is entirely silent on this world
of meaning. This is a strange omission for people who purport to be
interested in intellectual development. It is good that attention is given to
practical meaning – how mathematics is used in the world of work and
finance – and that internal meaning is recommended to facilitate the
learning of mathematics. But surely we should include something about
the biographies of mathematicians, the history of mathematics, and its
fascinating connections to art, music, philosophy, religion, literature, and
recreational puzzles. Given the wide diversity of interests among students,
we should provide connections that open many doors to meaning and,
thus, to intellectual growth as well.

A similar neglect may be detected in the standards for language
arts. We might praise the new emphasis on the reading of nonfiction,
especially the careful analysis of historical documents, but to achieve
real meaning from such labor students need some understanding of the
historical times and the personalities who produced the documents.
Again, the need for well-developed interdisciplinary study is pressing.
There is another caution to be observed here. Many of us, perhaps most,
find more existential meaning in literature than in nonfiction. We are
drawn to literature, too, because it is enjoyable; we become entranced by
it. We might do better to increase the reading of historically informative
fiction rather than simply concentrate on nonfiction. The English language arts standards are silent on the need for context and real cooperation across disciplines.

The commitment to meaning in teaching and learning is important, but
it must be both controlled and expanded. Not every student will achieve a
deep understanding of sophisticated mathematical relations, and unless the
range of themes is extended, many students will never associate mathematics with existential meaning.

MODELING AND ORDER

Another topic holding great promise is that of using mathematics and language arts to "model" various situations. In mathematics, the idea is to represent empirical events mathematically, to construct and solve our own work problems. This is time-consuming and challenging work, and most teachers are not prepared to arrange or to supervise it. It is an area in which academic math teachers could learn much from vocational teachers.[11] Working together, academic and vocational math teachers should be able to devise at least a few projects in which students might engage in mathematical modeling.

I want to shift now to what might be called modeling in the language arts. Under the core standards, students are required to read and analyze various historical documents. They are asked to read (observe) these documents and, through analysis, construct an interpretive document of their own. Just as math students learn to bring order to some collection of events and objects through the use of mathematical representation, students are asked here to use the language arts to create an interpretation and critique of written documents and the social events to which they are addressed. To do this effectively, students need to know something about the historical background of the documents, the biographies of their authors, and the language employed in the documents. The object is not just to recognize or memorize parts of these documents, nor is the required analysis simply a logical exercise. It really demands both the knowledge and skill to model or remodel a historical argument.

In Chapter 5, where we considered the idea of an intact morality, I suggested that students think about what the founders meant when they claimed that "all men are created equal." Why did it take so long to include black men among those "created equal"? Why were women not included? Are there parts of the document that we would write differently today? The language we use models the society we are trying to establish or maintain. I mentioned, too, the words "in God we trust" and when they first appeared on U.S. coins. Why were they added? If they had not been added then and their addition were suggested today, might there be a debate? Similarly, students should become aware of when and why "under God" was added to the Pledge of Allegiance. As we move toward a more secular society, might these expressions be removed? The day after writing this, an article appeared in a local paper reporting that a family working with the American Humanist Association is suing the regional school district to have the phrase "under God" removed from the pledge. An increase in developments of this sort underscores the need for greater emphasis on critical thinking in our schools and more attention to controversial questions.

In Chapter 3, we considered the centrality of the human search for order and how order in daily life supports the search for order in the wider physical and political worlds. Attempting to analyze a historical document, students need to ask what sort of order the writers were seeking, why they chose the language they did, and whether that language was effective. If it was effective, what made it so? Is it still effective today, or should the document be rewritten? Why? How? What role did emotion – such as religious or patriotic passion – play in inspiring various documents, slogans, or additions to them?

As an example, recall the comment made by Virginia Woolf to the male correspondent who requested help in preventing war: ". . . we can best help you to prevent war not by repeating your words and following your methods but by finding new words and creating new methods."[12] What might these words be, and how should we use them? Some words have enormous emotional power, while others seem logical but fail to move us. Words associated with patriotism, masculinity, warriors, and battles have had this emotional power. Words associated with women, peace, and daily order have inspired no vigorous emotion. Woolf tried to arouse emotion by calling attention to the history of England and its dismal treatment of women:

> Therefore if you insist upon fighting to protect me, or "our" country, let it be understood, soberly and rationally between us, that you are fighting to gratify a sex instinct which I cannot share; to procure benefits which I have not shared and probably will not share; but not to gratify my instincts, or to protect myself or my country.[13]

She then goes on to say that, as a woman, she really has no country and that she – along with all women desiring peace – should abstain from all "patriotic demonstrations; to assent to no form of national self-praise; to make no part of any claque or audience that encourages war; to absent herself from military displays, tournaments, tattoos, prize-givings and all such ceremonies as encourage the desire to impose 'our' civilization or 'our' dominion upon other people."[14]

Does this have emotional appeal? Is it going too far? Finding the new words sought by Woolf will not be easy. Peace – much loved in the abstract – can be boring. In *Candide*, Voltaire describes his characters who have decided to retreat from the world of battle to cultivate their gardens as suffering "a boredom so excessive" that they might welcome rape, flogging, imprisonment, or any violence rather than their current state of "doing nothing."[15] And if we identify peace with the good and war with evil, Simone Weil reminds us: "Nothing is so beautiful and wonderful . . . as the good. No desert is so dreary, monotonous, and boring as evil. This is the truth about authentic good and evil. With fictional good and evil it is the other way round. Fictional good is boring and flat, while fictional evil is varied and intriguing, attractive, profound, and full of charm."[16]

How, then, might students model with words the world sought by Woolf? Alternatively, how might they defend the world already modeled so effectively with the images of war and patriotism? Since Woolf's time, the status of women in the public world has changed dramatically, but the language to describe that world has not. It is still male dominated, and a woman's success is judged by how well she fares in that world. There is now an interesting movement under way to "reclaim" words used in the past to criticize or "put down" women who dared to assert power in the public world. "Ladylike" was used to describe women who remained quietly in the background of events, and "unladylike" was directed at women who dared to speak assertively. Now several female politicians are redefining "lady-like." Senator Claire McCaskill, for example, has said that "ladylike" means: "Speak out, be strong, take charge, change the world."[17] Some women even seek equality in the armed forces. Far from shunning everything related to military heroics, they want to be accepted in combat units. Would Woolf regard this as progress toward a world of peace?

In this discussion of modeling with words, I have granted that standards emphasizing critical reading and writing are important, but their statement is too simplistic, and too much is expected of students without careful analysis. For example, students are expected to assess, as part of their research, the credibility of sources. The expectation almost certainly asks too much of high school students. How are they to be prepared to do this?[18] Nor can they be expected to analyze historical documents in a purely logical fashion. They need context, and their sphere of study must extend well beyond the documents and their vocabulary. The standards are not at all helpful in establishing and studying contextual, interdisciplinary material.

THE NEW "SOFT SKILLS"

Along with the supposedly increased rigor set out in the Common Core, there is a new emphasis on so-called soft skills: the ability to listen, to work cooperatively in groups, to communicate effectively orally as well as in writing, and to appreciate cultural diversity. All of this is to be applauded. As discussed in the previous chapters, many of us would also put a renewed emphasis on moral understanding and conduct. But even with the addition of teamwork or cooperation, we are already in a linguistic world of contradiction.

Our national/social attitude on cooperation is close to schizophrenic. We want our students to learn teamwork in order to compete more successfully in a competitive world economy. The message seems to be that we should cooperate with those who can benefit us. Why, then, should high school students cooperate with each other in science and mathematics when they are often in a fierce competition for grades? Some teachers respond to this by awarding team grades for various projects, thus encouraging cooperation within teams and competition between teams. We are all familiar with this blend of cooperation and competition in athletics. However, is this the spirit we are trying to cultivate when we advocate the development of cooperation among our students? Perhaps it is. If so, we should be honest about it. But many of us would prefer to encourage cooperation to solve problems for the good of all rather than to compete more successfully with others for limited resources, and we would surely want to promote the attitude of cooperating for the common good on the global level.

We are talking here about a national conundrum. Do we value cooperation for the common good or to further national dominance? We talk both lines. Recall Goal 5 in Goals 2000 (adopted by Congress in 1994): "[B]y the year 2000, United States students will be first in the world in mathematics and science achievement." What great human purpose does such a goal promote? Not only does it offend the world – as does any statement by a swaggering braggart – it is not even a practical goal. In a world of competition, the rank of our students measured as an average means very little. In that world of competition, we should want to be sure that students in our top decile rank with the world's best and that all are functioning well enough to maintain a place in the nation's economy. If we managed to get all of our students to the current median score – no one higher or lower – we would be consigned to a dismal place in the world competition. But we should be looking beyond our competitive economic status.[19] Are our high school graduates prepared for work they have chosen under careful guidance? Are they prepared for parenthood and intelligent citizenship? Are they committed to lives of caring and integrity?

FURTHER WORDS ON THE LANGUAGE OF SCHOOL REFORM

Diane Ravitch notes that her thinking about several concepts related to school reform has changed. "Where once I had been hopeful, even enthusiastic, about the potential benefits of testing, accountability, choice, and markets, I now found myself experiencing profound doubts about these same ideas."[20] She should have had doubts from the start. From the beginning, some of us noted that "accountability" and "markets" do not belong to the deep structure of educational language at all, and "choice" should belong primarily to discussions of subject matter, student interests, and the professional decisions of teachers, not to parents' choice of schools for their children. "Testing" has, of course, long been an important feature of schooling, but the sort of testing over which teachers have no control is problematic. Professional teachers know what, when, and how to test.

"Accountability" comes to us directly from business, and I have argued that it tends to distort the project of educators:

> *Accountability* forces us to answer to authorities for what we have accomplished or failed to accomplish; it points upward in the chain of power, and it encourages compliance or the appearance of compliance. We have to satisfy some authority that we have met some specific goal. There is some evidence that emphasis on accountability may even invite corruption. People, so focused on showing that they have met a particular goal, may cheat or "fudge" a bit to avoid penalties and criticism. In contrast, *responsibility* points downward in the power chain; it asks us to respond to the legitimate needs of those placed in our care.[21]

Probably most human enterprises would be morally improved by establishing at least a balance between accountability and responsibility. When attention is focused entirely on doing one's job with little or no concern about its effects on those it impacts, a worker (at any level) may shrug off his or her own morally questionable behavior as "I'm just doing my job." Even medical doctors have had to be reminded that their first responsibility is to their patients, not to their agency or group employer. Here, too, responsibility is to be honored over accountability.

The problem is widespread in the current age of market fundamentalism. In a recent *New York Times* piece, Nicholas Kristof commented on the moral failure of General Motors executives in failing to correct faulty ignition switches: "I'm sure these G.M. executives were good people who helped out their neighbors and donated to churches and charities, but they also had a moral blind spot. That has been the history of business."[22]

The language of business has also infiltrated education with an emphasis on data. Educators are urged to develop policy that is "data driven." Again, there are certainly areas of policy that should be directed by data; we need data, for example, on finance, demographics, and the number of available subject matter specialists. However, policy decisions and directives on curriculum, pedagogy, diagnosis, and evaluation must be grounded in intellectual history, in a well-considered philosophy, in both the assumed and expressed needs of student groups, and in the first-hand knowledge of individual students that must be developed in relations of care and trust. Data should be collected, studied, and employed where needed. Educational policy at the deepest level should control the use of data; it should not be *driven* by data.

Along similar lines, there is much talk about "scaling up." Today's "reformers" are in a constant search for one best method that will work everywhere for everyone. Now and then, an example is located, and school people are urged to adopt its methods. It is rarely noted that the exemplar being urged on us has worked by getting rid of the kids (and teachers) for whom it did not work. Those of us who have raised families know that, even within a family, what works with one child may have disastrous effects on another. This is not to say that we cannot learn a great deal by watching others work and conferring regularly. Collegiality should be widely encouraged. Genuine education is deeply rooted in the shared responsibility developed in relations of care and trust.

Similarly, educators should be wary of the market-defined notion of choice. Choice, embedded in the deep structure of educational theory, pertains to well-considered selection of subject matter, student programs of study, the assignment of teachers, and, where feasible, student projects. Choice should not imply mainly that families should be allowed to choose their children's school. The fact that conditions in some of our schools are so bad that parents feel a desperate need to find alternative placement for their children is shameful. Those conditions must be improved, and perhaps we should remain open to the current debate over charter schools. But as we continue to discuss the matter, we should look carefully at the possible bad effects of supporting charters, not only at the desired positive effects.

An argument is often made that the use of vouchers would make it possible for poor families, not just wealthy families, to choose their children's school. But, under any voucher arrangement, the difference between elite schools available to the wealthy and those from which the poor must "choose" would likely be dramatic. In addition to enormous differences in the quality of school building, location, and resources, there is the element of stability to consider. Well-established private schools are unlikely to close during a given student's school days; charters and other alternatives may disappear with little notice. To claim that poor families will now have the same "right" as rich families to choose their school is shamefully dishonest. Worse, as concerned parents move their children out of failing public schools, those schools often become even worse for the students who remain in them. The problem is one that must be addressed on a level comparable to the World War II Manhattan Project. It is a challenge worthy of nationwide attention. The market-induced language of choice simply misdirects us.

Because my focus in this book is on a new vision for America's high schools, I want to move on to discuss matters that are central to education and to the language that belongs to its deep structure. There are ideas and aims in the Common Core that are part of that deep structure. But before moving on to one of those aims – the promotion of critical thinking – something should be said about the corruption induced by the money factor. Money is, of course, at the very center of market interests. Enormous amounts – billions – have been spent on constructing the Common Core, promoting it, and developing standardized tests for it. The Common Core has given a huge boost to the testing industry, and the results may either support or undermine the Core itself: "In terms of overall execution, how do the exams crafted by the two main state testing coalitions – the Smarter Balanced Assessment Consortium and the Partnership for the Assessment of Readiness for College and Careers, or PARCC – stack up to what they promised in their $360 million bids for federal funding?"[23] Some of us believe that the huge sums spent on testing might have been better used to fund school lunches, expand preschool and day care, build school gardens and kitchens, and finance interdisciplinary work on the curriculum.

It is not only the misuse of money, however, that should dismay – even alarm – us. It is also the distraction of educators from the central concerns of education. Too many fine scholars have turned their attention away from the analysis and development of the educational concepts they promote to their testing. Too many are deeply engaged in developing and promoting tests for critical thinking, cooperative communication, and problem solving when the most acute need is for further analysis and reflection on what these concepts mean, what school conditions support or weaken them, and how each is developed within and across the school disciplines. In education as well as medicine, advertising, and engineering, market fundamentalism has created moral blind spots.

In conclusion, from the perspective taken in this book, the Common Core is a disappointment, ignoring the great differences among students, the need for connections among the disciplines, and the unsatisfied longing for existential meaning. However, the standards do emphasize various aspects of critical thinking and, approached thoughtfully, that emphasis might be a bright spot.

7

Critical Thinking

The Common Core Standards are permeated by a concern for critical thinking: critical reading, the analysis of documents, editing for meaning, defining problems, solving problems, searching for order, and conceptual understanding. This emphasis is to be applauded, but questions arise not only about how to teach critical thinking but, more basically, about how to define its scope and application over a wide range of human activity. Must everyone learn to apply critical thinking to the foundations of mathematical operations? Must everyone become capable of using critical thinking in reading historical or scientific documents? And how is critical thinking related, if it is, to the moral dimension of life?

SOME BACKGROUND

Although philosophers and educators have long agreed on the importance of critical thinking, they have engaged in lively debates about how to define and teach it. Some forty years ago the debate centered on whether critical thinking is field dependent or a subject/skill that can be taught on its own.[1] Those who argued for its field dependence pointed out – rightly, I think – that one can hardly think critically in an area about which one has no knowledge. One can hardly criticize a taxonomy of flowering plants, for example, if one knows nothing about plants. Similarly, it would be difficult to argue the merits of a political proposal if one knows little about the purpose of the proposal and the context in which it is proposed.

However, strong counterarguments have been made for the centrality of logic in all forms of critical thinking, and symbolic logic can be taught without reference to a specific subject or field outside it. Certainly, all students should become familiar with the basic form of a syllogism: If all birds can fly and robins are birds, we may conclude that robins can fly. As a math teacher, I learned that many students find logic in both words and symbols fascinating and useful. I also learned that some students are totally befuddled by it, and even in the world of logic, it helps to stay grounded to a real-world field of reference.

I have recounted in several places the kinds of errors that students make when they suppose that logic is a special world that follows its own rules and shuns common sense. This question appeared on one of my tests:

1. All fish can swim. (Or, if it is a fish, it can swim.)
2. I can swim.
3. ?

What conclusion, if any, can be reached? A surprising number of students concluded: "I am a fish."

We had covered the territory carefully, discussing such errors as reasoning from the converse (the error made by the students who concluded that they were fish). If the first statement had been "If X can swim, X is a fish," the students would have been logically justified in concluding, "I am a fish." But they should have noticed that, in the real world, that statement is clearly false. Recognizing its falsity, they should have been led to examine their logic. The students were familiar with conjunction, disjunction, implication, inverse, converse, contrapositive, the law of excluded middle, and the law of contradiction. We had even studied and constructed truth tables. How, then, could any student conclude, "I am a fish"?

Here we might recall Brownell's hope that understanding the structure of meaning would safeguard students "from answers that are mathematically [logically] absurd."[2] But, clearly, some of my students thought that the world of formal logic contained or allowed conclusions that would be judged absurd in the real world. In the world of logic, they might indeed be fish!

Consider another example. In a pre-calculus class, we were doing problems involving rates and distances among ships on maneuvers. One very bright student, finishing a problem quickly, announced her answer: At the end of the given maneuver, the two ships in question were 39,000 miles apart. She had used the right formulas and techniques and understood them, but, still, having made an arithmetical error, she had arrived at an absurd answer. Anyone could have made her computational error, but what led her to accept the absurd answer? Her acceptance stemmed from a lack of practical, factual knowledge, not from a deficiency of mathematical understanding. Her error led to an interesting discussion about the circumference of the earth and various global distances. The ships, after all, were on the earth, not somewhere in space. Where *on earth* could they be? For immediate recognition of an absurdity, we needed to know something about the earth; the error did not arise from lack of mathematical understanding.

None of this suggests that we should abandon the teaching of mathematical and logical reasoning and get "back to basics." Meaning, understanding, and critical thinking must be broadly construed. Formal logic, mathematical structure, careful reasoning, and common sense all have an important place in teaching and learning. Should all students be required to master the rudiments of formal logic? Probably not. But all students should be introduced to it; they should have an opportunity to learn more about it if they wish to do so. This implies that we should distinguish between concepts or skills that will be required and those that are offered initially as "free gifts" to those who will pursue them further. I will say more about how this might work in Chapter 10, on planning and evaluation.

There is another thing to keep in mind as we consider what to include in a curriculum that emphasizes critical thinking. Logic and logical analysis can be fun! This is another consideration entirely ignored by the Common Core. Math and English teachers could work together, for example, to develop a theme based on *Alice's Adventures in Wonderland*. Using Martin Gardner's *Annotated Alice*, students can be invited to explore the variety of logical errors in the book.[3] Some of the errors come from faulty reasoning – often reasoning from the converse – and some demonstrate strictly logical reasoning from mad premises. Gardner's annotations include a fascinating collection of items such as passages from the Socratic dialogue *Theatetus*, a description of Bertrand Russell's physical resemblance to the Mad Hatter, a wildly confusing discussion of time and clocks, and all sorts of references to novels, poems, history, songs, and doggerel. Students might be asked to write a critical analysis of some part of *Alice* or of Gardner's notes, but there should be no test on the material. The point is to engage in critical analysis, not to memorize quotations or fictional events, and the critical analyses should be shared. This is a wonderful example of the use of interdisciplinary themes.

It is not likely that the debates over teaching critical thinking as a subject of its own or teaching it within each field will be revived, and it is even more unlikely that attempts – such as that made in an elementary science program "Science: A Process Approach" (SAPA) – to teach critical skills such as classifying, observing, measuring, and inferring as topics separate from the fields in which they are used will be reinvented. That day is behind us. But there is a remnant of that thinking in the present-day supposition that critical thinking can somehow be taught without attention to controversy. Diane Ravitch, for example, describes her disappointment in the 1995 loss of history standards over charges that the proposed standards were politically biased. She thought the standards might be revised, that all political bias might be removed from the document: "It shouldn't have a whiff of political partisanship from the left or right."[4] Later in the same book, she extends the recommendation by insisting that science and religion be strictly separated in our schools: "Education authorities must separate teaching about science from teaching about religion. They must clarify to parents and the public that these are not the same. In other words, science classes should teach science, as validated by scholarship, and religion classes should teach religion."[5]

But, of course, the question whether evolution is or is not science is still at the heart of the matter for some people. Further, if we want students to think critically, we must make them aware of such dramatic controversies. Can we expect students to believe one proposition in science class and a contradictory one in religion class without experiencing some discomfort? Probably, the contradictions should be discussed in both classes. The debate invites critical thinking, and, additionally, it is intellectually and politically exciting. It provides another vitally important opportunity to work across disciplines on an issue of deep human interest. Related historical events such as the exchanges between Thomas Huxley and Bishop Wilberforce are exciting, and students will enjoy hearing about the passions aroused in the debates. If students are inclined to judge the Bishop as a bit stuffy and antiscientific, they may broaden their thinking when they hear that his father, William Wilberforce, led the antislavery movement in England. It would be a shame to ignore all the fascinating historical/biographical stories that arise in connection with controversies, whether they are scientific or political. Where, then, should they be discussed? Wherever they naturally arise: in science, literature, history, or religion class.

Difficulties in handling controversial issues give rise to an exploration of pedagogical neutrality. Teachers have to find a way to give all reasonable sides of a controversy a fair hearing, and this requires pedagogical neutrality. The teacher's job is not to promote his or her own view (on this, I agree with Ravitch) but to get students thinking critically about the issue at hand. That does not mean that teachers should not reveal their own views. If asked, they should do so, but they should express their opinions with a reminder that opposing views exist and should be examined critically. In these discussions, everyone is invited to speak, and every position should be open to criticism.

Should teachers maintain pedagogical neutrality on every issue? Clearly, there are views that must be rejected on moral or democratic grounds. We cannot condone giving critical respect to obviously racist views, and I cannot imagine remaining pedagogically neutral if someone recommends a new "Hitler Youth" organization or one that condones a violent response to the "capitalists of Wall Street." Remember that, in our dedication to producing better adults, we are committed to the principles and values espoused by our democratic society. But just where the line should be drawn will always be somewhat problematic, and that problem should itself be part of the discussion, especially at the level of teacher education. We should keep in mind also – and I will say more about this a bit later – that a student who expresses a racist view needs our attention; we have to find a quiet moment in which we can ask why he or she holds the belief expressed, what the student has read that endorses the view, and whether he or she has been exposed to contrary views. We should not castigate or shame the student publicly, but neither should we simply accept his or her view as a legitimate opposing position.

I believe that genuine education for citizenship requires the examination and analysis of controversial issues. But there is also a variety of critical thinking involved in the ordinary study of all subjects, and the Common Core Standards are clear on this. We want students to use a critical eye on their own work – checking grammar, spelling, punctuation, paragraphing, and the clarity of their writing. We want them to consider whether or not they have made their points clear, supplied convincing evidence, and considered the views of others who have written on the topic. In mathematics, students should check the form of their solutions: Does it help to keep the "equal signs" in successive equations under each other? Have the capital letters been clearly distinguished from the lowercase letters? Is the work orderly so that someone else can read and make sense of it? Does the solution make sense in both mathematical and practical worlds? Are there alternative, legitimate ways of approaching the problem? Surely, the cultivation of a critical eye is a major objective in the teaching of critical thinking.

Critical thinking involves more, however, than the critique of form and the careful analysis of statements for truth or falsity. It also requires weighing complex arguments, listening respectfully to various interpretations and recommendations, and constructing one's own arguments in response. This is a lot harder than locating an error in the reasoning of the Mad Hatter.

CRITICAL ISSUES

If we are going to encourage critical thinking in our schools, we will have to cultivate an attitude of respect for opposing views. This is not to say that all critical thinkers are or have been respectful or generous to their opponents. On the contrary, many have used caustic wit and biting words to dramatize their arguments. But if we are to discuss controversial issues in schools, we must insist on language that respects all reasonable views. We cannot eliminate "a whiff of political partisanship" from our educational debates, as Ravitch hoped, because any view passionately expressed is likely to be interpreted as somehow partisan by opponents. But we can forbid nastiness and demeaning attacks. We should demonstrate in the conduct of our discussions that we cherish democracy as "a mode of associated living, of conjoint communicated experience," as John Dewey put it.[6] The idea is to demonstrate in schools how critical thinking and argumentation should take place in a democratic community.

As I mentioned in an earlier chapter, Jane Addams stands out as an example of generous critical analysis. In her discussion of the Scopes evolution trial, for example, she credits the fundamentalist mountaineers for their willingness to sacrifice their daily work and walk miles to present their view and stand by their convictions. Their energy and devotion opened the intellectual circle to a world many had forgotten existed:

> But suddenly there came from a group of remote mountaineers a demonstration of a vivid and sustained interest in matters of religion, resulting in a sharp clash of doctrine between themselves and thousands of our fellow citizens, who all hung upon issues of the trial with avid interest.[7]

Addams obviously disagreed with the mountain people, but she admired their energy and dedication, and she welcomed the resulting debate.

Addams also demonstrated her generous critical thinking in her continued invitations to Clarence Darrow to speak at Hull House. In his biography of Darrow, Kevin Tierney remarks: "To her eternal credit, Jane Addams tolerated and even encouraged Darrow's presence at the settlement, recognizing his talent even in his prevailing mood of discontent."[8] Addams wanted people to work together to make the world a better place; it was not her primary purpose to win arguments. She set a fine example for school people: Use disagreement to understand social problems more clearly and tie critical argumentation to moral purposes.

When it is morally impossible to respect another's views, discussion must either be abandoned or give way to confrontation. Sometimes, as mentioned in the case of a student's racist remarks, we have to close down the public discussion and find time to meet the offending student privately. In schools, we must avoid the sort of confrontation that threatens to harm members of the school community physically or verbally. We cannot permit the advocacy of racism, the denigration of women, or the abuse of children or animals. Morality trumps pedagogical neutrality on such matters. Still, we might – after making it clear that the defense of these practices will not and should not be tolerated – try to change the subject and work toward maintaining the sense of community. As pointed out earlier, teachers and schools bear responsibility for *all* of their students. We must try to involve morally weak students in cooperative projects that might lead them to reconsider the views we abhor as morally indefensible. Care ethics strongly advises such an approach, one that says a firm "no" to any student's expressed need to hurt others but tries nevertheless to maintain a caring relation with the culprit. Our best path to reform is not punishment but the steady influence exercised in relations of care and trust.

Before exploring some important themes that might be offered in our efforts to develop critical thinking, we should face the fact that some critics reject the very idea of encouraging critical thinking by high school students. We may recall fictional characters who warned against teaching children to think: Dickens's Thomas Gradgrind, who told his children not to *wonder* but just memorize facts, and the Professor of Worldly Wisdom in Butler's *Erewhon*, who advised, "It is not our business to help students to think for themselves. Surely this is the very last thing which one who wishes them well should encourage them to do. Our duty is to ensure that they shall think as we do, or at any rate, as we hold it expedient to say we do."[9] There are people today – not as extreme or rationally deficient as the fictional characters – who believe that the teaching of material that contradicts beliefs held deeply by parents and/or communities does harm to the cohesiveness of groups that are central in a democratic society.[10]

Eamonn Callan provides a generous (if critical) overview of "sentimental civic education" – the form of education designed to induce pride and national devotion in students – and notes that it has had powerful advocates, including Plato.[11] It is easier to maintain patriotic devotion to a nation or faith when people participate in laudatory exercises of the sort criticized by Virginia Woolf and hear no real criticism directed at it. Callan draws a useful distinction between "representative" democracy, in which loyal citizens pledge their allegiance in good faith to their official representatives, and "participatory" democracy, in which citizens join in intelligent, critical debate about the doings of government.[12] Critical participation risks confrontation, of course, and differences may deepen. Callan offers a mode of conciliation consonant with the recommendations of care ethics:

> [T]he fitting response to ongoing moral conflict is sometimes not renewed effort to achieve dialogical victory over our adversaries but rather the attempt to find and enact terms of political coexistence that we and they can reasonably endorse as morally acceptable.[13]

In the course of continued conversation, the one holding a questionable moral position may begin to rethink his or her views.

The difficulty here, of course, is that it can happen that our adversaries endorse practices that are morally unacceptable not just to us personally but to our society. When we include a young racist in cooperative school activities, we do not accept his or her racism; we accept our responsibility for the student's moral as well as intellectual growth. In contrast, when we must work as adult citizens with people whose moral views we reject, the situation is much more difficult. Still, it may be better to find situations in which the moral difference is not centrally involved; it is thus possible to work together on limited projects. It may even happen, then, that it will become unthinkable to harm this obnoxious other with whom we have been working successfully. At that time, it may be possible to return to the debate over central moral issues. D. C. Phillips notes that a solution like this was advocated by John Dewey, but the "solution" should be rejected, Phillips argues, because it does not address intractable cases in which people do not respect each other's viewpoints enough to communicate openly with them.[14] Phillips is right that we may never find a satisfactory conclusion to our political differences with some people, but we might nevertheless work with them to build a community garden, establish a preschool, or organize a center to distribute food. With Dewey, I would still try to find a situation or project on which we might cooperate despite intractable differences on political/moral issues, but to engage in such efforts we need participatory citizens, well educated in critical thinking.

Is something lost when we move away from sentiment-based civic education? The enthusiastic solidarity characteristic of military, patriotic, and religious communities may be reduced. The sort of celebrations deplored by Virginia Woolf may draw fewer participants, and many of us would regard this as an improvement; others would surely regret it and predict a loss of "true Americanism." There would be a loss of innocence as more people recognize the dark as well as the bright side of our affiliations. Such critical reflection could have a positive effect on our conduct in various groups. Along with the loss of innocence, there might also be an increase in suspicion and loss of trust in political representatives and other authorities. This might still be good if it leads to a greater sense of responsibility among authorities at the policy level. A positive result also depends on the application of reflection on the part of participatory citizens, and education will necessarily play a large role in inducing reflective-critical thinking.

Let us consider two topics that might be used to develop this thinking. Religion is one such topic. Certainly we should not teach (or preach) a particular religion or religious perspective in our public schools. But we can and should teach *about* religion and religious debates, and we can draw on all of the standard disciplines to do this. In an earlier chapter, I commented on the exchange between the mathematicians Laplace and Lagrange concerning the existence of God as creator. In science classes, evolution will of course be taught, but discussion might include material on Darwin's religious transformation. He preferred to trace the cruelty of the natural world to nature and evolution, finding it impossible to believe that a good God would have deliberately created a world in which its creatures must eat one another to survive.[15] Time should be spent in history classes on the debates in which Darwin and other scientists participated. In sharing their wonderment and arguments, we are not teaching for or against religion; we are teaching about religious belief, and it is a fascinating history.

In high schools, we cannot teach about religion and religious beliefs as we would in college classes in philosophy. But many people, even college graduates, will never experience these classes. Surely, they should all at least hear some passionate arguments for religion and some equally passionate arguments against it. They should hear something of the political-religious arguments made by Hobbes in opposition to religion and by Rousseau in favor of an enlightened Christian theology. In one view, we reduce the violence encouraged in passionate religious devotion by separating theology and politics; in the other, we work to perfect our political-religious views and use them to support peace, compassion, and fellow-feeling.[16]

In the past few decades, schools have made some progress in helping students to respect – if not to understand – differences in religious and ethnic perspectives. But they have done almost nothing to reduce the fear and distrust of atheism; by some accounts, atheists are the most feared and disliked of all minority groups, and it is generally agreed that a confessed atheist could not possibly be elected president of the United States. Knowledge about atheism, agnosticism, and deism should not be restricted to those who study liberal arts at the college level. Every citizen should be aware of what these terms mean and that many thoughtful, morally sensitive Americans might be so labeled. It is not my intention to develop a curriculum here; that is the job of subject matter specialists working together at the school level. However, all high school students should hear biographical stories documenting the beliefs of Charles Darwin, John Dewey, Robert Ingersoll, James Madison, Bertrand Russell, Thomas Paine, and many of America's Founders who are properly classified as atheists, agnostics, or deists. Just as we now teach something about the beliefs of our world's religions, we should also teach *about* well-argued positions that reject religion. Atheism is a topic that can provide a wonderfully interesting interdisciplinary theme.

Consider also what might be done with religion and art, religion and music, religion and politics, religion and war, religion and slavery, religion and women's rights, religion and child-rearing, religion and food, religion and poetry, religion and ecology, religion and language, religion and education – theme after theme begging to be addressed.

What other controversial topics might be considered for interdisciplinary study? I mentioned patriotism in an earlier chapter, and that remains high on the list. We should add poverty, housing, employment, advertising, incarceration, immigration, and economic inequality. Addressing these real-life issues does not require us to abandon teaching the fundamentals of each subject in the standard curriculum. It requires, rather, that we ask seriously how each subject can contribute to the understanding and improvement of real life, and it invites creative, as well as critical, thinking across the curriculum.

CRITICAL THINKING AND MORAL COMMITMENT

Critical thinking is an important aim for education, but it must be supported by moral commitment. There are, after all, very bad people who are also highly capable critical thinkers, and there are critical thinkers who think well but remain aloof to the problems they see quite clearly.

Jane Roland Martin challenged us some time ago to think seriously about "critical thinking gone awry":

> One need only look at public policy discussions on nuclear war where hawks and doves alike transform a problem of the fate of life on earth into questions of military technology and strategy about which they exercise their considerable powers of critical thinking. It is to be found also in discussions of medical ethics where expert physicians and philosophers turn real cases of birth and death that bring catastrophe into the lives of family members into abstract questions of "the patient's best interest."[17]

I, too, referred to this problem earlier in the discussion of caring at the policy level. There it was noted that the solution of social problems is often held back by arguments among policy makers over who has defined "the problem" accurately. When that happens, the living problem of actual sufferers is converted into an abstract problem that absorbs the attention and energy of policy makers. The hungry remain poorly fed; the homeless remain without homes; the parentless remain unparented.

It should be recognized also that critical thinking may leave moral agents emotionally unaffected. It is not unusual for bright people to observe the pain or hurt of another, analyze it correctly, even identify a solution, and do nothing. They become bystanders, leaving an active response to others. David Hume argued strongly that, as moral agents, we are moved by feeling, not by intellectual understanding. Referring to the intellectual work of moral agents, he wrote:

> But where the truths which they discover are indifferent, and beget no desire or aversion, they can have no influence on conduct and behavior. What is honorable, what is fair, what is becoming, what is noble, what is generous, takes possession of the heart, and animates us to embrace and maintain it. What is intelligible, what is evident, what is probable, what is true, procures only the cool assent of the understanding; and gratifying a speculative curiosity, puts an end to our researches.[18]

Hume reminds us that it is *feeling* that motivates us to act, and this observation should reinforce our decision to address controversial issues in our attempts to teach critical thinking. Controversial issues arouse feeling in our students, and feeling encourages interest. Addressing these issues in educational settings performs a public service by bringing critical thought to feelings already aroused. Such issues, carefully and generously presented, may inspire students to study further, feel something more deeply as a result, and act on what they conclude.

Charles Sanders Peirce, in his discussion of logic and the scholarly pursuit of truth, argued that logical analysis is only one "phase of the summum bonum which forms the subject of pure ethics."[19] Ethics provides the foundation for other branches of philosophy, and a moral commitment underlies the search for truth and understanding. That search is badly corrupted when the commitment to moral good is sacrificed.

As we teach for critical thinking, we should draw attention to how easily the process can be corrupted. One huge arena for moral corruption is located in global politics. In this arena, patriotism may encourage moral corruption, and sentimental civic education aggravates the tendency.

Reading David Fromkin's account of the machinations of England and France in the creation of today's Middle East, thoughtful readers should be both astonished and disgusted at the ease with which otherwise moral men lied, cheated, and betrayed others across national lines – and sometimes even within national lines.[20] Apparently, sentimental patriotism helps to create moral blind spots in international affairs.

Blind spots are sometimes the result of ignorance or thoughtlessness. Not long ago, I talked with a group of graduate students who told me about city teachers who "assisted" their students on standardized tests. They were not critical of the teachers' conduct. Indeed, one young man praised them for their act of "civil disobedience." I was astonished. I held up a warning finger, and we had a discussion about the meaning of civil disobedience. Those who commit civil disobedience purposely and publicly disobey a law they consider unjust, and they suffer the penalty for doing this in order to uphold the Law, the agreed-upon legal system on which our civil society is founded. Martin Luther King, Jr., and other Americans committed civil disobedience to promote the rule of just law. The city teachers simply cheated. They did not admit publicly what they did or planned to continue doing, and they set a bad example for their students. Our educational aim to produce better adults is corrupted by their example.

Civil disobedience is an excellent example of an interdisciplinary theme to be studied. Another is advertising, and a critical study of advertising offers an opportunity to examine moral blind spots in an occupation.[21] We should not brand the whole advertising enterprise as immoral, but we might ask students to consider whether they would accept a position that required them to create advertisements promoting the use of tobacco by teenagers. Would they regard such work as morally acceptable? How about promoting the economic gain of corporations known as polluters of the environment? If you work for organizations such as these, are you just doing your job – making a living – or have you compromised your moral integrity?

Consider another example. Teachers in a middle school in Chicago were worried about reports that some of their students were engaged in shoplifting. Their school was fairly upscale, and the teachers were baffled by their students' behavior. They were not stealing out of need, and they were not apologetic about it; indeed, they sometimes bragged about their prowess in shoplifting. When I talked with the students about their illegal acts, they said that they stole only from "big" stores, never from local "mom and pop" shops. The implication was that the big stores ripped people off and would not miss a few things. The students thought of their thievery as vengeance for the thievery of corporations. As we talked, it became obvious that the guilty students had little regard for an absolute moral rule against stealing. They did, however, express a commitment not to cause deliberate pain or harm, and that is why they would not steal from local, neighborhood shop owners. We talked about the possibility of their doing harm to their own character, but this possibility seemed to cause little concern. Then we talked about the retaliation of corporations with higher prices to offset their losses and the effects the higher prices might have on people who are struggling financially. This *did* produce some moral concern. Some said they had not thought of that, but – even so – they were quick to blame the corporations more than themselves for the harm done. These young people were learning to think critically, but they needed to engage in further discussion to weigh the results of their thinking.

When I left, I hoped the teachers would follow through with further discussion about moral issues, but I heard one teacher say, "I'm a math teacher, not a moral educator," and I thought once again that we in education simply must get past this prime example of bureaucratic thinking. The idea that every problem, every issue, every area of study is the responsibility of one agency or occupational specialty must be jettisoned. The contemporary world is too complex and interconnected to be governed in this piecemeal fashion. In education, *every* teacher is a moral educator, and our primary aim is to educate better adults – "better" described over an amalgam of intellectual, physical, emotional, civic, social, and moral traits.

Educators need to engage in vigorous and persistent critical thinking directed at ourselves and our work. Our critical thinking must be reflective. What are we trying to do? Why? Is the method we have chosen for one purpose likely to retard our progress toward an even more important aim? The teachers whose students were unashamedly engaged in shoplifting needed to talk, to reflect on what they were doing. Their students needed to consider questions such as: Should I accept an absolute rule against stealing? Why? Is it morally acceptable to steal from the rich? Have I advanced the sense of community by stealing from a corporation? Have I hurt anyone? Should I worry about the state of my own character when I steal, cheat, or lie? If I were asked to name a moral exemplar, who would I name? Would he or she condone stealing? All of these questions are central to the main categories of moral thought. We need not engage in formal study of Kantian rationalism, Aristotelian character education, religious doctrine, care ethics, and utilitarianism, but by addressing questions such as these, we will introduce students to the moral issues of continuing concern to moral philosophy and to thoughtful persons generally.

As we become reflectively critical of our own beliefs and practices, we call into question many views that we have often accepted as politically correct. To use myself as an example, I have become critical of the slogan "All children can learn"; it is essentially meaningless, but it is used constantly to remind us that we have a deep responsibility for the growth of all children. I agree whole-heartedly that we are responsible for the growth of all children. But we would do better to say exactly that. As it is shouted now, many teachers seem to believe that all children can learn whatever the school offers, and when students fail to learn what is prescribed, it must be the teacher's fault. But not all children can learn algebra or physics at an academically adequate level. Not all children can master music theory nor attain the linguistic mastery to understand Plato, Augustine, or Jean-Paul Sartre. Our task as teachers is to help students find out what they might be good at, what they want to do in life, how to evaluate that enterprise, and then help them to succeed at it. We should remind ourselves constantly of our main aim – to produce better adults.

Believing – or pretending to believe – that all children can learn whatever we set out to teach them is one example of unreflective thinking in today's educational world. Another comes dangerously close to out-and-out hypocrisy. We say, as Americans committed to participatory democracy, that we respect all people regardless of race, ethnicity, religion, or class and that we respect and appreciate the full range of human talents. But when we are faced with the possibility that children are inclined to mechanical or physical work of some kind, we "generously" insist that they should go to college. Our actions speak clearly: Go to college or be nothing. The appropriate response to this attitude, I have been arguing, is a renewed commitment to truly excellent vocational education and, at the societal level, to a universal standard of living that reflects our genuine appreciation for all human abilities and contributions.

I will return to the exploration of reflective critical thinking in the coming chapters on collegiality, continuity, intellectual vitality, and teacher preparation.

8

Collegiality, Caring, and Continuity

In addition to an emphasis on critical thinking, the Common Core advocates attention to such "soft skills" as collegiality, cooperation, communication, teamwork, and social skills. This chapter will discuss how we might promote these skills for both students and teachers. I will start with collegiality, then discuss the need to establish relations of care and trust in order to support the whole array of social skills, and conclude with an argument in support of continuity of subject matter, people, and place in our high schools.

COLLEGIALITY

"Collegiality" conveys the notion of shared responsibility. In Chapter 1, I commented on the collegial organization used at Columbia University in planning and implementing its freshman core course. Its benefits, described by Andrew Delbanco, include the mixing of students from various departments, socio-economic backgrounds, and social clubs.

> The Core also counters the provincialism of the faculty. Senior and junior professors, along with graduate student instructors, gather weekly to discuss the assigned texts – a rare opportunity for faculty from different fields, and at different stages of their careers, to consider substantive questions. And, not least among its benefits, it links all students in the college to one another through a body of common knowledge; once they have gone through the core, no student is a complete stranger to any other.[1]

I am not sure the claim that "no student is a complete stranger to any other" can be sustained, but the random assignment of students to small core classes is certainly valuable in extending both friendships and information on various programs at the university. I have already suggested that such a mixture of students be used in the four-year social studies classes designed to treat collegially planned interdisciplinary themes. High school English teachers might also adopt this process and use random assignment of students to small discussion groups as they promote the interdisciplinary knowledge required for contextual understanding of the documents students are now expected to analyze. The idea of collegiality – shared responsibility – is valuable for students as well as teachers. Small groups – four or five students – in English language arts classes might be encouraged to work together in mastering standard language as they tackle the analysis of various documents. They should accept responsibility for reminding each other to use the "formal" language of schooling, and this should be done with generosity and good humor. Both teachers and students can joke a bit as they do this, but teachers will have to watch carefully lest the criticism get out of hand. If, for example, only one student in the group has not yet mastered standard English, the teacher should not promote student criticism. It would likely be too embarrassing and might even discourage participation by the criticized student. If the groups are well balanced racially and linguistically, they might be encouraged to criticize each other in a friendly way. Everyone needs help. When a student makes a good point using bad grammar, a student-critic might respond "great idea – now can you put that in a way the teacher will approve?" A group might invent a fictitious "great critic" or even a "sourpuss critic" to whom they will regularly defer in employing standard language.

We are talking here about genuine collegiality in student groups. Much of the research on small groups has concentrated on the formal structure and operation of groups, and teachers have been encouraged to assign students to formal roles within the groups.[2] This is important work in itself, designed to further competence in teamwork. But I am talking here about a less formal collegial arrangement that supports the conversation of people exploring ways to pursue common aims. Such conversation is open, informative, friendly, and creative. It may, by general agreement, sometimes become more formal to pin things down. Teachers supervising these groups have social aims as well as academic aims in mind. They attend to the tone of conversation and remind students to address each other with respect. As they move from group to group, listening – gently correcting when necessary – they become familiar with the ways in which students interact. They find out who the leaders are, who might be left out, who might be a bully, and who might be the victim of bullying. Sometimes a reminder such as "We don't talk to each other that way in here" is necessary.

As in the example just mentioned, informal group work can provide a natural transition to valuable instruction. While walking about the room, listening to student interaction, a teacher may hear the same mistake or misunderstanding repeatedly. It is time then to interrupt the group work and clear up the misunderstanding. Obviously, the brief lesson motivated by student conversation has powerful potential; it is presented in response to expressed student need. As a math teacher, I found these short, spontaneous lessons useful and well received. My students and I were, during these intervals, in a real collegial relationship – one of shared responsibility.

I want to say a few cautionary words here. Not every class is ready for the sort of informal, collegial work I am describing. To make some of the problems clear, and to be as explicit as possible, I will confine my remarks to math classes. To get started, a teacher might say, after assigning the night's homework, "You can work together." There might be only ten minutes or so left in the class period, so things are unlikely to get out of hand. In that short time, the teacher will find out whether the students will talk with the people nearest to them, whether they are pleased to have this opportunity, and whether they will actually address the homework. If chaos ensues, a more structured approach will have to be sought.

Let us suppose all goes well. What are we trying to accomplish? We are trying to show that our common object is to master the material at hand and to help one another to do so. I advise strongly against grading math homework or even collecting it. Too often, students do their homework in order to get a passing grade recorded or to avoid a zero for failing to do it. This is an enormous distraction from the real purpose of doing homework, which is to practice the skills involved or to explore alternative ways of handling the tasks assigned. I never collected homework or assigned a zero if a student turned up without his or her homework. The message continually given was that homework is an opportunity to learn, to make mistakes, to raise questions, and to share solutions. Every day began with a lesson invited by students' questions and observations on the assignment. As some students demonstrated their solutions on the blackboard, I would walk up and down the aisles noting the work students had done. Occasionally, a desk-top might be empty, and I would ask quietly, "No homework?" Usually there was a good reason for this and nothing more needed to be said. If the lapse occurred often, a conference was scheduled.

We should say a bit about what to do if students are too unruly to work together as I have suggested. Keep trying! We have to remember our unitary purpose – to produce better adults. Time spent talking with students about their responsibilities to each other, about the value of working together, is not time wasted. Further, we can point out to them that time spent working together in class will reduce the time they must spend alone on homework. If many of the students in an unruly class do not do their homework, cooperative class time is even more important, and working together may convince some students that they can, after all, do the required work. We do not help lagging students by "getting tough," giving lots of zeroes and referrals for discipline.

We could spend much more time on a discussion of homework. Some would argue, rightly I think, that its merits have been exaggerated and that we force elementary school children to suffer under an unreasonable load of homework. Alfie Kohn has made a convincing argument against homework for young children, and his argument for a reduction of homework for secondary school students is equally persuasive.[3] Educators must use reflective critical thinking on the issue. What are we aiming to accomplish? Does homework contribute to the accomplishment of this aim?

As a former math teacher, I would argue that a reasonable amount of homework provides the practice necessary to consolidate learning. Some might respond that my description of collegial work among students should be called "classwork," not "homework." But it is both. A certain amount of homework should be done in class, collegially, and the problems that arise in that setting contribute substantially to fruitful instruction. Some of a teacher's very best lessons are presented as a result of students' questions – another lovely form of collegiality. Too often today teachers are urged to plan every lesson starting with a well-stated learning objective drawn judiciously from the established curriculum. All of us teach such lessons when we introduce new material. But these lessons are rarely as powerful as those taught in response to genuine questions from students, although we seldom have time to prepare them in detail; they must be produced spontaneously. Indeed, when invitational lessons are presented, it is the *teacher* who must be prepared, not the specific lesson. Teachers must be very well prepared in their subject matter to respond with these "invitational" lessons. Such lessons are offered in response to the expressed needs of students, and I will say more about them in the following section on "Care and Trust" and in Chapter 9, on curriculum. One of the worst pedagogical errors we commit today is to work from the supposition that the teacher must decide on each day's learning objective based on the a priori, assumed needs of the students as described in the standard curriculum. Combining homework and classwork provides an opportunity to learn something about the *expressed* needs of students.

I have not, and will not, argue for the merits of homework in itself. I do not believe that homework does much to encourage diligence and responsibility. Indeed, such an emphasis on the merits of homework may distract us from its real purpose: to hone skills, make mistakes, deepen understanding, and underscore the value of shared responsibility. I would, therefore, neither give formal credit for work submitted nor penalties for work undone. This work – some done in class, some at home – is central to both individual growth and the sense of shared responsibility. That is where its value lies. If things have become so warped over the last three or four decades that students will simply not do homework without credit or threat of penalty, we must start over – encouraging students to try the assigned exercises in preparation for sharing their results with both the class and the teacher. And again, if things are really that bad, we are wasting our time with talk of raising academic standards; we should be concentrating on raising the moral sensitivity, intellectual curiosity, and morale of our students.

There is another important point to be considered before leaving the topic of homework. Teachers today seem to expect the home and parents to do much of the school's work. Education should, of course, be a cooperative enterprise – schools, homes, and communities working together. But as I argued earlier, today's schools may not be doing enough to support healthy family life; the purported cooperation has become too nearly a one-way process. When we transfer some homework to classwork and emphasize the social/moral learning inherent in collegial work, we support the work of families in raising socially responsible children. We should do much more, of course, including the recommendation already made on the teaching of parenting, but it is worth pointing out here that the handling of homework can support or undermine the quality of home life.

Not all homework serves the same purpose. Special projects and long-term writing assignments, for example, are homework because they must be done outside of class at times chosen by the students. The math homework described above could be done in class or at home, and it is properly thought of as a continuation of classwork. Teachers should consider the burden that math homework often puts on parents, especially if the work is to be graded. Most of the nightly battles over homework could be avoided by reminding students that their questions will be answered – and honored as contributions – in tomorrow's class session and by assuring parents that the order of home life is respected. Parents, in turn, should remind kids that homework is their responsibility as students, and both parents and teachers should talk about the centrality of order in daily life, how essential it is for students to think about their own work habits and choose the time at which they will do their homework. That time should not be chosen for them.

Let us return now to the issue of teacher collegiality. Most high schools have regular departmental meetings, and so teachers within a given department enjoy at least some collegiality. However, if we are to take seriously the task of teaching themes that connect the disciplines to each other and to life itself, it will be necessary for interdisciplinary teams to meet regularly. E. O. Wilson points out that we are living in an age of interdisciplinary investigation – that biology, for example, "has expanded to the borders of the social sciences and humanities, and they to it."[4] He describes a "middle domain" in which disciplines come together to share investigative work:

> The middle domain is a region of exceptionally rapid intellectual advance. It, moreover, addresses issues in which students (and the rest of us) are most interested: the nature and origin of life, the meaning of sex, the basis of human nature, the origin and evolution of life, why we must die, the origins of religion and ethics, the causes of aesthetic response, the role of environment in human genetic and cultural evolution, and more.[5]

Wilson also notes that "religion and science are the two most powerful forces in the world today," and he urges them to unite "on the common ground of biological conservation."[6] In this dedication to the project of saving the Creation – living Nature – he overlooks what is possibly the greatest force of all – money – but his invitation to cooperate is still worthy of our attention. Here is an ideal interdisciplinary theme – environmentalism – and it is closely connected to a theme already mentioned – religion. Wilson, a secular humanist, has paved the way by casting his plea for cooperation on the natural environment as a letter to a Southern Baptist pastor. We can learn something about collegiality from his choice of language: "Earth is a laboratory wherein nature (God, if you prefer, pastor) has laid before us the results of countless experiments. She speaks to us; now let us listen."[7]

CARE AND TRUST

Caring, as defined in care ethics, is not simply a matter of having or expressing concern. It is best described as a *relation*. A caring relation, in simplest terms, involves two parties, a carer and a cared-for; the carer attends to the expressed needs of the cared-for, is moved affectively by what he or she detects in the other's situation, and is prepared to respond in some appropriate way; the cared-for completes the relation by recognizing – showing in some way – that the attempt to care has been received.[8] Much more must be said to fill out the roles of carer and cared-for, but for present purposes it may be enough to note that *caring* basically describes the quality of a relation, not the virtue of an individual; it may, however, be applied to an individual who regularly establishes and maintains caring relations. It is fundamental in care ethics to remember that the relation is not properly defined as *caring* unless the cared-for somehow shows that the attempt to care has been received as caring.

In education, the relational definition is crucial. We often hear adults – parents, teachers, policy makers – claim that they are employing certain methods because they care. In some cases, students who are supposedly the recipients of this care say of their situation, "Nobody cares!" The traditional response to this disappointing claim is that the young people do not know what is good for them, that someday they will understand and appreciate the "care" they are now receiving, and that the adults in charge will eventually be credited with the virtue of caring. This is not an altogether empty claim. Most of us have experienced moments of enlightenment when we admitted to ourselves that Grandma or our high school science teacher was right after all. But care ethics advises us to take seriously claims that we do not seem to care and to work toward building relations of care and trust. Again, *caring* is best construed as a quality of relation, not primarily as a virtue belonging to an individual.

Care theorists in education share the emphasis on dialogue characteristic of all forms of relational ethics. Martin Buber, for example, writes of a "dialogue which never breaks off" even in the dark of lonely night. To the child, this dialogue in relation provides assurance, protection:

> Trust, trust in the world, because this human being exists – that is the most inward achievement of the relation in education. Because this human being exists, meaninglessness, however hard pressed you are by it, cannot be the real truth. Because this human being exists, in the darkness the light lies hidden, in fear salvation, and in the callousness of one's fellow-men the great Love.[9]

Buber's language is romantic, but his view of education and teaching is utterly realistic. The teacher is a real person: "He need possess none of the perfections which the child may dream he possesses; but he must be really there."[10] There is mutuality, but it is not the mutuality of equals. In the language of care ethics, the teacher acts as carer – receiving what is there in the student, hearing expressed needs, standing ready to respond; the student acknowledges the caring with a sparkle in his or her eyes as an approved project is pursued, with the disappearance of a frown as a problem is solved. For Buber, and for care theorists, the teacher must see things from the student's side. If he or she cannot do this, the educational enterprise "may degenerate into arbitrariness, and ... the educator may carry out his selection [of subject matter] and his influence from himself and his idea of the pupil, not from the pupil's own reality."[11] As we have already noticed, the very best lessons are those motivated by students' questions, interests, and responses.

One can find examples of responsive teaching in many biographical accounts. Scott Nearing described Simon Patten teaching economics at the Wharton School. In an introductory lesson, Patten spoke "haltingly, almost bashfully," but then a student interrupted apologetically with a question. "Patten turned toward the student. His face lit up. He smiled engagingly and gave a clear, concise definition, adding a few examples to make his meaning clear."[12] Nearing gained a whole new sense of what it means to teach from Patten: "questions and answers – the exchange of ideas – were woven into the course"; "he was at home in history, social philosophy, sociology, and political science"; "there was never a dull moment in Patten's classes."[13]

Recall the earlier quote from Nearing about his own teaching: "With several hundred new students each year it is difficult to establish and maintain personal relations, which are an essential feature of all good teaching. However, I always tried to know students personally..."[14] Nearing and Patten were engaged in university teaching, and they used evening gatherings and social settings to maintain both personal relations and continuing intellectual dialogue. In the next section, on continuity, I will suggest some ways in which this might be done in our high schools.

Mark Edmundson, too, has discussed the power of relations and conversation in teaching. We need not reject the wonders of technology in planning our lessons and units, but we should not depend too heavily on them. Edmundson emphasizes the need for face-to-face encounters rather than (or at least in addition to) online instruction:

> Why does the encounter need to take place face-to-face...? Because the student and teacher need to create a bond of good feeling, where they are to speak openly with each other. They need to connect not just through cold print but through gestures, intonations, jokes. The student

needs to discover what the teacher knows and what she exemplifies about how to live; the teacher needs contact with the student's energy and hopes. That kind of connection happens best in person; perhaps it can only happen that way.[15]

Thus, it is not only care theorists who argue for the centrality of relation in education. There is widespread agreement among thoughtful educators on questions of collegiality, mutuality, and the need to establish relations of care and trust. I have been arguing that, as we concentrate on establishing those relations, we should also revive and renew the true language of education and place the language of business – "accountability," "data-driven," "scaling up" – on the periphery. We can use this business language sparingly and wisely, but we should not let it displace language that belongs to the deep structure of education.

As care ethics has become increasingly popular, an important issue has arisen that needs clarification. The word "caring" itself is widely used in everyday conversation, and it is necessary to distinguish its meaning in care theory from these many everyday uses. It is especially important to explain the distinction between *caring-for* and *caring-about*. Caring-for is identified as the form of caring characteristic of the caring relation. It is described in terms of the attitudes and activities of the one caring or carer. It is attentive, receptive, empathic, and responsive, and it is in direct communication with the cared-for. Caring-about may be identified with concern. To say that we "care about" something or someone is tantamount to saying that we are concerned. To care-about is sometimes the initial step in the business of caring, but it may or may not lead to caring-for. Consider contrasting examples. I care-for my own children directly – moved by love and a feeling response to their needs. I care-about starving children in war-torn Africa; I am concerned. But my concern may or may not lead to some genuine form of caring-for – by either me or the people I sponsor.

Caring, at the policy level, almost always starts with caring-about, or concern. If the concern is sustained, there will be recommendations for action. Now the big question is whether the recommended action will produce or support genuine caring-for. The transition from caring-about to caring-for is crucial. Recall the example cited earlier in which school administrators defended a policy in the name of caring-about children: We invoke this rule or practice because we care about our students! But the students, when consulted, insisted that "Nobody cares!"

The example of the impoverished family with eight young children living for three years in a city-run shelter is a powerful case in point.[16]

The community and its governing agents care-about the homeless; there is concern for their welfare. But the transition from caring-about to caring-for verges on the tragic. The family does not feel cared-for, there is no sign of caring-for among the other occupants of the shelter, and there is little reason to predict that the future will be better for them. If care theory is to have a positive effect on social outcomes, meticulous attention must be given to the difference between caring-about and caring-for, and especially to the transformation of caring-about to caring-for.

In today's schools, the "arbitrariness" Buber warned against is now standard practice. We justify many policies in the name of caring-for our students, but in doing so, we ignore the students' reality. Without the recognition of the cared-for, there is no caring relation. What might be done to fulfill our commitment to relations of care and trust?

CONTINUITY

Let us turn now to a discussion of continuity and how it might contribute to the establishment and maintenance of relations of care and trust. Continuity of purpose, of subject matter, of place, and of people (classmates and teachers) are all important. I will start with continuity of purpose.

With the current emphasis on test scores at the pre-college level and graduates' salaries after college, we seem to have forgotten the main purpose of education: to produce better adults. Exactly how the better adult should be described is the matter under discussion in this book, and it is one for continual discussion. Perhaps, however, we can agree that the description should include consideration of the main attributes and aspects of human life: intellectual, physical, emotional, social, aesthetic, and moral. Further, whenever it is reasonable to do so, we should connect material on the aspect under present emphasis to the others. We are working with whole people – not sharply segmented components.

When a social or moral question arises in a class session, it should be addressed. This is not an excuse to neglect or brush aside a planned lesson; it is an imperative reminder to embed the current lesson in what really matters in a fully human life. Let us say, for example, that a bullying incident has occurred on campus. In math class, we are reviewing homework on the graphing of ellipses. We can certainly spend a few minutes talking about the difficulties students experienced with the problems and how to help one another. We might even joke a bit about how difficult the problems are and how even a good-hearted student might give way to nastiness in frustration with the doggone ellipses. We can stop for a bit and discuss how we might help students who are tempted to bully or who may be the victims of bullying. Is the bully trying to hide a fear or weakness? Is the victim afraid to ask for help? Is either in need of a friend? And what is a friend? Here is another excellent topic for a school-wide theme, and the math teacher – judging from reactions in the class – may suggest "friendship" as a theme to be considered by the interdisciplinary team.[17] If the discussion in math class becomes so interesting that the teacher does not have time to explain the current material adequately, homework should still be assigned and the students be told to read the text and give it a try. (An aside: Students will not try to distract teachers with imaginary moral and social problems if they know the assignment will be made anyway.) Their independent effort will set the stage for a powerful invitational lesson on the next day.

This may be a good point at which to return to the exploration of homework and invitational lessons. The formal curriculum provides a logical continuity of subject matter, but the teacher's response to student problems and questions facilitates intellectual continuity. A lesson that introduces a new topic does not end with a homework/classwork assignment. It comes to culmination with a review of the homework that satisfies questions students may raise about it. We have to consider the intellectual continuity of each student.

Supporting the intellectual continuity of each student is a difficult task and is made even more so by the standard practice of moving a whole class along when most of the students seem ready for the next step in the prescribed curriculum. The hope is that slower students will, with help and hard work, catch on and catch up. But usually things just get worse. Math teachers refer to cumulative ignorance – a massive lack of knowledge that continues to grow. Students who cannot work with one variable are unlikely to succeed with problems in two variables. Youngsters reading at the fourth grade level will be helplessly frustrated faced with Shakespeare or Dickens. The solution suggested is often to retain such students in grade. At the high school level, retention in grade nine frequently results in the student's dropping out. Retention rarely helps at any level. I suggested earlier that high schools should provide a preparatory ninth grade in which students' skills might be upgraded. This is much to be preferred over retention, which may retard the growth of cumulative ignorance slightly but at the severe cost of separation from former classmates and lowered self-esteem. Continuity of people, of classmates, is probably more important – certainly more treasured – than continuity of subject matter.

There is a better solution. In sequential subjects, we must group and regroup students for part of each class session according to the material they have so far mastered. In math, students do not go on to Chapter 3 until they have passed at least a rudimentary test on Chapter 2. This process does not require a sharp separation or exclusion from all of the class's activities and discussions, but it does require the assignment of different homework and the construction of several variant forms for tests on each chapter or unit of study. For some students and in some topics, online programs are available that will allow students to move at their own pace. A system of this kind is easier to run with a team of teachers, but it can be done in a single-teacher classroom. Students moving more slowly through a text or well-defined curriculum may never catch up; that is, they might not complete the standard course. But what is the point of "completing" a course if one has learned virtually nothing in doing so? Paradoxically, supporting students as they move at a slower pace brings a reward in results on standardized tests. In my own experience, students who managed to complete six chapters successfully scored higher on the test than students who failed their way through twelve chapters. Very few of the slower moving students will score in the bottom quintile; they will all have learned enough to answer some questions correctly. Notice that this approach is a variant of mastery learning.[18] We need not believe that every student can master every subject the school offers; I certainly do not. We can, nevertheless, learn from and adapt the powerful ideas of mastery learning, the most important of which is that a reasonable foundation must be provided and achieved for everything we teach.

The plan just described raises questions about grades and credits. Should students who have successfully completed half of the standard course receive full credit for it? What grade should they be given? These are questions that must be answered locally. If it is a terminal course (for example, the student does not intend to take more mathematics), I would simply grant a year's high school credit. If more math is needed, another year of individualized pacing should probably be arranged. There are various ways to handle grading/credit in these courses, and the faculties involved should explore them carefully. I confess here that I have never found a satisfactory answer to this problem. The traditional system of grading is so deeply entrenched in our schools that it is enormously difficult to make even small changes. Perhaps, when enough educators realize that the system actually impedes pedagogical progress and almost destroys educational creativity, we will get rid of it and find a more genuine and informative way to assess the work of students and teachers.

Continuity of place should also be considered. We know how hard it is for students to adjust when they move from one community to another. It can also be difficult to move from elementary school to middle school and from middle school to high school. One might reasonably argue that it was a mistake to create the junior high school – now renamed the middle school. As first envisioned, the junior high was to be a place where students would be sorted into those suited to the academic work of the college preparatory high school and those better fitted to a vocational program.[19] Even then, there were those who emphasized the exploratory role of junior high education and those who concentrated on its sorting function. That debate continues, with some modifications, to the present day.[20] "Sorting" is frowned on today, and the recommended alternative is to prepare everyone rigorously for the academic program of the high school. One can understand and sympathize with the seemingly more generous attitude dominant today, but it ignores the real talents and interests of many children, and there is a viable alternative that rejects both the sorting function and the uniform concentration on preparation for college.

That alternative is to define middle school as an exploratory educational experience. As such, it would indeed be a time of sorting – a period in which students could begin to sort themselves by interest and innate talent. Under this plan, all students would be required to participate in a wide variety of introductory courses ranging over the entire curriculum, such as algebra, shop, music, fine arts, computer science, and literature. There would be no formal grades given in this exploratory period, but teachers, students, counselors, and parents would work collaboratively to help students identify their own strengths and weaknesses. I am not suggesting that students would start high school with a sure, unchangeable life-plan in place; our lives today are properly open to continued, reasoned change. But students should enter high school with a tentative plan that excites them and is clearly respected by the educational community. They should be given the opportunity to make well-guided choices.

The plan for middle school education just described seems to give little attention to continuity of subject matter. Indeed, it seems to allow, even invite, discontinuity and intellectual wandering. There *should* be a time and place for such exploration. The plan holds to continuity of unitary purpose, and it requires continuity in the teacher–student relationship. Every student should have the continual guidance of a teacher who will "stay with" the student through this period of exploration.

Because the caring relation is so fundamental in education, we should consider ways in which to support it in our high schools. Instead of having a different "specialist" for every year of mathematics, for example, students might work with the same teacher throughout their high school years. Teachers working this way would have to know the entire math curriculum very well, of course. But they should! There is something disturbingly wrong with a system of teacher preparation that produces high school math teachers who know only first-year algebra and introductory geometry. I will say more on this in Chapter 11, on teacher preparation.

When teachers and students stay together for several years, there are advantages for both. With continuing students, teachers can pick up in September where they left off in June. There might even be a summer reading assignment from the math teacher: Gardner's *Annotated Alice*, Hofstadter's *Gödel, Escher, Bach*, Kahn's *Pythagoras*, Abbott's *Flatland*, Mazur's *Imagining Numbers*, Best's *Damned Lies and Statistics*. There are fewer new student names to learn. Student learning styles and idiosyncrasies are familiar. The teacher's ways and expectations are also familiar. And if there is a gap in general student learning, the teacher can trace it to his or her own failure to follow up in last year's lessons. The teacher also knows what to emphasize this year because he or she knows what is coming in the next year. Not least important, the teacher has established relations of care and trust with the students and among them. They will help each other and treat each other with respect. Their grades will not depend on their doing better than their classmates.

Collegiality, caring, and continuity lie at the heart of education; they support and enrich each other. Continuity of purpose is fundamental, and caring relations promote the growth and development of the better adult we seek to produce. Emphasis on collegiality reminds us that shared responsibility is inherent in the concept of genuine education. We need to say more now about the complicated matter of transforming the curriculum in ways that are feasible given the constraints imposed by college requirements, standardization, and commercial interests in testing.

9

The Curriculum and Its Setting

In this chapter, we will consider more closely the ideas so far discussed and see what might reasonably be done to bring the curriculum and extracurricular activities into line with these broad recommendations. This is to be done without insisting on a sweeping transformation that would eliminate, or even threaten, the traditional academic program. As pointed out throughout this book, such a transformation would be both utopian and hopeless. What follows, then, should be practical. We will look first at some modifications of the curriculum, then at the importance of extracurricular activities, and finally at the physical setting for high schools of the future.

THE CURRICULUM

It seems entirely feasible to expand existing courses with the theme and interdisciplinary team approach already described. The challenge, of course, is to apply the concepts of intellectual continuity and shared responsibility to the whole enterprise. Where possible, we want to connect the themes not only to central human questions but to each other and, certainly, to the subject matter of the standard classes. It is not suggested that the officially prescribed work of mathematics, science, or literature be suspended but, rather, that it should be enriched to include the chosen themes. The use of biography and literature can enrich the curriculum in every subject.

For example, in discussing the centrality of law, power, and economy of expression in mathematics, Barry Mazur departs from formal mathematics briefly to describe the use of dactyls in poetry. He asks us to consider the power of W. S. Merwin's "Elegy," a one-line poem ("Who would I show it to") consisting of two dactyls.[1] As we learn about imaginary numbers from Mazur, we also hear all sorts of things from Rilke, Ashbery,

Wordsworth, Yeats, and Coleridge. Mazur also reminds us that – for some odd reason – the later letters in the alphabet are considered somehow harder than the earlier ones, and he gives an example of this thinking from Virginia Woolf's *To the Lighthouse*. Mr. Ramsay is described as moving more deeply into abstractions as through the alphabet: "Z is only reached once by one man in a generation. Still if he could reach R it would be something. Here at least was Q."[2] Algebra students might react to this with appreciative recognition: Of course! x, y, and z's are way harder than a, b, and c's. Just as Mazur's discussion of imaginary numbers is enriched by his occasional discursions into art and fiction, so might our math classes be enlivened.

In addition to enriching each of the standard courses in the disciplines, we might begin to develop parallel courses in some subjects. Science would seem to present wonderful opportunities for such courses. Many students find the usual courses in biology, physics, and chemistry both difficult and dull, and, unless they plan to major in college programs that require these courses, they will avoid them if possible. Courses in human biology (growth, nutrition, disease prevention, sex, child development) are often received with some enthusiasm, and they should be more widely offered. Schools will have to be careful to describe them in ways that meet college admission requirements, but they should also be made attractive and available to students in vocational programs. Indeed, the vocational faculty might take the lead in developing courses in human biology, environmental science, plant growth and gardens, community planning, and home construction. Whereas the usual academic science program consists of courses designed to prepare students for further work in a particular discipline, these parallel courses would prepare students for life in the real world. Courses planned and taught cooperatively across academic-vocational lines would contribute genuine preparation for both college and career.

A major difficulty standing in the way of developing parallel courses is the power exercised by higher education. Students who aspire to a college education must take the high school courses required for admission. It should not be inordinately difficult, however, to develop parallel, college-acceptable courses – a series for students likely to continue study of a particular discipline in college and a series for those unlikely to do so. The result of such differentiation should be students better prepared for further study in the discipline and students better prepared to make wider connections to the disciplines on which they will concentrate.

At present, schools are being pressed to put more and more emphasis on the so-called STEM subjects (science, technology, engineering, and mathematics). We should think carefully about this emphasis. It is certainly reasonable to work continually to improve courses in these subjects and to identify and encourage students whose talents lie in this direction. But there is little justification for pushing all students toward uniformly higher standards in these subjects. More attention should be given to non-STEM subjects and talents and to well-informed student choice.

The Common Core, as it appears now, assumes that linguistic and mathematical skills are fundamental in the curriculum, that they provide the foundation for all other studies. They clearly are important, but we might again raise a finger of caution. In a participatory democracy, perhaps no area of study is more important than social studies, but no subject in the curriculum has been more contentious. With the growth of the social sciences – political science, sociology, economics, and anthropology – the central place of history in the school curriculum was challenged.[3] In many schools, it had already been supplemented by civics, a study of government, and by geography. At the high school level, geography was usually included in history, and civics sometimes appeared as a second course in American history, for example, "Problems of Democracy." Understandably, historians feared that the study of history would suffer a loss as the social sciences were accommodated in the curriculum.

The controversy was not limited, however, to arguments over how much time should be given to each of the social sciences. There was a livelier debate between the two large categories called *social science* and *social education*.[4] Supporters of social education advocated an organization of curriculum around social problems, not established disciplines. It is a view that has similarities to the theme approach I have been advocating in this book – except that I have so far suggested themes and problems as additions, as expansions, to the traditional disciplinary subjects, not as replacements. It may be that the optimal organization differs from subject to subject. For example, a sequential subject such as mathematics might best be organized by mathematical concepts and skills, with social problems added occasionally through themes, whereas social studies might better be organized around social problems (themes). We need not insist on a uniform mode of organization.

Even within social education, however, disagreements arose, and some are still with us. Some social educators advocated that social justice should be the aim of social education and that it should be pursued directly and actively. However, a basic, highly controversial, question arises immediately: What do we mean by "social justice"? We discussed earlier the position of George Counts on this matter. Others, Dewey among them, advocated the teaching of critical thinking on social issues; citizens skilled in critical thinking should be better able to find ways to promote social justice in the wider world. I mentioned also that this problem is still with us because it seems hard to separate entirely clear, critical thinking on an issue from partisanship on that issue. Recall Ravitch's hope that social education should (or could) be taught "without a whiff of political partisanship." There are those who will cry "partisanship" if certain topics are even mentioned. (This is something to keep in mind as the removal of teacher tenure is recommended by some reformers. We too easily forget a main reason why tenure was granted initially.)

Consider how difficult it might be, for example, to propose and teach a unit on the attractions and dangers of sentimental civic education. The evidence is overwhelming that enthusiastic forms of religious, tribal, racial, ethnic, and national allegiance are deeply implicated in genocide and violent discrimination. Hatreds and feelings of contempt may simmer for years, but if those in power give those feelings approval, violence may ensue. Many examples can be cited: the Nazi systematic extermination of Jews, the murder of Tutsis by Hutus in Rwanda, the massacre of Armenians by Turks, the current threat of Sunni-Shiite violence in Iraq and Syria. Loyalty and pride in the group to which they belong have often led people to harbor ill will toward others, and when those in power call on that pride and approve of the hatred they feel, violence becomes an acceptable response. In America, riots and murders during the struggle for civil rights were sometimes encouraged by leaders and supported by law officers. It is hard to imagine what might have happened during the upheaval over civil rights without the benign and eloquent leadership of Martin Luther King, Jr.

But even when there are no group hatreds bubbling, pride and loyalty – patriotism – may prepare people to accept and participate in war if the nation's leaders respond to events and encourage it. And then hatred may follow. Arguments for and against the promotion of patriotism in our schools were discussed in Chapter 7, on critical thinking. The answer, I think, is to teach *about* patriotism. This can be a tricky business. Neil Postman, for example, decries the failure of today's schools to teach patriotism; too often, he writes, they neglect to include "respect, let alone affection, for America's traditions and contributions to world civilization."[5] He shares, however, the worry discussed earlier that "the idea of love of country is too easily transmogrified into a mindless, xenophobic nationalism..."[6] It is necessary, at least, to read and discuss accounts of mindless nationalism and its consequences.[7] Was Virginia Woolf right in her refusal to participate in patriotic-military ceremonies, or did she go too far? Should we discuss pacifism and spend some time analyzing it critically? Should we examine reflectively how hatred is aroused and encouraged during war? Were Americans encouraged to hate the Japanese during World War II? Did the Japanese express hate for Americans?

Critics often express dismay because Americans seem to know so little about their own history and government structure. As Stephen Thornton has pointed out, however, most of the material about which Americans are so ignorant *does* appear in the formal curriculum. Presented chronologically, by famous names or political categories, it just does not register with students. He advises us to teach "social studies that matters," and this suggests that we blend the interests of students with the recommendations of experts in the field.[8] The experts can help us to understand which concepts are essential to understanding what "social studies" is about, and student interests can guide us in how to present this material.

In addition to the use of themes, we should probably make far greater use of biographies to make historical material come alive. In a popular American history text, Jane Addams is mentioned several times, but the brief allusions give us no sense of the issues with which she wrestled or the courage with which she approached them. The text mentions her role in establishing the Women's International League for Peace and Freedom, but it says nothing about the abuse she suffered for opposing World War I. It tells us that she fought poverty in her work at Hull-House but says nothing about her commitment to help immigrants succeed in American society and, at the same time, to retain pride and interest in their original cultures. It tells the story of the Scopes trial, but it says nothing about Addams's generous response to the hill farmers with whom she disagreed. It discusses Clarence Darrow's role in the trial, but it is silent on the disagreement and cooperation of Darrow and Addams in work at Hull-House. Her association with Darrow – with whom she often disagreed – could serve as a model of critical thinking. Unfortunately, the treatment of history in most existing texts is just a recitation of facts with occasional pictures and one-liners. We do not get a sense of the importance of the events in the lives of real people.

Think what we might do if we decided that all high school students would experience four full years of social studies and that these courses would be offered across programs; that is, every class in social studies would be carefully composed of students from vocational, art, and academic programs. These carefully constituted high school classes would, in their diversity of students, resemble that of the Columbia University core course described earlier. Students would experience what it means to live in a participatory democracy, what it has meant in the past, and what the absence of such experience has meant to those deprived of it.

The proposed four years of social studies could serve as a model of curriculum planning and enactment. One or two of the years – whatever is required by the state in which the school is located – would be given to American history, and the other years should give some attention to the neglected histories so important in real human life, for example, of childhood, housing, sanitation, disease, agriculture, industry, advertising, entertainment, and transportation. A list of possible histories might be presented by the teacher, who would consider not only their importance overall but his or her own interests and expertise. After a brief (and one would hope fascinating) introduction to the possibilities, the students would be invited to choose a suggested number of them for study. A given year's curriculum would change from year to year depending on student interests, faculty competence, and financial requirements. Notice that faculty collegiality and choice would be paramount in this arrangement.

To get started on our lessons, we should turn to what I have called the educational treasure chest, the wonderful collection of methods that should be neither accepted as panaceas nor discarded because they could not succeed as panaceas.[9] Teachers, carefully prepared as critical thinkers, should be able to employ or draw on projects, role playing, Socratic questioning, Pestalozzian object lessons, group work, discovery, the five-step lesson, mastery learning, online exercises, inquiry, mock courts, games, and films. And, of course, the teacher should introduce relevant stories, poetry, music, and art. Today we have become so mired in worries over test scores and the perceived failure of teachers to follow a fixed, prescribed lesson plan that we have almost forgotten the array of various methods available to us. Seen as work, work, work for both teachers and students, many of our class sessions have become dismally boring and intellectually impoverished. Four exciting years of social studies, collegially planned and enacted, could stimulate the whole high school curriculum.

As we try to restore some vigorous interest in our studies, we should keep our unitary purpose in mind: to produce better adults. We want our students to become aware and appreciative of the full range of human abilities and interests. Classes composed of students from the whole spectrum of programs will surely contribute to this aim. We want also to emphasize moral goodness as a primary quality in our conception of better adults. The human struggle for moral goodness should be a guiding theme as we consider stories, biographies, and historical accounts. In the sort of social studies envisioned here, we need not fear distraction from the prescribed curriculum when we address moral and other existential issues because they lie at the very heart of the collegially constructed curriculum. Educators and policy makers interested in putting together a social studies program along these lines should be prepared for criticism. Every curriculum plan that has deviated from the prescribed curriculum and systematic instruction has been embraced by some enthusiasts and condemned by vociferous critics. In the 1920s and 1930s, as we have seen, critics of the very idea of social studies deplored the whole movement. William Chandler Bagley, for example, described it as "the primrose path of least resistance" and "an educational pablum."[10] Critics today would not dare to use the language Bagley employed in condemning every form of progressivism, when he claimed that education needed theories that are "strong, virile, and positive not feeble, effeminate, and vague."[11] Still, despite the poor results from programs of instruction that concentrate on historical facts, critics will continue to press the case for such courses.

In this section, I have suggested that four years of social studies might serve as a center or fulcrum for the high school curriculum. Collegially planned and conducted, social studies courses would bring together students from vocational, arts, and academic programs; address central issues of human life; and help to connect the disciplines to each other.

So far, in addition to the discussion of social studies, several recommendations have been made for the high school curriculum. In general, the curriculum should be constructed collegially, attending to the strengths of teachers, the interests of students, and the nature of each subject as it has been described by experts. No one of these should rule the day for all subjects. What is presented in each course will be heavily influenced by interdisciplinary committees and the use of themes designed to connect the disciplines to each other and to real life. In mathematics, for example, the sequential nature of the subject and well-established topics, skills, and vocabulary suggest the use of semi-individualized instruction – a plan under which students would be required to demonstrate at least minimal competence on a given unit of study before passing on to the next. But even with such a plan – different assignments for different small groups moving at different paces – there would be whole class discussions and regular attempts to connect math to the other disciplines. Again, the recommendation is to avoid a single method of instruction and keep in mind our unitary purpose.

In science, teachers and advisors might develop parallel courses (in, e.g., environmental science, health and nutrition, human development, or psychology) that would supplement the standard academic biology, physics, and chemistry, thereby allowing students who are not interested in a science major to make an alternative college-acceptable choice. Here, too, in both the traditional academic courses and the parallel courses, themes central to homemaking, parenting, moral life, happiness, and civic life would figure prominently.

In English language arts, there should be strong emphasis on clear, grammatically standard English. The Common Core emphasis on critical thinking in reading, writing, and analysis should be encouraged, but the need for contextual knowledge in the analysis of documents should be recognized. Students cannot be expected to analyze historical documents without considerable knowledge of the events, persons, and needs of the times when the documents were written. Remember that, although some knowledge of logic can contribute substantially to it, critical thinking cannot be taught effectively by itself. We must think critically about *something*, and the documents and themes should themselves be chosen by a process of reflective critical thinking. Further, we should consider carefully the new emphasis away from fiction toward the reading and analysis of nonfiction material. Some of us would argue that we have learned more about historical times and human predicaments from literature than from documentary accounts.

It is clear from what has been said so far in this chapter that attention must be given to the physical component of our schools and campuses. Before turning to that topic, however, something should be said about extracurricular activities in high school.

EXTRACURRICULAR ACTIVITIES

Extracurricular activities and activities similar to them in the regular curriculum have long been a bone of contention among critics of education. In the 1930s, with the country in deep economic depression, some critics wanted to eliminate all "frills" from our schools, and they included art, music, manual training, kindergarten, sports, and pedagogical games in the list of frills.[12] As Dewey noted, "It is proposed to eliminate from the schools such things as health service, work with wood, metal, tools, domestic arts, music, drawing, and dramatics, on the ground that they are 'frills' and costly frills at that."[13] Dewey pointed out that these additions to the curriculum in the new comprehensive high schools were largely responsible for the huge rise in high school attendance from about 200,000 in 1890 to more than 4,000,000 in the 1930s. High school had become more relevant to the new industrial world and more accessible to its young citizens.

Nevertheless, there were articulate critics of the new high school. These critics, often using derogatory language directed at the New Pedagogy, argued for a return to the fundamentals – reading, writing, arithmetic, and spelling. H. L. Mencken, for example, wrote of the new education "experts":

> With them there flourished the doctrine that children ought to be kept in school as long as possible, regardless of their tastes or capacities, and that those who were obviously too stupid to master the common branches should be entertained by various forms of play...[14]

He strongly condemned the resulting larger schools, with their additional "gymnasias, laboratories, *ateliers* [studios or workshops], and shops."[15]

Today scarcely anyone would argue against laboratories, art studios, or craft shops, but laboratories have been absorbed into the most prestigious level of the curriculum, while arts and crafts have frequently been pushed into the realm of extracurricular activities. There are still arguments over kindergarten and pre-primary education, and – without a great stir of opposition – many schools have reduced or even abandoned regular courses in art, music, and shop. Still, we must differentiate between "frills" in the curriculum and acceptable frills as extracurricular activities. Few people are urging that extracurricular activities at the high school level should be dropped. Probably the main reason for their continued health is that colleges have put a high premium on participation in these activities as part of the college admission process. By and large, however, these high premium activities were not the elements that originally attracted students who were not academically oriented to the new high schools.

We should remind ourselves that there are better reasons to support extracurricular activities than their power to influence college admissions officers. First, many of these activities offer an opportunity for students to practice the procedures so highly valued in a participatory democracy. In the vision of high school education described here, these activities – well planned and supervised – will bring together students from all programs and major interests. Besides providing opportunities to practice democratic procedures, the careful constitution of their groups should increase appreciation for a wide range of talents and interests. Too often today, in trying to accommodate different interests (when such attempts are even made), we establish "magnet" schools that physically separate our future citizens from each other. There must be another way, one more consonant with democratic life. Notice that, if we value these activities, they should not be regarded as "frills" whether they appear in the regular curriculum or in extracurricular opportunities. The curriculum is not the sole purveyor of education in our schools.

Second, wisely chosen extracurricular activities can help to develop social consciousness. Students have an opportunity to consider problems discussed in their social studies courses and to participate in voluntary, charitable activities.

Third, the choice of activities to be supported says a lot about what we value in individual and social life. Consider sports, for example. Some of the most reactionary critics of the 1930s wanted to eliminate even physical education from the school's activities. Physical education a frill! Today, however, things have perhaps gone too far in the opposite direction. Physical prowess and team competition have been highly valued since the high days of the Greeks, and we need not deny that value. But we should exercise some critical thinking on it. Remember that for the Greeks courage was identified with manliness, and both were closely linked to strength and aptitude in physical competition and combat. Even today, many people admire – get a thrill from – the spectacle of men boxing, wrestling, or smashing others in contact sports. Remember, too, Woolf's cautionary words about "manliness" and "womanliness." We need not reject everything identified with these words, but we should think critically on them and have the courage to reject practices that are known to cause many injuries. Schools should *not* sponsor football or boxing. There is nothing admirable, attractive, or manly in one man's knocking another unconscious. "What does it mean to be a man?" is a fundamental existential question that should be discussed in our high schools, and the schools should lead the discussion with action – the elimination of sports that incur great and lasting harm through deliberate action.

We should also pause to think critically on the actual benefits of extracurricular activities. Clearly, as pointed out, their potential benefits are great. But many young people do not or cannot participate in them because they are needed at home or because they work after school at part-time jobs. The scheduling of extracurricular activities as well as the almost exclusive concentration on academic courses works against the interests of many of our students. Further, the sort of activities that might be of help in real life – cooking, childcare, plant and pet care, household repair – are either missing entirely or scorned by colleges. The one major extracurricular activity open to the nonacademically oriented students – sports – is, sadly, one in which they are too often exploited. Time should be made in the regular school day for extracurricular activities; they should not be relegated to after-school hours.

There is another bit of irony in this matter. Happily, critics no longer refer to our nonacademically oriented students as "too stupid" to master the traditional college preparatory curriculum. Now we generously insist that "all children can learn" and that all of them should go to college. We still have not acknowledged the wonderful range of human talents and interests, and, as a society, we have done not nearly enough to improve the lot of those who must do unskilled labor. Schools can do little on the latter problem but could do much to prepare students for highly skilled vocational jobs. We should be honest, too, in admitting that, at present, about one-third of our college graduates are employed in work that does not require a college education.

THE PHYSICAL SETTING OF THE SCHOOL

In her discussion of school architecture, Rena Upitis notes that schools all over the world look disconcertingly alike: "Why should a school in urban Montreal look just like a school in northern Alberta? The fact that many schools are virtual clones of one another is, I think, a central flaw of school architecture."[16] Upitis would like schools to reflect their natural and social settings – to encourage the study and appreciation of both their natural environment and the sort of work done in the area in which they are located. That this so rarely happens is, in part, due to a lack of conversation between architects and educators. Upitis notes, "Architects and educators, at some level, speak entirely different languages," and to add to the confusion, they sometimes use the same word to refer to entirely different concepts. For example, architects use the word "program" to talk about square footage, the number of students to be accommodated, and storage space, whereas educators use "program" to refer to a curriculum and associated activities.[17] Upitis draws attention to a point made repeatedly in this book: the need for interdisciplinary, collegial conversation.

Karsten Harries also comments on the sameness of buildings all over the world and charges this sameness to the legacy of functionalist architecture.[18] Because the function of schools is everywhere the same, it is only natural that all school buildings should be the same. With functionalism and bureaucracy, all functions, needs, problems, and issues can be neatly divided up and assigned to particular agencies, bureaus, or departments. As we begin to challenge some of these sharp separations, however, our thinking changes; we begin to see differences and to seek connections.

Consider the dramatic change in our thinking about the environment. Not long ago, we saw and acted on a sharp difference between wilderness and lived places. Our thinking was not all bad; we did act to preserve vast areas of wilderness. But we are beginning to see that we must look beyond the wilderness if we are to preserve Earth as a habitat for life. Ted Steinberg wrote appreciatively of Rachel Carson's contribution to the new way of thinking:

> Although she used the word sparingly in her book, Carson helped to transform *ecology* into the rallying cry of the environmental movement. Unlike *wilderness*, conceived as a world apart, the word *ecology* suggested, in a sense, the reverse – that all life was bound up in an intricate, interconnected web. Human beings, she believed, were thus part of the balance of nature, not divorced from it in the way that some wilderness advocates implied.[19]

Probably we should always have paid greater attention to the physical setting of our schools, but we now have a thriving ecological movement to support the idea. Schools and the education to which they are dedicated are designed to enhance everyday life, not to help us escape from it. Where not more than a century ago, education was aimed at discovering the mind of God and increasing abstraction as studies progressed, we are now more awake to physical and social surroundings. Rejecting the sharp separations that characterized earlier conceptions, Larry Ford comments, "We seek some sense of community, sense of place, sense of belonging, sense of history, or feeling of involvement and participation."[20] These *senses* are cultivated not by patriotism in the traditional national mode but by increased sensitivity to our life spaces. Speaking eloquently on what this means for education, Wendell Berry writes:

> I believe that for many reasons – political, ecological, and economic – the best intelligence and talent should be at work and at home everywhere in the country. And, therefore, my wishes for our schools are opposite to those of present-day political parties and present-day politics of education and culture. Wes Jackson has argued that our schools – to balance or replace their present single major in upward mobility – should offer a major in homecoming.[21]

To conclude this heartfelt reawakening to life in our lived-places, we should consider the advice of Sara Stein:

> [L]et's look at something smaller than Colorado. Let's look at seeps, rivulets, sumps, hollows, bogs, ditches, frog ponds. Let's examine the face of the continent through a magnifying glass, noticing less the large protuberances and declivities than the fine texture of its skin, its pores,

its wrinkles. Let's get down to the minutiae of puddles. Let's look at our own back yards and ask where butterflies can drink.[22]

This is a nice vocabulary lesson, too.

No part of the preceding discussion should be taken as a rejection of our commitment to preserve and extend wilderness. After all, many wild animals cannot survive in city parks and rooftop gardens, nor can acres of majestic trees and shrubs. We must attend to both wilderness and our back yards. In agreement with one of the main points stressed in this book, David Orr emphasizes *connectedness*:

> There is an architecture of connectedness that includes front porches facing onto streets, neighborhood parks, civic spaces, pedestrian-friendly streets, sidewalk cafes, and human scaled buildings...there is an economy of connectedness...

> There is an ecology of connectedness evident in well-used landscapes, cultural and political barriers to the loss of ecologically valuable wetlands, forests, riparian corridors, and species habitat.[23]

Connectedness certainly applies to the human community as well and to the specialized occupations within that community. In her discussion of school architecture, Upitis draws our attention to the topics that should be part of the conversation between educators and architects. Important among them is the place-based education discussed above, but she also draws our attention to broader conversation on play, romance, bodies, value, the nature of dwellings, and the central importance of conversation itself.[24]

As we consider the physical setting of our high schools, we must think about the social and moral aspects affected by that setting. In the last decades, we have sometimes given support to different interests and talents among our students by separating them physically. For example, large cities and districts have established magnet schools that serve students with interest in the arts or some other specialty. Certainly the provision of vocational schools and schools specializing in the arts is consonant with my recommendations for serious attention to interests other than the traditional academic. However, we should be concerned not only with the knowledge base of the curricula offered but also with the effects of our decisions on the growth of our students as participants in a democracy. It is not enough that each separate school involve students in the shared exercise of democratic procedures. Athens introduced the world to democratic processes, but Athens was by no stretch of the imagination a participatory democracy.

In planning our schools to provide for a variety of intellectual and practical interests, we must also think about their role in preparing students for active life in a participatory democracy and deeply satisfying home life. Students from all of the accepted specialties should have opportunities to study and work together. Therefore, it would make sense to plan our schools as community-like campuses, with, say, a vocational building, an academic building, and an arts building. Each student's work would be mainly in one of these buildings, but he or she would also take an occasional course in a different school, and at least one course – I have suggested social studies as the required common heart of the curriculum – would involve students from all of the schools. Further, extracurricular activities would be collegially organized across all of the schools.

The school buildings and grounds should, ideally, reflect the most loved physical characteristics of the community, but they should also encourage working together. Gardens provide a wonderful opportunity for students to learn about growing food and flowers, to work together, to learn about nutrition, to get some exercise, and to come to a greater appreciation of working with their hands. They may even come to enjoy insect life. When urban middle school students visit my garden, I always have to assure them that most bugs will not bite them – that they should just hum along with the bees but be careful not to grab them. Here again is a chance to talk about community – the community of plant and insect life. Many current writers on the ecological theme urge us to adopt more natural ways in our gardening. Speaking of these writers, Eric Grissell comments:

> Not surprisingly, they endorse the concept of the interdependency of organisms, thus allowing all creatures a share of the garden. These authors seem to suggest that the garden needs a whole lot more diversity and a lot less stuffiness. Perhaps they have not gone so far as to invite in all the insects, but that is what they mean to say. I say, "What's good for the garden is good for the bugs."[25]

Grissell advocates for ecology what I am advocating for education: community, connection, balance, and diversity.

In this chapter, we have discussed some modifications of the standard curriculum, the democratic importance of extracurricular activities, and the need to attend to the physical setting and arrangements of our schools. Given these additions to the preceding ideas about interdisciplinary themes, collegiality, homemaking, parenting, moral development, vocational preparation, and critical thinking, how might teachers prepare their courses and lessons?

10

Planning, Enacting, Evaluating

Given the emphasis so far on a unitary purpose, collegiality, continuity, and broadly selected themes that reflect concern for connections to real life, how might individual teachers plan their courses? How should they select content, decide on pedagogical methods, and evaluate the performance of their students? How should they evaluate their own performance? We will start this chapter with an exploration of planning, then move to carrying out our plans in the classroom, and conclude with a critical look at evaluation.

PLANNING

Planning is part of the ideal aspect of teaching. For me, it has always been a special pleasure because it presents an opportunity to review and extend my own knowledge and to reformulate it more articulately. Everything is possible at the first delightful stage of planning – all the material that is prescribed, all the material I know beyond what is prescribed, all the new things I would like to learn before facing my classes. My own preference is to overplan, that is, to include in my initial plan far more than I will eventually accomplish because such planning prepares *me*; it facilitates spontaneity and invites student participation and choice.

All public school teachers are required to maintain a plan book in which daily lessons are briefly described in case the teacher is absent and a substitute is required. These notes are not really plans; they merely direct a substitute teacher to a page in the text, a homework assignment, or a suggestion for student activity that will fill the class period. Clearly, I am not talking here about that sort of planning. Real planning does more to prepare the teacher than the lesson. Well prepared teachers can invite student questions and engage in invitational lessons – lessons shaped in large part by the problems and interests of students. Teachers who have limited knowledge of their subject are likely to be restricted to a tightly organized plan from which they will not deviate. Unfortunately, it is exactly this sort of planning that is widely advocated today.

Sound planning begins with an overview of the course to be taught. Usually there will be a text and/or syllabus from which teachers are expected to work. But a teacher must scrutinize this material carefully. Which concepts or skills are of central importance? For which ones might students be poorly prepared? Which are crucial for work in a following course? This is where continuity plays an important role. A good teacher, a well-prepared teacher, must know the material that precedes the current course and the material that comes after it. He or she must anticipate backing up now and then to fill in likely conceptual gaps. How will he or she rearrange the teaching calendar to do this?

At this stage – looking at the course as a whole – teachers should consider where and when the broad collegially chosen themes might be engaged. If there are no such agreed-on themes and the school has not yet adopted interdisciplinary, collegial planning, teachers should still consider possibilities along the lines discussed here in earlier chapters. All teachers should consider applications and enrichment topics from literature, biography, music, art, ecology, religion, history, practical science, homemaking, social justice, parenting, and other areas. A particular teacher's interests and competence are important here. None of us can be conversant with every area of legitimate interest. However, as I will argue at length in the next chapter, every high school teacher should be at least minimally competent in every subject that students are *required* to take. Beyond that universal, basic knowledge, teachers should use their own special knowledge to enrich the prescribed material through themes. When the course plan or syllabus has been modified with these suggestions, we are ready to begin unit and lesson planning.

Supervisors today put tremendous emphasis on *learning objectives* as the heart of lesson planning. They want teachers to specify exactly what students will learn (be able to do) as a result of their instruction. Many lessons should, of course, be planned this way. But what teachers do has the potential to produce a great deal more than specific "learnings." By sharing material in which he or she delights, a teacher may bring some student to delight in it also, but the teacher need not state this as an objective nor should he or she insist on it. It should be all right, after all, for students to reject the teacher's expanded interests as "not for them." In teaching, we convey ourselves, intellectual vitality, a view of the world, and a way of relating to it. Further, there are desirable outcomes to be sought beyond specific subject matter objectives: increased self-esteem for some students, ability to relate socially, increased collegiality, a deeper understanding of and commitment to moral life, and, in general the establishment of lasting relations of care and trust.

Daily lesson plans can be greatly enhanced by the teacher's previous work in reviewing the text, syllabus, and general unit plans. Consider a few examples. When a social studies (or history) teacher spots the first mention of Jane Addams in the text, he or she should be prepared by earlier review to include discussion of Addams's life and many contributions. The teacher should talk to the class about how Addams worked to improve the living conditions of immigrants in Chicago. Not long ago, I heard a graduate student dismiss Addams as "an assimilationist." This is simply untrue. What is an assimilationist? And why should that label not be applied to Addams? The teacher should make it clear that, while Addams worked hard to help immigrants succeed in American society, she also encouraged them to retain pride in their original cultures. She supported a textile museum in which artifacts, tools, and products of the original cultures were displayed. Students will perhaps be shocked to learn that Addams and a few of her classmates at college tried opium (then widely available) to enhance their understanding of the books they were reading. It did not work, and a sympathetic teacher put an end to the experiment.[1] They may also be interested to hear her reactions to the advice of Leo Tolstoy and why she rejected it, deciding not to spend hours on kitchen work for the good of her soul. These stories will help students to see Addams as a full human being. They should also hear, of course, about her pacifist commitment and opposition to World War I. As a result of that opposition, she suffered greatly from public accusations that she was unpatriotic. This is an opportunity, too, to engage students in a discussion of the effects of sentimental civic education, good and bad. Again, students may see some irony in the fact that Addams shared the Nobel Peace Prize in 1931 with Nicholas Murray Butler, the president of Columbia University who dismissed two faculty members for actively opposing the war. All of this can be told in a short talk that should engage students and plant Addams firmly in their memories. Biographical accounts such as this one make it more likely that students will remember the events presented in the documentary accounts.

I mentioned in Chapter 1 a story that might profitably be used by math teachers. Somewhere in every math class there should be at least a brief discussion of the origins of mathematics. Is it discovered or invented? The story of Laplace and Lagrange told earlier illustrates the differences of opinion and provides an opportunity also for teachers to talk a bit about the debates over religion and creation. Perhaps mathematics is neither totally discovered nor totally invented. Perhaps, as Leopold Kronecker put it, "God made the integers. All the rest is the work of man."[2] Building on this belief, Kronecker insisted that all true mathematics must be based on the integers.

English teachers conferring with social studies teachers might challenge students to read a bit of *Plutarch's Lives*, with which Jane Addams was so familiar. Will anyone volunteer to read and report on Crassus, Pompey, Caesar, Demosthenes, Cicero, Antony, or Marcus Brutus? Addams had read many (perhaps all) of *Plutarch's Lives* as a child, and her father had paid her five cents for each one.

In science, when evolution is discussed, there are many biographical stories to tell. Some students may well be unimpressed by "Soapy Sam" Wilberforce, but they should enjoy hearing something about his father, William, who, as a Member of Parliament, led the battle against England's participation in the slave trade. When that succeeded, he mounted a campaign to eliminate slavery entirely. The law abolishing slavery in the British Empire passed three weeks after Wilberforce died in 1833. When did the United States abolish slavery? Why was America so far behind Britain in rejecting slavery?

In discussing the life of Charles Darwin, his reasons for abandoning religion should at least be mentioned. Why, he wondered, would an all-good God deliberately create a world in which so much cruelty and misery exist? Why would such a God create a world in which its creatures must eat one another to survive? Darwin preferred to charge all this to nature and evolution.

Let us turn now from the intellectual delights of planning, from the classical fantasy of encouraging students to read *Plutarch's Lives*, to the practical problems of planning daily lessons. To decide on a lesson form, teachers must consider themselves – their own levels of competence, interests, personalities, and values. They must consider their students, the material to be addressed, and the situation – size of class, physical setting, time of day. Let us consider briefly some of the problems we encounter when planning lessons for students who have great difficulty with the basic skills of schooling. This discussion may add urgency to my earlier recommendation for a preparatory high school year.

As a math teacher and department chair, I always taught the basic class in "general" math in addition to my favorites in algebra, geometry, and calculus. I believed then, and still believe, that the task of teaching remedial math should be handled by experienced teachers, not new teachers. I am talking here about the sort of general math course often required for high school graduation – not classes specially designed for vocational or commercial programs. As I argued earlier, there should be no "general" program, and the course I taught should have been part of an intensive remedial/preparatory year for incoming freshmen.

The first thing to recognize is that there really are high school kids who can barely read, cannot add fractions, and resolutely avoid anything resembling a word problem. I liked these kids. I remember with great appreciation what a guidance counselor said to me: "I send these kids to you because you love them." But that does not mean that I was successful in teaching them what the curriculum prescribed. I was not, and I am still trying to figure out how to do this.

What are we up against? In the mostly middle-class, regional high school where I taught, we could not let these remedial students take textbooks home because the books would regularly disappear. We could not assign homework because many students had no place to work at home. Recall the earlier discussion of conditions in city-run shelters for the homeless. Nearly similar situations exist in many of the homes in which these youngsters live. Visiting one of them, I noticed that the kitchen table served as a storage place. There was barely room to eat at it – certainly no room for doing homework. So, practically, classwork had to take the place of homework, but that is not a disaster. I have already argued against too much homework. But too much and none at all are both extremes.

The kids did not come to class prepared with notebooks, pens, and pencils. I kept a steady supply available on my desk. They were often reported as having unexcused absences for which they were supposed to get zeroes on the day's work. I ignored this, and although I urged them to arrive at class on time, I also ignored their occasional tardiness. Often, when work (say, ten math exercises) was assigned in class, I would mark their papers on the spot and enjoy the ensuing announcement to the class: "Hey, I got 100!"

All of this sounds pretty good, but I know that I really did not come close to solving their academic problems. One day we were working on travel problems – miles driven, gasoline prices, and the cost of various trips. Hoping to make the work more interesting, I asked the class to suppose that we were planning a cross-country trip from New Jersey (where I was then teaching) to California. As we leave New Jersey, what state do we enter? I was flabbergasted at the responses. I heard everything from Tennessee to city names such as Chicago. I needed a pull-down map, but my "math" room had only a giant old Keuffel & Esser slide rule on the wall. My students were not immigrants; they were born in America, but they knew almost nothing about the geography of their native land. We spent the rest of the period talking about our make-believe trip, but I ended the session feeling somewhat helpless.

Many things have changed since I was in the classroom. There are no longer slide rules hanging on the walls. We now have computers and i-Pads to help with our computations. But the overall condition of our most deprived students does not seem to be better. More students are graduating from high school, but some of these graduates – even some college students – are still reading at a grade school level and demonstrate severe deficiencies in basic mathematics. The preparatory high school year recommended earlier is a real necessity and should make a difference, but academic help and steady guidance should continue throughout the high school years. A basic program, supplemented by participation in inclusive classes in social studies, the arts, and physical education, should be developed. Instead of satisfying ourselves with slogans such as "All children can learn," we should face the fact that many have great difficulty in doing so and that we should provide the steady, realistic support so obviously needed. Renewal and enrichment of vocational programs should also get top priority.

Readers should take note that I am not recommending a return to the useless, shameful "general" track that was offered for years. The basic preparatory program suggested would be incorporated into a larger organization that would include students from all of the programs, and universal participation in extracurricular activities would be encouraged. Most important, the basic program would be sustained until students have mastered the defined basics. It would not be a mere holding pattern.

Preparation for these basic classes requires the usual analysis of subject matter and potential methods for teaching it. But it also requires observation of social needs: Can we encourage students to work together without inviting chaos? If not initially, that should become a major, lasting objective. Should we use incentives such as grading papers on the spot and recording credits immediately? Should teachers find out more about how students are doing in the inclusive classes, especially social studies? From the experience I have recounted here, I would suggest that a parent/–teacher–mentor be assigned to the students who need remedial help and that that person remain with them throughout their high school experience or, at least, until they have mastered the skills required to move on. In my experience, one period a day for one year was not nearly enough.

ENACTING

In an earlier chapter, I mentioned the treasure chest of pedagogical methods available to us. I also cautioned against choosing any one of them as the only way to teach. Choice of a method depends on several factors: the topic, student readiness, availability of materials and devices, relevant social issues, time, and teacher preparation and preference. I suppose I should add supervisory pressure to this list; I am keenly aware that many teachers today are forced to use a standard lesson form. But to give way to this tyranny is to sacrifice our professional souls. Supervisors can properly question the choice of methods and make suggestions, but the ultimate choice belongs to the professional doing the teaching.

It is important to keep in mind, as we choose a method, that teaching is a collegial activity, one in which responsibilities are shared. Students have a responsibility beyond obedience or mere acquiescence, and they should be encouraged to act on this responsibility. When students come to class prepared through a completed assignment, they can be instrumental in initiating what I have called an "invitational" lesson, one invited by student questions and comments. A well-prepared teacher welcomes these lessons. Some of the material alluded to earlier – on Jane Addams, Laplace and Lagrange, Virginia Woolf, the Nobel Peace Prize, the Wilberforce family – might be presented either as a planned lesson or as a spontaneous response to student comments. Good teachers have volumes of material up their mental sleeves ready to pull out on invitation.

As we plan and enact lessons, we want to keep the unitary purpose – to produce better adults – in mind. We will be concerned with moral and social issues, not simply academic objectives. If the class is ready for group work, we will encourage it; if not, we will work toward it gradually. If the topic is suitable, we might design a discovery lesson, but we probably should avoid asking students to "discover" things that can easily be simply told and applied. I heard teachers once urging students to discover the names of various star constellations. Well, once we know the names, it is fascinating to see why the names were given, but students – many unaware of the underlying stories – are unlikely to "discover" these names. When I suggested to the teachers that they just tell their students the names and then go on to the relevant stories, they responded that this was not the "constructivist" way. How about, then, at least telling the stories first so that the kids have a hint about what they should discover?

Today we do not often talk about the holistic pedagogical theories that once were so loved and debated. We now talk about strategies, standards, and tests. But no strategy will work with every topic, every class, every child – or for every teacher. There are strategies (or methods) to which some of us are philosophically opposed; we would never use them. Looking over the possibilities, including those in our educational treasure chest, I think Lee Cronbach got it exactly right when he declared:

> I have no faith in any generalization upholding one teaching technique against another, whether that preferred method be audiovisual aids, programmed instruction, learning by doing, inductive teaching, or whatever. A particular educational tactic is part of an instrumental system; a proper educational design calls upon that tactic at a certain point in the sequence, for a certain period of time, following and preceding certain other tactics. No conclusion can be drawn about the tactic considered by itself.[3]

If we agree with Cronbach on this, planning becomes even more important. We do not choose one pedagogical method for all topics or all students. But this does not imply that we have no overall attitude or moral commitments to which we will be faithful. Our moral commitment may rule out certain methods, such as harsh punishments, grubby incentives, or sarcastic "inducements."

When we think about what to do in our classrooms, we could do worse than explore the "seven Cs": choice, critical thinking, caring, connectedness, continuity, collegiality, and creativity. We have touched on all of these at some point in this book. In this section, I want to say more about choice and continuity and their role in classroom activity.

Student choice is, or should be, a fundamental component in education. Teachers are officially in control of what goes on in their classrooms, but good teachers recognize student choice as part of collegiality in the best education and also as a basic element in evaluation. We learn a lot about student progress by observing students' choices and how they act on them. Further, education for life in a participatory democracy must necessarily aim at producing people who will make well-considered choices. David Hawkins comments:

> Once you are committed to the belief in the primacy, the priority of children's choice-making capacities as the main thing that education is after, then there are many things that follow which likewise run afoul of traditional stereotypes. . .[4]

Commitment to this belief leads to changes in assignments, in companions for group work, in evaluating student work, in deciding what to do next in the classroom. "In fact," Hawkins tells us, "I think the familiar phenomenon called 'The Test' is largely a crutch to replace the good means of evaluation we have when we don't suppress children's capacity for choice."[5] I wish more people understood this today.

There have always been those opposed to student choice because they have misunderstood or distorted it. In the views of responsible educators, it has never meant letting students run wild to do whatever they wish. Student choices interact intelligently with teacher choices. If the teacher has suggested a set of topics for projects, students may choose one from the set. Before the set itself is finalized, the teacher may invite students to make suggestions, and he or she may rightly accept or reject suggestions on the grounds of the teacher's own expertise. Unless there is another competent adult to help, a teacher unacquainted with the suggested topic should not post it on the list. Students might also sometimes be allowed to choose how their work will be evaluated – by formal test, written paper, or oral exam of some sort. Certainly, in the universal social studies courses suggested, students should be involved in the choice of topics.

Teachers obviously make vital choices not only about subject matter but also on how the class is conducted. I have put great emphasis on conversation and the establishment of relations of care and trust. To establish such relations, teachers must get to know a bit about their individual students. But this does not mean "shooting the breeze" or encouraging all sorts of verbal distractions. We talked in an earlier chapter about order and its importance in organizing our lives. Teachers teach something about order by the ways in which they organize their classes. Classroom order is not a matter of authoritarian order. It is a matter of putting everything into the task of educating in an orderly fashion. The class should start on time – no messing around, no pointless banter. If students are late, the teacher should simply nod in acknowledgment and continue the lesson he or she has launched. If one student is absent or late often, a conference should be scheduled. An intellectually enthusiastic teacher will not be derailed by incidents that have nothing to do with either the subject at hand or a relevant social/moral issue. From such a teacher, students learn how to value order. Order makes possible what is important in life and in education; it is not an end in itself.

Conversation is essential in building relations of care and trust. Students are encouraged to ask questions and to make comments. The teacher listens and gets some sense of how well the students are doing. She notes their choices, detects worries, returns to those students who seem troubled. As the students work together, the teacher listens to their remarks and, if necessary, reminds them that the purpose of working together is to help one another. No cussing, no bullying, no dirty jokes.

Good high school teachers do not need to post the standard rules of decent behavior in writing on a bulletin board. The kids already know these rules, and teachers should not get bogged down in stating them repeatedly. When there is a minor infraction, the teacher should use the Martin Buber–like technique of raising a finger, momentarily stopping everything, and reminding everyone: We don't talk to each other that way in here. We don't throw things in here; please pick it up. Hold on – we'll get to you. Order serves the educational purpose. It is not the purpose of education.

If there is to be a homework assignment, the teacher usually prepares the class for it. In the event that the preparation is interrupted by an important social/moral issue, the teacher might advise the students to "Give it a try." With some assurance, the teacher suggests that they can figure it out but, if not, it will be explained on the next day. I have told the story before, but it may be worth repeating here. On the few occasions when a moral issue completely interrupted my math class and students were put on their own with homework, they often came in the following day with even better work than usual. This was somewhat humbling to my pride as an explainer, but it was deeply satisfying to my sense of developing relationships.

EVALUATING

One of a teacher's hardest jobs is to evaluate student work and assign a grade. This is another area in which I must confess ambivalence and a lack of certainty. There are a few things I definitely reject: the normal curve (there are no "normal" classes), giving zeroes as punishment, giving As for trying hard. Let me try first to explain my aversion to giving zeroes. Would I never put a zero in the grade book? Any math teacher knows what a zero will do if the final grade is established by adding a string of scores and dividing by the number in the string. We could, of course, argue against this way of establishing the grade, but let us put that off for a bit. After observing the dismay of students who saw a "20" or "30" (let alone a "0") on their returned test, I decided it would be better to omit the score and simply write "not passing"; that designation signaled a standing invitation to try the test again (an equivalent, not identical version). For a variety of reasons – such as a test at the end of a marking period – this was not always possible. But students were informed that "50" was the lowest grade I would enter. A "50" is clearly a failing grade, but one can recover from it more easily than a zero. A zero is really devastating to one's average.

But what about a case of cheating? Would I not enter a zero for a proven infraction? I might if it happened more than once, but in the few cases I encountered – after expressing disappointment so deep that it approached disgust – I simply made the culprit retake the test. I admit ambivalence on this. However, there is no ambivalence on the importance of honesty in academic life, and I would discuss it often. Why is plagiarism in scholarly life so universally condemned? High school students should hear regularly about the interdependence of work in all forms of research. We *depend* on the honesty of our colleagues in advancing every form of study. One who betrays the trust of his or her academic/research colleagues does not rightly belong to that community. Instead of advancing knowledge, the cheater has set it back. Forgiving a high school cheating incident should be accompanied by a frank discussion of what is at stake – not just for the cheater but for the entire community. It is too important to risk losing the commitment of a young person who has made a bad mistake. With generous understanding and persistent conversation, he or she may dedicate himself or herself to the community of honest effort; without it, the student may simply decide to act so as not to get caught the next time.

Without punishing, we need to find ways to help our students think critically about moral matters. Of course we want them to join the community of honest inquiry. We should also want them to consider a host of moral questions about adult life: Should I accept a job at a company that advertises tobacco when I know its effects on human health? Should I be comfortable with actions that are legal – such as granting large mortgages – but risk the financial welfare of people who can ill afford the effects of my actions? Should I be comfortable with an executive position in a company that exploits its hourly workers? What forms does this exploitation take? Should I endorse programs of welfare that seem to undermine the independence and work ethics of their recipients? How should I think about these things? It is especially important to talk about these matters in an age that seems to value education only for its economic value. We have to show by our continual critical conversation that there is more to education than this.

The preceding discussion is illustrative of what happens in good classrooms. The day usually starts with academic (subject matter) topics or questions. When a moral issue arises, however, the conversation shifts to focus critical attention on it. When it is resolved or temporarily put aside for further thought, discussion returns to the subject matter topic. Let us return now to the topic of grading.

The task of grading is particularly difficult when we are working with students who have great gaps in their learning or who hate the subject we are teaching. Again, I will direct my remarks largely at mathematics where the problems are often deeply embedded. In working with students who are just "not getting it," I suggested that teachers might use a variant of mastery learning.[6] Simply put, it means that students do not go on to chapter 2 until they have shown at least minimal mastery of chapter 1. Here again, teachers must know their subject matter well. What material in chapter 1 is essential to that of chapter 2? If a student has failed the test on chapter 1 because of one error repeated several times, it is sensible to spend some time with the student, correct the error, and let him or her proceed to chapter 2. (If a test is failed because of a repeated error, it is probably a bad test.) But if the errors are a result of wide or deep lack of understanding of the basic concepts in chapter 1, the student should stay with that material, get further instruction, and complete assignments on the topic.

Working this way – an organized modification of self-paced instruction – I have seen enormous differences in what students will accomplish. Some go well beyond the assigned test, completing as many as eighteen chapters in the year. Others struggle to complete six chapters (one per marking period). On a standardized test at year's end, very few students score in the bottom quintile. Virtually everyone learns something.

But how should we assign grades under such an arrangement? In the classes with which I worked, we set it up so that grades went up with the number of tests passed in a marking period and tacked on "plus 1's" for each test passed at better than 90 percent. This encouraged excellence and made it possible for a student to make the top score, 99, for the marking period. Notice that, theoretically, it is possible to get a 70 for one marking period and a 99 in the next. It does not matter where you start; your grade is a result of how many chapters you complete. However, I never saw this happen. Mathematics is a highly specialized, sequential subject, and if students are having difficulty at the start, they are likely to experience continuing difficulty. Obviously, that does not mean that they cannot learn at least the rudiments of the material. It just takes longer.

Educators need to think critically about the problems just outlined. Must all college-bound students take three years of academic mathematics in high school? Must all college freshmen show competence in whatever is regarded as the basic math required for admission? Why? If a student plans to major in, say, music or literature, why must the student prove competence in college algebra?

We might consider offering academic math courses in three categories for our high school students: minimal, standard, and advanced. I would like to see these courses open to student choice. The choice should be guided, of course, but participation should be by choice, not by faculty assignment, and there should be no stigma attached to choosing the minimal course. It should be understood to mean that mathematics is not the main interest of students who choose the minimal course, and, as in many college courses, the final grade should be "passing" or "no credit." Similarly, I think our advanced courses would be much more exciting if they were known as courses for those especially interested, not for those specially qualified. Advanced Placement courses, for example, might be renamed "courses for the passionately interested," and no extra high school credit should be granted for them. Too much of what we do in our high schools today is aimed at honors, credits, and penalties; not nearly enough is done to encourage genuine intellectual vitality. Perhaps we need to find new names for all of our courses.

I have spent quite a lot of time on the problems teachers face in grading because the task and its complications demand so much of our attention. In my remarks, I have not said "do this" or "do that" – except for the admonition to insist on at least minimal competence before moving on in sequential subject matter – but I have confessed my own ambivalence about the ways in which we grade and have invited teachers to work on the problems collegially. I find myself largely in agreement with writers such as Derek Stolp – thoughtful teachers who would like to get rid of grades entirely.[7] But he, too, sees many obstacles in the way of doing this. Even with the policy of allowing (perhaps requiring) students to retake tests they have failed, problems arise. Should those who do well on the second or third try get the same high grade as those who excelled on the first try? Stolp and I both say yes to this. The point is to learn the material, not to outscore one's classmates. Our purpose is to produce better adults: more competent, more rational, more morally conscious.

Moves similar to those described in this last section should be made in all subjects. In English, for example, a poorly written paper should be resubmitted. It should not merely be supposed that failing students will profit from the teacher's remarks on the poor paper and, thus, do a better job on the next one. Just as minimal competence is required in mathematics before moving to the next unit, so should it be required in every subject a student chooses – or is forced – to take. And we have to manage this form of mastery learning without resorting to the socially devastating practice of retention in grade.

Looking over the material discussed so far on evaluation, I want to add a few more thoughts. The first is that the new global interest in cooperation should prompt educators to review and critique everything we do in light of this interest. To move from an emphasis on competition to one on cooperation will be especially difficult for a society such as ours steeped in the love of (and faith in) capitalist competition. The new interest in cooperation demands careful thought and modification, not the complete overthrow of a way of life. Perhaps the first step is to reject the current hypocrisy of talking about cooperation but acting on competition.

Now we must face the question of how to evaluate teachers. The current trend is toward more and more emphasis on students' standardized test scores as the main measure of teacher effectiveness. Many of us believe that this is a bad mistake. Not only is it too narrow a measure by which to evaluate teachers' effectiveness, it is not very useful in promoting the growth of students. For those who agree that our main purpose in education is to produce better adults, we will want to know how students are doing with respect to growth in all of the great aspects of human development: intellectual, moral, social, physical, aesthetic, emotional, and spiritual. Scores on standardized tests will not help much with this enormous educational task.

But we need not throw out these tests entirely. Some years ago in mathematics education – it seems almost like ancient history – standardized tests came with most of the major text series. There was built-in alignment between curriculum and test. Through the years of the New Math some major text publishers even provided two tests, one directed at the New Math and one on the traditional material. My math department decided to give both tests because we hoped to show that our students were not somehow deprived by studying the New Math. Results confirmed our informal assessment. Students did well on both.

This brings up an essential point of understanding. Standardized test results are *confirmatory*: They tell us what good teachers already know. Every competent teacher should be able to predict with a fair degree of accuracy how each student will do on these tests. Good teachers are rarely surprised by the scores. The results of a well-aligned standard test merely supply numerical support for the teacher's judgment. Indeed, one factor in evaluating teachers' competence is their ability to make such accurate judgments. The results can be used as factors in a host of tasks involving public comparisons and corrective planning for the future, but they contribute very little to the diagnostic capabilities of teachers.

Good teachers continually ask themselves questions about their own performance: Are my students engaged and reasonably happy in our work together? Am I contributing to their social and moral growth? To what positive signs can I point? What else might I try? Am I making interdisciplinary connections? What do my colleagues think I might do? What might they learn from me? What books have I read recently? Any impressive op-ed pieces? Should I share some of my reading? Would this be a good way to find out which publications are available to my students in their homes? Have I gone to any cultural events? Museums? Sporting events? Movies? Are any of these worth sharing? What do the kids want to share about their lives? Are the kids willing to help one another? Are there signs of bullying? Is anyone regularly left out of classroom discussions? Have I provided opportunities for students to make choices on what they will study and how they will demonstrate what they have accomplished? Do we at least occasionally have fun with our work? Would I like to continue working with these kids? Would they like to continue working with me?

In this chapter, we have looked at the tasks teachers undertake in planning, enacting, and evaluating their educational activities. We have also considered briefly how teachers might evaluate their own accomplishments. Now it is time to think about how teachers might be prepared for their work.

11

The Professional Preparation of Teachers

Teachers in the United States have long struggled for professional status. In this chapter, we will revisit some of the history of that struggle and try to identify both promising recommendations and discouraging mistakes that were made in that effort. Then, working from the chapters preceding this one, we will explore what a strong secondary-teacher education program should look like. In that section, we will consider both the major subject to be taught and the subject matter of education more widely construed. In the last sections, we will consider how teachers can be prepared to define and sustain the ethos of their schools and how that work and their daily interaction with students might contribute to a more genuinely moral civic society.

THE STRUGGLE FOR PROFESSIONAL STATUS

Formal teacher training began in the United States with the establishment of normal schools, the first of which appeared in Massachusetts under the urging of Horace Mann in 1839.[1] It was obvious to Mann and other supporters of public education that well-trained teachers were needed if the public schools were to succeed and grow. As the school population grew, and especially when more children began to attend high school in the early twentieth century, the normal schools gave way to teachers colleges, and these schools began to offer college degrees. But although the degrees were bona fide BAs, some organizations – the American Association of University Women (AAUW), for example – refused to admit women whose degrees were earned at teachers colleges. The status problem persisted.

A huge change occurred at the end of World War II. Hordes of returning veterans, supported by the GI Bill, sought admission to higher education. The teachers colleges were ready to expand. They had subject-matter departments similar to those in liberal arts colleges and universities, and most of them were eager to welcome the influx of new students. Almost overnight the low-status teachers colleges became state colleges. Montclair State Teachers College, for example, became Montclair State College and, after several decades and the addition of specialized schools, Montclair State University. Teacher education took its place among the many accepted departments, schools, and centers typical of institutions of higher education.

But the story was not without its downside. Whereas subject matter departments in the teachers colleges concentrated on how their students would eventually teach the subjects they were learning, the expanded departments were more interested in a presentation of the subject that would prepare students for a variety of future occupations. Predictably, this led to a concentration of each subject on itself and added to the growing trend toward separation of the disciplines. Then, of course, status problems rose again. What sort of mathematics should be studied by those who intended to become high school math teachers? Why should they not have exactly the same background preparation in mathematics as future mathematicians and scientists? Not only were courses designed mainly with pure mathematics in mind, courses especially aimed at pedagogy were often disdained. This tendency has persisted. In California, for example, as recently as the 1980s, there was a concerted effort to remove or deny credit for courses (even at the master's level) labeled as "methods" courses. Teaching, it seems, was to gain status by forsaking itself. But, at least, a college major in education was now acceptable, if not admired, as a choice in undergraduate education. Today, we know that research has persuasively shown the value of subject matter methods courses. For teachers already reasonably well prepared with subject matter knowledge, a methods course is more positively related to student gains than another course in subject matter.[2]

The effort to achieve professional status has been complicated by a contest between *professionalism* and *professionalization*.[3] Teaching, like nursing, traditionally put a high value on altruism and service as central indicators of professional life. The natural desire for professional recognition, however, has sometimes challenged this devotion; a *professional* rightly expects commensurate social respect and financial security. Because the public school system needs so many teachers, it is hard to raise the status of teaching by requiring a higher standard for all teacher candidates. At one meeting of the Holmes Group, for example, it was suggested that candidates for teacher education programs should be chosen from the top quartile of college students. When it was pointed out that such selection would absorb almost all of that quartile, the person who had made the suggestion backed off to recommend that candidates should at least come from the top half. Still too many! Finally, dismayed, the speaker pleaded that, at least, few should be chosen from the bottom quartile. Perhaps we should concentrate more enthusiastically on the attitudes and virtues originally associated with *professionalism*. Then, with people who exhibit such qualities, we can work industriously to shape them as professionals.

We need not, however, give up on the effort to elevate the professional status of teaching. If it cannot be accomplished from outside – raising salaries of teachers in general – it might be accomplished from within; that is, it should be possible for teachers to rise in rank to more prestigious and well-paid positions as teachers. A plan along these lines was suggested by the Holmes Group.[4] This idea should be revisited. It should be possible for good teachers to achieve higher status and pay by qualifying for and receiving positions of leadership that do not require them to leave teaching for administrative positions. Qualification for such positions might require a higher degree or credential – National Board Certification should be encouraged and its tests should be continually improved – but certification and/or a higher degree should not be the sole requirement, nor should the acquisition of the degree guarantee assignment to the higher rank. In addition to successful teaching (and that needs much further discussion), we might consider participation in interdisciplinary teams, mentoring new teachers, participation in professional activities at the state or national level, and contributions to school governance and curriculum development. Who would make final judgment on the candidates to be promoted? Once a cadre of "advanced" or "lead" teachers has been established, this group should probably have the most influence on the decision, but knowledgeable administrators and the local board should also have a part.

Teachers might worry about undue influence and partisanship in such a plan, but the alternative – a fixed structure involving a degree and automatic promotion – does not guarantee the excellence we seek. Certainly, such a plan of collegial and administrative review must itself be under continual review – as it is at the university level. But if we want both excellence and recognition for our best teachers, we must do something along these lines. It may be worth repeating a paragraph I wrote twenty years ago to motivate such a move:

Whether we look at *professionalism* or *professionalization*, mathematics teachers – in fact, all teachers – fall short of professional status. At present, teacher-led organizations have little control over standard-setting for the profession. There is no consensus on the knowledge that teachers must have, and control over teacher-knowledge does not rest with teachers. Devotion to service, to the lives and well-being of students, has become a mark of semi-professional rather than professional life. There is little prestige or status attached to teaching. Teachers still labor in isolation, lacking the collegiality necessary for rich professional life. Finally, external regulation has severely constrained individual teacher autonomy.[5]

Sad to say, in regard to teacher autonomy, advancement, and collegiality, things are even worse today than they were twenty years ago.

We should note that there is a move afoot today to eliminate teacher tenure. Thoughtful people should oppose this move strongly. We should remember that tenure is provided to protect the intellectual autonomy of teachers. It is hard enough to introduce controversial topics as part of our mission to increase critical thinking. Imagine how much more difficult it would be without the protection of tenure. The system should be improved; tenure should not be granted, for example, after only one year of practice, and the pre-tenure years should be richly guided by expert lead teachers. A strong system of tenure is essential to teaching.

Another interesting recommendation advanced by the Holmes Group aimed at the establishment of Professional Development Schools, public schools that would work closely with teacher education schools and departments in the training of teachers. It was understandable that the Holmes Group would want the best possible sites in which teacher candidates would observe and practice for their profession. These schools would, in a sense, replace the elementary and secondary schools that once had a place on the campuses of teachers colleges. But designating some public schools as "professional development schools" creates an unhealthy separation among schools in a district, city, or county. It would be better to establish a professional development *center* in every school and a district or city-wide council to oversee and guide the centers. That council would consist of teachers from the advanced ranks, administrators, and representatives from the teacher education institution. The purpose would be dual: expanded collegiality and focused concern on teacher quality in every school.

Consideration of the possible negative effects of designating only some schools as professional development schools may trigger similar worries about the recommendation to establish an avenue for teacher advancement.

That worry should not be brushed aside. A sound, workable plan for teacher advancement will very likely bring with it disappointment, jealousy, and resentment among teachers who want to advance but fail to receive appointment to the higher rank. It is for this reason that some advocates of an advanced rank would prefer a system by which teachers can advance by meeting a specific criterion – earn an advanced degree, for example, and be automatically entered into the advanced rank. This, too, would be a mistake. There should be a well-defined set of criteria for advancement including student test scores broadly considered. By this last, I mean that the scores should be reviewed for anomalies such as sudden drastic drops under a change of teacher assignment or a dramatic difference between the scores of one teacher compared with those in a similar situation. In general, the criteria should be clear and not too numerous. Is it possible, with an excellent system of promotion, to avoid all challenges and disappointments? Probably not. But few of us at universities would give up the three-pronged system of advancement in professorial life. There are ways to make reasonable judgments about professional prowess in secondary schools, and if we want to attract excellent candidates to the profession, we should muster the courage to codify such judgments.

WHY TEACH?

The altruism, love of children, and dedication that have long been associated with teaching should be celebrated. This spirit need not – should not – be given up in the quest for professional recognition. Subject matter expertise is important, surely, but devotion to young citizens, to a nurturing school environment, and to a better society in the making is even more important. Gerald Grant and Christine Murray write that every teacher must, at least implicitly, answer three questions concerning lifelong relationships to students, school community, and future society:

> [W]hat balance do I strike between expertise and nurturance? . . . What
> is my responsibility for shaping the ethos of the school? Am I primarily
> a transmitter or a transformer of my society's values?[6]

All three of these questions point to the moral dimension of education and to what I have called the "unitary" purpose of education to produce better adults. This means that topics and problems in moral philosophy, ethics, and moral education should have a central place in programs of teacher education. It does not imply that adding a course in moral philosophy will satisfy the need, although, if designed carefully for educators, it might be useful. It would be better if topics involving social/moral life appeared in every course in the teacher education curriculum, and, as I have argued, teachers should be encouraged to include such material in the high school courses they will teach.

It is, perhaps, a bit odd to contrast expertise and nurturance as Grant and Murray suggest in their discussion of balance. By "expertise" they mean both a high level of achievement in students and a sure command of subject matter and method in their teachers. Expert teachers can sometimes be torn between pressing for high levels of achievement in their students and supporting – nurturing – their students along the lines of their expressed needs. This does require balance. Expert teachers, exercising their expertise considerately and democratically, may almost automatically be perceived as "nurturing" by the students most talented and conscientious in their subjects. But every good teacher has to know when to back off on the push for achievement and respond to an array of expressed needs. Students often need and appreciate praise for their work in other subjects or school projects, and a good math teacher will recognize outstanding work in art, sports, or school governance. It is also important to remind students who are working hard for a grade – a higher GPA – that it is more important in the long run to find something they really love than to grit their teeth and grind away at grades. Caring teachers build relations of care and trust with their students, and it is within these relations that decisions on balance are made.

Before exploring Grant and Murray's second and third questions, let us look at the important issue of teacher expertise. Teachers should be well prepared in the subjects they will teach, but they should also be knowledgeable about their profession – about what might be called the subject matter of education. Teacher expertise involves both fields of knowledge.

SUBJECT MATTER PREPARATION

In the old teachers colleges, the subject matter for secondary teachers concentrated on the material they would be expected to teach; subject matter and pedagogy were fairly well connected. Usually the subject matter courses went a bit beyond advanced high school courses but not far beyond. Many math majors, for example, got a healthy dose of calculus but often no advanced calculus. One could argue that math majors from the best teachers colleges were well enough prepared in mathematics, but they were certainly not prepared to do the interdisciplinary work discussed in this book. In my own undergraduate preparation, I heard almost nothing about the biographies of great mathematicians. We heard of Pythagoras, of course, but nothing of Pythagorean religious beliefs, their vegetarianism, or their strange aversion to beans. I think we heard the story of Gauss inventing (discovering?) the formula for the sum of an arithmetic series as a child when his teacher – in an act of pedagogical vengeance – assigned the class to find the sum of the integers from one to one hundred. Gauss, constructing the formula on the spot, was the only one to get the right answer.

Unfortunately, the same dull emptiness pervades most college math classes. The material sometimes appears in courses on the history of mathematics or in the philosophy of math, but there is rarely an integration of this content. What is needed for genuine interdisciplinary study is not only the incorporation of historical and philosophical study in regular math classes but also liberal mention of fiction, poetry, art, and music associated with mathematics. This is not to say that specialized courses in the history and philosophy of mathematics should be dropped but, rather, that interest in these courses would be encouraged and enriched by the inclusion of powerful elements in the standard courses. Such inclusion would contribute richly to the search for meaning in the curriculum.

A similar argument can be made for including historical and biographical material in the preparation of English language arts teachers. We have already noted the need for English teachers to have strong contextual knowledge if they are to guide the critical thinking of their students in reading historical and political documents. Again, this is probably not best accomplished by requiring every prospective English teacher to take a strong course in American history. We can endorse such a requirement but still argue that some of this material should be embedded in the language arts curriculum itself. It is the connections that enhance meaning.

The subject matter preparation of biology teachers should include the arguments on evolution and religion discussed in an earlier chapter. How will students find meaning in their education if they hear one story in science class and an entirely different one in religion class with no discussion of the debate – its history, current status, and central thinkers? And how should teachers conduct lessons on the debate without resorting to indoctrination? They need extensive knowledge of the debate and powerful examples of work that attempts to bridge the differences.

The work of Simon Conway Morris illustrates the possibilities. Conway Morris, a professed Christian and professor of evolutionary paleobiology, offers an "evolutionary theology." He warns his readers early on that "if you happen to be a 'creation scientist' (or something of that kind) and have read this far, may I politely suggest that you put this book back on the shelf. It will do you no good. Evolution is true, it happens, it is the way the world is, and we too are one of its products."[7] He then goes on to present a detailed study of evolution compatible with a belief in God.

Teacher candidates and their prospective students may enjoy exploring a question raised by Conway Morris: Because wheels are such an efficient means of moving about and evolution seems to be directed at greater and greater mastery of the environment, why haven't living creatures developed wheels?[8] Is there something about the natural environment that discourages such an evolutionary development? Well-prepared teachers should have a wealth of material from which to choose in helping students to think critically about issues central to human life. And as I have suggested often in this book, these connecting stories are fascinating; they bring some fun to the classroom. Perhaps we should add intellectual fun to our list of aims consonant with producing better adults.

A teacher must know not only the subject to be taught but the subject matter of the profession, that is, teaching. The teacher should be well informed in psychology, the history of school reform, the traditionally accepted purposes of education and various disputes about them, and why views on moral education have always been central to educational thinking.

In recent discussions of the teaching of subject matter, great emphasis has been put on pedagogical content knowledge. This emphasis is entirely compatible with the recommendations made in this book, but we should be concerned that most advocates of pedagogical content knowledge do not object seriously to the formal separation of subject (say, math) and courses on its teaching – one typically taught in the college of arts and science, the other in the school of education. They should be connected under one roof. We will return to this controversial issue, but let us first consider why psychology is so important in teacher preparation.

Psychology should be considered part of the subject matter preparation of teachers. I am not referring here to what might be called the everyday psychology of classroom management and instruction. Rather, my recommendation points to historic episodes such as the debate between cognitivists and behaviorists and opportunities to read some of Frederic Bartlett, Jean Piaget, B. F. Skinner, Jerome Bruner, William James, Lev Vygotsky, and Abraham Maslow. What from these writers have educators applied and how? Have our ideas about discovery, intuition, translation, and readiness changed over the past several decades? Do we now talk at all about intuition? About stages of cognitive development? Stages of moral development? Are there issues on these matters that deserve further debate?

It is not only for practical knowledge that psychology should be included in teacher preparation. Teachers without this knowledge are not wholly literate in their profession. How is it, for example, that Piaget was at the center of teacher knowledge in the 1960s and 1970s but scarcely mentioned today, although the theory of knowing he endorsed – constructivism – is still important in pedagogical theory?[9] Teachers are in an intellectually impoverished position to judge current recommendations and even mandated methods when they have little knowledge of earlier theories and disputes and why some ideas keep recurring.

Along the same lines, teacher candidates should be well informed about previous attempts to "reform" public education. The history of education is a fascinating subject, but if it cannot be addressed comprehensively, at least the story of public schooling from about 1900 to the present should be studied closely.

LEARNING FROM PAST EFFORTS AT SCHOOL REFORM

The study of previous reform efforts is essential in the preparation of teachers. Every effort at reform has given rise to enthusiastic support and equally enthusiastic opposition, but for the most part schools have remained stubbornly the same over the years. As I have argued, the most useful approach can be found by critically analyzing and synthesizing the ideas generated in reform movements; that is, we can usually find something of lasting value in a reform movement, and we can almost always find something to which we should object on reasonable grounds. The problem here is that supporters and opponents too often hold their positions on political or ideological grounds. We need to study these movements in order to bring a more rational, critical approach to the evaluation of current movements.

In the early part of the twentieth century, the great school reform movement was directed at the extension of secondary education to a large population and culminated in the establishment of the comprehensive high school. We have already discussed both the positive and negative effects of this move, and we have noted that a similar debate over the expansion of college education continues today. The main issues underlying the debate fall into the same two categories: concern about intellectual quality and concern about social and economic equality. Every school reform movement has generated a struggle between these two great aims of education.

Progressive education as it was described by John Dewey (there are other definitions of "progressive") was designed to promote both intellectual quality and social equality, although strong critics argued that it failed on both aims. Those, such as George Counts, who wanted to push strongly for social justice, found the Deweyan approach too dependent on an idealized view of critical thinking. Others, including Hutchins and Adler, found it far too weak in intellectual quality.

On the second issue, the progressive approach might have been vindicated and continued to grow if more attention had been given to the Eight-Year Study, which came out in 1942. The results of that study showed convincingly that graduates of thirty progressive high schools (1,475 students) did at least as well by the usual college-success measures as counterparts from traditional schools. Indeed, graduates of the most progressive schools did the best. But strong critics insisted on challenging the results. Joseph Kahne remarks, "Both the critics and those who defended the study from these attacks took mainstream measures of academic success as unproblematic proxies for desirable outcomes."[10] Kahne expresses some surprise at this attitude, and his disappointment with the quality of debate provides an important lesson for prospective teachers. He suggests that the debate should have centered on such questions as: "Should schools really focus on democracy as a way of life? Were the measures proposed for students' interests and social sensitivity reasonable? Does teacher/pupil planning undermine teachers' authority or the ability to focus students' attention in productive ways?"[11] These are the kinds of questions I hope teachers and researchers will ask in considering programs that focus on collegiality, connectedness, choice, and critical thinking.

Debates on the foundations of education almost faded away during the years of World War II, but they revived in the 1950s. In part, this revival might be credited to the explosion of knowledge in the disciplines encouraged by the rapid growth of colleges and research universities. The early 1950s saw the creation of curriculum study groups in math and science at the university level, and these studies were directed at changes in the secondary school curriculum.[12] There was an unparalleled profusion of new curricula in mathematics, science, English, and social studies.[13] The movement started in the early 1950s, but it was pushed along by the launching of *Sputnik* in 1957. With the focus on new curricula, most invented by university professors and researchers, emphasis was clearly on the intellectual, but the new emphasis on cognitive (constructivist) psychology also played a role. The key word at the center of the new curricula was *structure*, the foundational concepts of the disciplines. It was believed that a basic grasp of structure, compatible with mental stage, would make it possible to teach the disciplines in an organized, "spiral" fashion, and Jerome Bruner's *Process of Education* raised the hopes of both scholars and secondary school teachers that this could be done.[14]

As a high school math teacher and curriculum supervisor, I loved the new curricula. But, as I have already confessed, I had not found a satisfactory way of working with academically disinterested and deprived students. In embracing the new curricula and enthusiastically teaching the new math, I moved even farther away from our "lost" kids. It was predictable that the social aim of equality – the longing for equality – would cast doubt on the overemphasis on structural understanding of the disciplines. (Remember that *Brown v. Board of Education* took place in 1954.)

But it was neither the democratic devotion to equality nor justified doubts about their intellectual emphasis that undermined the new curricula. It was conservative political rage at the cultural permissiveness of "Man: A Course of Study," a new social studies program for middle schools, that triggered a successful campaign to end government sponsorship of curriculum development.[15] Critics were outraged at the idea that our children should learn about cultural customs different from, even morally repugnant to, our own without hearing strong condemnation of those customs. That outrage flowed over to condemn all government intervention in or attempts to control the school curriculum.[16] Future teachers should critically consider the recent history of changes in citizens' attitudes toward involvement of the federal government in the public school curriculum and operation. How is it that we have moved from outrage over the sponsorship (but not endorsement) of curriculum creation to acceptance of huge government expenditures on "standards," testing, and charter schools?

The lesson for prospective teachers is to understand the power of both political/social thinking and money on public schooling. Again, as in the report of the Eight-Year Study, the challenge addressed to the new curricula of the 1960s missed the main educational points, and questions still need to be asked. Of the new math, physics, and chemistry: Are these the best curricula for all students? How might they be modified? Of the movement in general but especially in the social studies: How are we to teach critical thinking without arousing the wrath of political opposition? Can we do a better job in balancing the quest for intellectual excellence with that aimed at social/economic equality? And, perhaps most important of all, can we do a better job of instilling moral sensitivity and dedication in our future citizens?

The new curricula were aimed almost exclusively at college preparatory programs. Meanwhile the number of courses offered in high schools proliferated madly. Oddly, students in the academic track had far fewer choices than those in the general and vocational tracks; their choices were constrained by college admission requirements.[17] Criticism of the proliferation seems legitimate, but we should exercise some critical thinking on it. We should not simply clamp down and eliminate choice in the high school curriculum.

I have been advocating choice in this book, but I have also recommended eliminating the largely useless and demeaning "general" track. Schools should still offer academic (college preparatory), vocational, and arts-centered programs. Within both vocational and arts-centered programs, there are and will continue to be justifiable choices. I have suggested that choice within the college preparatory program be increased, and in an earlier chapter, I wrestled with the problem of naming the courses that might be chosen within a particular discipline. We certainly do not want to label an algebra course "for dummies," "standard," and "for gifted." Both "dummies" and "gifted" are divisive – demeaning to either those taking the course or those left out of it. It must be made clear that the "minimal" course in algebra is for those whose interests lie outside the science, technology, engineering, and mathematics (STEM) world. Carefully guided choice is, again, central.

The criticisms directed at the course proliferation era fell into a familiar pattern, some directly critical of the perceived intellectual poverty of the courses and some more deeply concerned about the inequality embedded in the wasteland of choice. What should be done? Unfortunately the decision often made has been to force more and more children into college preparatory courses ready or not, interested or not. "Tracking" became a bad word, a practice to be avoided. Here, again, is an opportunity to look carefully at suggested reforms and work to sort out the beneficial from the pernicious, the practical from the idealized unworkable. I have already argued that "streaming" and organizing courses by interest are valuable practices, but that does not imply that the critics of tracking as it has been implemented in America are wrong.[18] They are clearly right that significant changes must be made if we are seriously dedicated to the preservation and progress of our democracy, to social justice.

Teacher candidates should be asked to study and analyze the critiques and recommendations of the various reform efforts in American education. The brief discussion here is meant to underscore the importance of such study. Let us consider how knowledge of past reforms might guide our analysis of today's Common Core. Does the current movement focus on intellectual achievement or social justice? I have already pointed out that it is a perversion of equality to force everyone into a uniform curriculum. But surely there are elements – ideas, concepts, attitudes, and skills – that should appear in every curriculum. Some of the most promising aims in the Common Core emphasize cooperation, conversation (dialogue, communication), and critical thinking. But keep a critical eye on testing. Is it consistent with the aims just mentioned? Here is an example from a sixth grade test being developed by Smarter Balanced testing. It is called a "performance problem," and students will be allowed 45–90 minutes to complete it:

> A cereal company uses boxes that are regular prisms. The boxes have the following dimensions: 12 inches high, 8 inches wide, 2 inches deep. The managers of the company want a new size for their cereal boxes. The new boxes have to use less cardboard than the original boxes. The new boxes have to hold the same or greater volume of cereal as the original boxes. Design a new cereal box for this company: give the dimensions of your box. Explain how your box meets each of the requirements for new boxes.[19]

The test is computerized. The students have been asked (in earlier parts of the problem) to find the volume and surface area of the original box. Finally, in the last part, they are to enter their answer in a designated text box.

One could argue – as both critics and test makers are already doing – about the use of scratch paper that is not collected and how difficult it would be to read even if it could be collected. Worries have been expressed, too, about scanning the scratch papers and their handling, which might make "it easier to cheat."

Must everything in today's schooling be made subordinate to technology and testing? Look at the problem! It is a natural for cooperation. It is just the sort of problem on which a *group* of students should work cooperatively. How would we know what they learned in the process or what skills they applied to its solution? Well, we would join them in the classroom, watch them, listen to them, perhaps record their conversation. We would be listening for communication skills and cooperation as well as mathematical knowledge and skill. This problem and its treatment by Common Core advocates represent a contradiction of the standards published by Common Core. We talk a good line on cooperation but ignore it when an excellent opportunity arises. Teachers and teacher candidates should watch for such contradictions, publicize them, and oppose them vigorously.

In concluding this section, we might decide that the tension between intellectual rigor and social justice in reform movements has been marked by either neglect of deep moral issues or a reduction of social justice to an artificial form of equality as sameness. Children are not all alike, and forcing them into one uniform curriculum is a travesty of democratic equality.

SHAPING THE SCHOOL ETHOS

Students are, of course, the first responsibility of teachers, but their schools also need support and confirmation in their mission to educate. Teachers help to develop and maintain a school's ethos. How will that ethos be described? It should be characterized by devotion to the unitary purpose of producing better people, and that means attention to the full range of positive human attributes. Good teachers are aware that their influence reaches beyond the effects they have on individual students. Both students and teachers are affected by the school's atmosphere. I mentioned earlier that, in concern for my students, I sometimes ignored rules that I thought were unfair or unhelpful. I did not hide the fact that I did this (I was not engaged in a fake form of civil disobedience), and I do not regret it, but I now think that I should have done more to get the rules changed.

Collegiality is essential in establishing a school ethos that makes the unitary purpose a living ideal. Teachers must work together not only on curriculum but also on school conduct – on the attitudes and practices that characterize social interactions in the school community. Recently, several accounts have appeared describing schools in which students are forbidden to talk in the hallways while changing classes. One school principal even bragged that he and his teachers were working toward silent lunchrooms! Teachers, working together, should oppose such antisocial policies unequivocally. In our dedication to the development of better adults, we should be concerned with how students are talking to each other, what they are saying, and with what effect. Occasional reminders on volume, bad language, and inconsiderate treatment of others are consonant with the unitary purpose. What is gained by insisting on silence? Certainly, a multitude of opportunities for social education are lost.

A similar attitude might be taken to tardiness. As a habit, tardiness is certainly to be discouraged, but an atmosphere that conveys both an expectation that people will be on time and an understanding that occasional tardiness is not a sign of incipient lawlessness is the sort of atmosphere in which most of us prefer to live. Again, collegial agreement is vital in establishing this climate.

Strong, reflective collegiality might have prevented acceptance of zero-tolerance rules. The use of specific penalties for specific infractions is not entirely rational. We want our students to exercise critical thinking in their studies, and we should encourage its use on their conduct and social interactions. Good teachers will, of course, remind students that "we don't talk to each other like that in here" when they use nasty language; they will raise a cautionary finger when things get too noisy or stop a lesson if a moral issue arises and needs discussion. But before assigning a penalty for a rule formally broken, good teachers will examine the reasons for the infraction, the possible harm done, the likelihood of repetition, and alternatives to punishment in order to avoid that repetition.

Anyone who has taught in our public schools knows that there will be debate over these issues. Private schools have an advantage over public schools in that a publicized ethos is their very foundation. Teachers who subscribe to that ethos are selected for their faculties, and families who agree with it seek admission for their children. In most of our public schools, teachers will differ on social and disciplinary issues. Teachers who agree with the attitude I have advocated may be described as "soft"; those who insist on more rigidly enforced rules will be described as "tough." Continual reflective, collegial dialogue is necessary, and a wise administration will respect a reasonable range of faculty positions. Teachers in preparation should think deeply about the kind of school atmosphere in which they would like to teach, and they should certainly ask about the school ethos when they are interviewed for a position. Will there be at least a cadre of teachers with whom you can work to establish and maintain an ethos of care and trust?

Shaping and maintaining such an ethos is, again, a work of collegial devotion. The faculty committees that suggest and develop interdisciplinary themes will continually reflect critically on their own work. Do the proposed themes encourage conversation, community, critical thinking, choice, connectedness, and creativity? Are they meant to contribute to the development better people? Are they effective in doing so?

Before leaving the topic of ethos, we should consider the significant role that lead teachers might play in promoting a highly competent faculty. Instead of spending thousands of dollars in legal efforts to get rid of incompetent teachers and/or paying them to do nothing in so-called rubber rooms, we should put our lead teachers to work in reeducating failing teachers. Steady collegial support, team teaching, and constant observation and evaluation could certainly move most incompetent teachers to a state of at least acceptable competence. We should exercise the judgment and practices on struggling teachers that we have recommended for students. Help them to do better; insist that they do better. We might even consider providing alternative forms of job-training for those unwilling to accept collegial reeducation, and these people would leave the profession voluntarily. A highly competent faculty is at the very core of a good school's ethos.

TRANSMITTER OR TRANSFORMER?

Grant and Murray urge teachers to ask the interesting question: "Am I primarily a transmitter or a transformer of my society's values?"[20] We should probably try to avoid extremes in either choice. Most of us, as teachers, want to improve our society. If we accept the unitary purpose of producing better adults, we might easily and enthusiastically declare ourselves "transformers." But recall our discussion of George Counts and his recommendation that we put aside our reservations about indoctrination and imposition. With Counts leading the way, we might feel tempted to do this. But recall, also, the concerns of John Dewey, concerns with which I expressed definite agreement. We should not risk producing enthusiastic, uncritical followers of any charismatic leader. Rather, we want to educate careful thinkers who will use strong critical thinking even on their own positions.

On the opposite end, teachers are pressed hard today to think of themselves as transmitters, even if they are not branded with that label. Their job, they are told, is to teach a specifically prescribed curriculum and see to it that students learn the material. Proof of that learning is revealed in test scores. This way of thinking, I have argued, is a travesty of teaching. No true teacher wants to be a mere transmitter. But "transmission" is surely part of the job, and it is not simple. At every stage, we have to examine critically the material to be transmitted and the methods by which it will be transmitted. As soon as we agree to that necessity, we are drawn back toward our obligations as transformers.

What we are talking about here applies to every subject we teach, but it is especially important whenever we are considering social and political issues. As cautious transformers, we want to encourage students to think critically about controversial issues, but we know that it is impossible to do this as Ravitch would like, "without a whiff of partisanship." If we reject the exclusive use of sentimental civic education – and, as critical thinkers, we must – we can still employ elements of that approach. We can point with patriotic pride to the written ideals of our nation, at the heroic acts of our patriots. But we must also acknowledge our mistakes and betrayals of those ideals. Dewey gave us good advice on how to move toward a better society: "The problem is to extract the desirable traits of forms of community life which actually exist, and employ them to criticize undesirable features and suggest improvement."[21]

As citizens we look, for example, at what is written in our Constitution; then we look at what is happening in our current society. On the basis of our examination, we may have to suggest improvements in our ways of interpreting and implementing the written ideals to which we are committed. At other times, we examine the real effects of a written law and decide that the law itself must be changed. Similarly, in shaping educational policies, we must analyze both our stated commitments and their apparent effects on actual students and teachers. It is a never-ending process of critical reflection, commitment, and caring.

We should press tirelessly for the advancement of teaching as a profession and prepare new teachers thoroughly in both the discipline they will teach and the general subject matter of education. Tenure laws should be retained and improved, not discarded, and a reasonable plan for advancement in the profession should be developed and implemented. If we are serious about producing better adults and a better society, we should commit ourselves to producing better teachers.

12

Reflecting on the Brighter Vision

Many of the ideas and recommendations I have offered in this book are not new in themselves, but examining them in light of current conditions may encourage a *renewal* – a richer, brighter vision for our high schools. The hope is to produce better adults, a better country, a better world. In his work on excellence, John Gardner suggested that a richer view of education might encourage this hope: "We should be painting a vastly greater mural on a vastly more spacious wall. What we are trying to do is nothing less than to build a greater and more creative civilization."[1]

One important factor in building a better world is the education of people who will be thoughtful and willing to work in a participatory democracy. I have suggested that a four-year sequence of social studies courses be implemented and that its classes be carefully composed of students from all classes and programs. We often hear complaints from well-educated critics that our society is divided not only into economic classes but also into social-thought classes. It seems almost impossible for people from these two opposing groups to engage in dialogue. If we are to achieve constructive political dialogue in our adult society, that dialogue must start earlier; high school students should have regular opportunities to study and discuss controversial issues with their teachers and one another. Providing such opportunities will not be easy because the introduction of controversial issues requires the very critical competence we are trying to induce. That means that we must start with the preparation of teachers as highly competent critical thinkers.

I have suggested that the education of teachers should integrate preparation in the discipline they will teach with comprehensive preparation in the subject matter of education itself. Further, teachers should continue to study and analyze the history of their profession, particularly its central concepts and efforts at reform. I have also recommended not only that the system of tenure be retained and improved but that we should create a pathway of advancement within the teaching ranks and place "lead" teachers where they rightly belong – at the steering wheel of planned progress toward a richer vision of schooling.

Restoring the comprehensive high school or, alternatively, organizing high schools in small clusters on unified campuses would be helpful in promoting democratic participation. Cooperative work on campus gardens and community projects would contribute to the sense of collegial citizenship. Active participation in the concerns of community ecology should also encourage the sort of discussion that will spill over into interdisciplinary work in each of the subject matter classes. Ecological study of the school building, grounds, and community should inspire further ecological study of the wider world.

As students and teachers from all of the major programs work together, respect for the full range of human talent should grow. An investment in the expansion of vocational education should pay off in more generous and appreciative attitudes among our future citizens. Paradoxically, an excellent vocational program may actually contribute to an increase in college attendance and attainment of at least a first degree. Indeed, doing well in work they *choose* may inspire vocational students to continue their education in a four-year program.

A strong ninth grade program of remediation was recommended. Two central ideas were emphasized. First, students in the remedial program should be included in the social studies program, various electives, and extracurricular activities. Second, a highly competent, dedicated teacher should work with these students throughout their high school years. Continuity is required to build relationships of care and trust. Among the fundamental tasks to be achieved is the acquisition of competence in standard oral language.

A brighter vision of secondary education opens eyes and minds to both the promise and the limits of education in the liberal arts. Surely, we should renew our dedication to an exploration of the great existential questions and insist that they be addressed in every course through the study of biographies, fiction, poetry, puzzles, religious commentaries, music, and art. We should not, however, insist on a restoration of traditional programs in the liberal arts with their prescription of specific books and materials that tend to become ends in themselves. (That does not mean that these books should be discarded or ignored.) An education that fails to ask about the meaning of life, of truth, beauty, and goodness is no education at all. A richer, brighter secondary education will keep the spirit of the liberal arts alive.

That spirit expresses interest in the whole of human life. It draws our attention to homemaking and parenting. It reminds us that, as Bachelard put it, our original homes are somehow – for better or worse – "inscribed" in us. The house (home) shelters daydreaming, he wrote, "and it is because our memories of former dwelling-places are relived as daydreams that these dwelling-places of the past remain in us for all time."[2] The study of homes and homemaking cannot be omitted from any true education.

Similarly, true education must include a deep and appreciative study of parenting. Why do we ignore careful consideration of the most crucially important work that many of us will ever undertake? When our students study *To Kill a Mockingbird*, for example, their attention is drawn rightly to the antiracism of Atticus Finch. But what about Finch as a model parent? What role does conversation play in good parenting? What role does order play? As the work of parenting is studied, special attention should be given to maternal thinking and its powerful application to peace studies. Students should become aware of the progress women have made in a world still defined by male traditions, but they should also be invited to think what the world might be like if it were more greatly influenced by women's traditional thought.

The sharp separation of the disciplines in secondary and higher education has induced a pervasive loss of meaning for many students. An emphasis on interdisciplinary themes should help to restore that meaning. Education should give increased meaning to every aspect of human life. It should not be thought of merely as preparation for a well-paid occupation.

In the discussion of ways in which education should contribute to the production of better adults, nothing is more important than moral growth and commitment. I have suggested that moral "betterment" is best pursued not through courses in moral education but, rather, through critical attention to moral issues in everything we do in our schools. A richer, brighter view of education in our high schools is necessarily a moral view, an enterprise guided by critical thought and moral commitment.

To make this brighter vision of education a reality, a competent, dedicated teaching force is required. That force, equipped with a substantial cadre of lead teachers, should oversee a curriculum rich in interdisciplinary themes, supervise new and weak teachers, and work to maintain an ethos of excellence, democratic collegiality, and respect for the full range of human talents.

I have not said much about recreation or the "worthy use of leisure" as recommended by the Cardinal Principles, but I have mentioned *fun* several times, and I urge teachers to seek activities that are fun and share them with students and colleagues. Fun and creativity are close relatives.

Throughout the book, I have emphasized choice as the stimulus for creativity, connectedness to generate meaning, critical thinking to promote democratic participation, collegiality to define and execute our plans, and continuity to support relations of care and trust. In a commitment to the unitary purpose of producing better adults, we do not seek or try to invent one uniform ideal; we celebrate the best of diversity. But we hope for a unified commitment to living fully moral lives – lives devoted to integrity, generosity, and care.

Notes

INTRODUCTION

1 See the chapters on aims in Nel Noddings, *Happiness and Education* (Cambridge: Cambridge University Press, 2003), *Philosophy of Education* (Boulder, CO: Westview Press, 2012), and *Education and Democracy in the 21st Century* (New York: Teachers College Press, 2013).

2 On the use of the expression "better adults," see Jerome Bruner, *The Process of Education* (Cambridge: Harvard University Press, 1960).

3 See Laura M. Desimone, Pilar Bartlett, Madeline Gitomer, Yasmin Mohsin, Danielle Pottinger, and Jonathan D. Wallace, "What They Wish They Had Learned," *Phi Delta Kappan*, April 2013: 62–65.

4 See Andrew Delbanco, *College: What It Was, Is, and Should Be* (Princeton: Princeton University Press, 2012).

5 See Matthew Ronfeldt, Susanne Loeb, and James Wycoff, "How Teacher Turn-over Harms Student Achievement," *American Educational Research Journal*, Feb. 2013, 50(1): 4–36.

CHAPTER 1: UNITY OF PURPOSE

1 The letter is from Jerry White and Cathy White to the *New York Times*, September 19, 2013.

2 Andrew Delbanco, *College: What It Was, Is, and Should Be* (Princeton: Princeton University Press, 2012), p. 41.

3 Andrew Hacker and Claudia Dreifus, *Higher Education?* (New York: Times Books, 2010), p. 35.

4 Robert Maynard Hutchins, *The Higher Learning in America* (New Haven: Yale University Press, 1999/1936), p. 66.

5 Hacker and Dreifus, *Higher Education?*, p. 101.

6 John Dewey, *Democracy and Education* (New York: Macmillan, 1916), p. 318.

7 Ibid., p. 319.

8 Hutchins, *Higher Learning*, pp. 97–119.

9 Ibid., pp. 60–61.

10 E. O. Wilson, *The Creation: An Appeal to Save Life on Earth* (New York: W. W. Norton, 2006), p. 137.

11 E. M. Forster, *Howards End* (New York: Barnes and Noble, 1993/1910), p. 101.

12 Quoted in Matthew Crawford, *Shop Class as Soulcraft* (New York: Penguin Press, 2009), p. 12.

13 See, for example, Richard Arum and Josipa Roksa, *Academically Adrift: Limited Learning on College Campuses* (Chicago: University of Chicago Press, 2011). Also Charles Murray, *Real Education* (New York: Random House, 2008).

14 Jerome Bruner, *The Process of Education* (Cambridge: Harvard University Press, 1960), p. 52.

15 Hutchins, *Higher Learning*, p. 66.

16 Herbert Kliebard, *The Struggle for the American Curriculum 1893–1958* (New York: Routledge, 1995), p. 12.

17 Charles W. Eliot, "Industrial Education as an Essential Factor in Our National Prosperity," *Bulletin No. 2 of the National Society for the Promotion of Industrial Education* (New York: The Society, 1908), p. 13.

18 Arthur Bestor, quoted in Kliebard, *Struggle for the American Curriculum*, p. 222.

19 Murray, *Real Education*, p. 21.

20 Ibid., p. 168.

21 Quoted in David L. Angus and Jeffrey E. Mirel, *The Failed Promise of the American High School: 1890–1995* (New York: Teachers College Press, 1999), p. 113.

22 See Nel Noddings, *Education and Democracy in the 21st Century* (New York: Teachers College Press, 2013).

23 Bruner, *Process of Education*, p. 52.

24 Ibid., p. 52.

25 Isaiah Berlin, *Four Essays on Liberty* (Oxford: Oxford University Press, 1969), p.167.

26 See Nel Noddings, "On Community," *Educational Theory*, 46 (3), 1996: 245–267.

27 Commission on the Reorganization of Secondary Education, *Cardinal Principles of Secondary Education* (Washington, DC: GPO, 1918).

28 Arthur Bestor, Jr., *Educational Wastelands: The Retreat from Learning in Our Public Schools* (Urbana: University of Illinois Press, 1953).

29 Richard Dawkins, an outspoken atheist, acknowledges the "outstanding merit" of the King James Bible and adds, "But the main reason the English Bible needs to be part of our education is that it is a major source book for literary culture." Dawkins, *The God Delusion* (Boston: Houghton Mifflin, 2006), p. 341.

30 C. S. Lewis, *The Problem of Pain* (New York: Macmillan, 1962).

31 Delbanco, *College*.

32 Mary Somerville, quoted in Leslie A. White, "The Locus of Mathematical Reality: An Anthropological Footnote," in *The World of Mathematics*, vol. 4, ed. James R. Newman (New York: Simon & Schuster, 1956), pp. 2348–2364.

33 David Noble, *A World without Women* (Oxford: Oxford University Press, 1993), p. 280.

34 See the biographies in E. T. Bell, *Men of Mathematics* (New York: Simon & Schuster, 1965).

35 Ibid., p. 181.
36 On the discovery–invention debate, see Rueben Hersh, *What Is Mathematics Really?* (Oxford: Oxford University Press, 1997).
37 Dewey, *Democracy and Education*, p. 308.

CHAPTER 2: VOCATIONAL PROGRAMS

1 Charles Murray, *Real Education* (New York: Random House, 2008), pp. 92–95.
2 John W. Gardner, *Excellence* (New York: W. W. Norton, 1984), p. 102.
3 See Frank Achtenhagen and W. Norton Grubb, "Vocational and Occupational Education: Pedagogical Complexity, Institutional Diversity," in *Handbook of Research on Teaching*, ed. Virginia Richardson (Washington, DC: American Educational Research Association, 2001), pp. 604–639.
4 Edward Bellamy, *Looking Backward* (New York: New American Library, 1960/ 1897). Other utopias: Frances Bartkowski, *Feminist Utopias* (Lincoln: University of Nebraska Press, 1989); Samuel Butler, *Erewhon* (London: Penguin, 1985/1872); Charlotte Perkins Gilman, *Herland* (New York: Pantheon, 1915/1979); Lewis Mumford, *The Story of Utopias* (New York: Viking Press, 1962).
5 See Robert Maynard Hutchins, *The Higher Learning in America* (New Haven: Yale University Press, 1999/1936).
6 See Mike Rose, *The Mind at Work: Valuing the Intelligence of the American Worker* (New York: Viking Penguin, 2004).
7 See Ken Koziol and W. Norton Grubb, "Paths Not Taken," in *Education through Occupations in American High Schools*, vol. 2, ed. W. Norton Grubb (New York: Teachers College Press, 1995), pp. 115–140.
8 See the discussion in Nel Noddings, *Education and Democracy in the 21st Century* (New York: Teachers College Press, 2013).
9 Thomas Frank, *What's the Matter with Kansas?* (New York: Henry Holt, 2004), p. 6.
10 Matthew Crawford, *Shop Class as Soulcraft* (New York: Penguin Press, 2009), p. 82.
11 See B. June Schmidt, Curtis R. Finch, and Susan L. Faulkner, "The Roles of Teachers," in *Education through Occupations in American High Schools*, vol. 2, ed. W. Norton Grubb (New York: Teachers College Press, 1995), pp. 82–101.
12 See, for example, Jeannie Oakes and John Rogers, *Learning Power: Organizing for Education and Justice* (New York: Teachers College Press, 2006).
13 See the comments on this in Achtenhagen and Grubb, "Vocational and Occupational Education."
14 See Anna K. Chmielewski, Hanna Dumont, and Ulrich Trautwein, "Tracking Effects Depend on Tracking Type: An International Comparison of Students' Mathematics Self-Concept," *American Educational Research Journal*, 50 (5), 2013: 925–957.
15 Ruby Payne, *A Framework for Understanding Poverty* (Highlands, TX: Aha! Press, 1998).
16 Ibid., p. 29.
17 Payne also recognizes the need to develop such relationships. See ibid.

18 Scott Nearing, *The Making of a Radical: A Political Autobiography* (White River Junction, VT: Chelsea Green, 2000).

19 Alexander McCall Smith, *The Minor Adjustment Beauty Salon* (New York: Pantheon Books, 2013), p. 180.

20 John Baugh, "Linguistic Considerations Pertaining to *Brown v. Board*: Exposing Racial Fallacies in the New Millennium," in *With More Deliberate Speed, 105th NSSE Yearbook*, ed. Arnetha Ball (Malden, MA: Blackwell, 2006), part II, p. 100.

21 Ibid., p. 100.

22 Sonia Nieto, *The Light in Their Eyes: Creating Multicultural Learning Communities* (New York: Teachers College Press, 1999), p. 60.

23 James Comer, *Leave No Child Behind* (New Haven: Yale University Press, 2004), p. 78.

24 The conversation appears in Ruth Rendell, *No Man's Nightingale* (New York: Scribner, 2013), p. 37.

25 See F. Clark Power and Ann Higgins-D'Alessandro, "The Just Community Approach to Moral Education and the Moral Atmosphere of the School," in *Handbook of Moral and Character Education*, ed. Larry P. Nucci and Darcia Narvaez (New York: Routledge, 2008), pp. 230–247.

26 See John H. Lounsbury and Gordon F. Vars, *A Curriculum for the Middle School Years* (New York: Harper & Row, 1978).

27 On the Eight-Year Study, see Joseph Kahne, *Reframing Educational Policy* (New York: Teachers College Press, 1996).

28 John Dewey, *Democracy and Education* (New York: Macmillan, 1916), p. 55.

29 Ibid., p. 55.

CHAPTER 3: WHAT MIGHT HAVE BEEN:
WOMEN'S TRADITIONAL INTERESTS

1 Witold Rybczynski, *Home: A Short History of an Idea* (New York: Viking, 1986), p. 17.

2 Ibid., p. 17.

3 See the five-part series by Andrea Elliott, "Invisible Child," *New York Times*, December 9–13, 2013.

4 Norman Crowe, *Nature and the Idea of a Man-Made World* (Cambridge: MIT Press, 1997), p. 7.

5 Quoted in Gail Collins, *America's Women: 400 Years of Dolls, Drudges, Helpmates, and Heroines* (New York: Harper Collins, 2003), p. 294.

6 See Jean Bethke Elshtain, *Jane Addams and the Dream of American Democracy* (New York: Basic Books, 2002).

7 Collins, *America's Women*, p. 92.

8 Rybczynski, *Home*, p. 161.

9 Ibid., p. 171.

10 For a history and assessment of the home economics movement, see Patricia J. Thompson's Hestia Trilogy: *The Accidental Theorist* (New York: Peter Lang, 2002), *In Bed with Procrustes* (New York: Peter Lang, 2003), and *Fatal Abstractions* (New York: Peter Lang, 2004).

11 Gaston Bachelard, *The Poetics of Space*, trans. Maria Jolas (New York: Orion Press, 1964), p. 6.

12 Ibid., p. 7.
13 Ibid., p. 14.
14 See, for example, Lizabeth Cohen, *A Consumers' Republic* (New York: Vintage Books, 2003).
15 Jacques Hadamard, *The Psychology of Invention in the Mathematical Field* (New York: Dover, 1954).
16 Ibid., p. 148.
17 Most of this work is conducted at the elementary school level, however. See John P. Miller, *Whole Child Education* (Toronto: University of Toronto Press, 2010).
18 Virginia Woolf, *To the Lighthouse* (New York: Harcourt Brace/Harvest, 1955). See the very interesting discussion of reactions to the Ramsay character in Brenda R. Silver, "Mothers, Daughters, Mrs. Ramsay: Reflections," *WSQ: Women's Studies Quarterly* 37 (3–4), 2009: 259–274.
19 Virginia Woolf, *A Room of One's Own* (New York: Harcourt Brace, 1929), p. 94.
20 For suggestions on how to plan curriculum by themes, see Clive Beck and Clare Kosnik, *Growing as a Teacher: Goals and Pathways of Ongoing Teacher Learning* (Rotterdam: Sense Publishers, 2013).
21 Virginia Woolf, *Three Guineas* (New York: Harcourt Brace, 1966/1938), p. 11.
22 Ibid., p. 11.
23 Ibid., p. 142.
24 Ibid., p. 143.
25 Elshtain, *Jane Addams*, p. 77.
26 Sara Ruddick, *Maternal Thinking: Toward a Politics of Peace* (Boston: Beacon Press, 1989), p. 176.
27 See my discussion in Nel Noddings, *Peace Education: How We Come to Love and Hate War* (Cambridge: Cambridge University Press, 2012).
28 See "Education by the Current Event," in *Jane Addams on Education,* ed. Ellen Condliffe Lagemann (New York: Teachers College Press, 1985).
29 George Counts, *Dare the School Build a New Social Order?* (Carbondale and Edwardsville: Southern Illinois University Press, 1932/1978).
30 Isaiah Berlin, *Four Essays on Liberty* (Oxford: Oxford University Press, 1969), p,172.
31 Elizabeth Cady Stanton, quoted in Geoffrey C. Ward and Ken Burns, *Not for Ourselves Alone: The Story of Elizabeth Cady Stanton and Susan B. Anthony* (New York: Alfred A. Knopf, 1999), p. 9.
32 See David F. Noble, *A World without Women* (Oxford: Oxford University Press, 1993).
33 Pearl Buck, *The Exile* (New York: Triangle, 1936), p. 283. See also my comments on this in Nel Noddings, *Critical Lessons: What Our Schools Should Teach* (Cambridge: Cambridge University Press, 2006).
34 See Dorothy Day, *The Long Loneliness* (San Francisco: Harper & Row, 1952).
35 See Simone Weil, "The *Iliad*: Poem of Might," in *Simone Weil Reader*, ed. George A. Panichas (Mt. Kisco, NY: Moyer Bell, 1977), pp. 153–183.
36 See Merlin Stone, *When God Was a Woman* (New York: Dial Press, 1976).
37 Nel Noddings, *Educating for Intelligent Belief or Unbelief* (New York: Teachers College Press, 1993), p. 135.

CHAPTER 4: A BETTER ADULT: CONTINUING THE SEARCH

1 See the account in E. T. Bell, *Men of Mathematics* (New York: Simon & Schuster, 1965).
2 Kenneth Howe, *Understanding Equal Educational Opportunity* (New York: Teachers College Press, 1997), p. 77.
3 Quoted in Thomas Frank, *What's the Matter with Kansas?* (New York: Henry Holt, 2004), p. 139.
4 Quoted in Sissela Bok, *Lying: Moral Choice in Public and Private Life* (New York: Vintage Books, 1979), p. 34 and p. 48.
5 Ibid., p. 48.
6 James Terry White, *Character Lessons in American Biography* (New York: The Character Development League, 1909), p. 1.
7 See Matthew Davidson, Thomas Lickona, and Vladimir Khmelkov, "Smart and Good Schools: A New Paradigm for High School Character Education," in Larry Nucci and Darcia Narvaez (eds.), *Handbook of Moral and Character Education* (New York: Routledge, 2008), pp. 370–390.
8 Ibid., p. 373.
9 See Paul Tillich, *The Courage to Be* (New Haven: Yale University Press, 1952).
10 Eric Hoffer, *The True Believer* (New York: Harper & Row, 1951), p. 92.
11 See Nel Noddings, *Women and Evil* (Berkeley: University of California Press, 1989).
12 Ibid., pp. 104–105.
13 See Andrew Delbanco, *The Death of Satan: How Americans Have Lost the Sense of Evil* (New York: Farrar, Straus and Giroux, 1995).
14 Ibid., p. 235.
15 George Counts, *Dare the School Build a New Social Order?* (Carbondale and Edwardsville: Southern Illinois University Press, 1932/1978), p. 5.
16 Ibid., p. 7.
17 See Vanessa Siddle Walker and John R. Snarey, eds., *Race-ing Moral Formation: African American Perspectives on Care and Justice* (New York: Teachers College Press, 2004).

CHAPTER 5: PARENTING

1 Shirley Brice Heath, *Ways with Words* (New York: Cambridge University Press, 1983), p. 369.
2 See Reay Tannahill, *Food in History* (New York: Stein and Day, 1973).
3 See Bruno Bettelheim, *The Uses of Enchantment: The Meaning and Importance of Fairy Tales* (New York: Alfred A. Knopf, 1976).
4 Kenji Miyazama, *Once and Forever*, trans. John Bestor (Tokyo: Kodansha International, 1993), pp. 25–26.
5 There are also interesting disagreements on the history of childhood. See, for example, Philippe Aries, *Centuries of Childhood*, trans. Robert Baldick (New York: Vintage Books, 1962). Contrast this account with that of Nicholas Orme, *Medieval Children* (New Haven: Yale University Press, 2001).

6 Sara Ruddick, *Maternal Thinking: Toward a Politics of Peace* (Boston: Beacon Press, 1989).
7 See Diana Baumrind, *Child Maltreatment and Optimal Caregiving in Social Contexts* (New York: Garland, 1995); also Dana Goldstein, "...And Don't Help Your Kids with Their Homework," *The Atlantic*, April 2014: 84–85; and Hanna Rosin, "Hey! Parents Leave Those Kids Alone," *The Atlantic*, April 2014: 75–86.
8 See Rosin, "Hey!"
9 See Nel Noddings, *The Challenge to Care in Schools* (New York: Teachers College Press, 2005).
10 Elliot Eisner, *The Educational Imagination: On the Design and Evaluation of School Programs* (New York: Macmillan, 1979), p. 16.
11 Ruddick, *Maternal Thinking*, p. 104.
12 Martin Hoffman, *Empathy and Moral Development: Implications for Caring and Justice* (New York: Cambridge University Press: 2000), p. 30.
13 See Jean Decety, ed., *Empathy: From Bench to Bedside* (Cambridge: MIT Press, 2012).
14 Simone Weil, *Simone Weil Reader*, ed. George A. Panichas (Mt. Kisco, NY: Moyer Bell Limited, 1977), p. 51.
15 On the importance of listening, see Sophie Haroutunian-Gordon, *Interpretive Discussion: Engaging Students in Text-Based Conversations* (Cambridge: Harvard Education Press, 2014).
16 For discussion at the global level, see Jeremy Rifkin, *The Empathic Civilization* (New York: Jeremy P. Tarcher, 2009).
17 Paul Bloom, "The Baby in the Well," *The New Yorker*, May 20, 2013: 118–121.
18 George Orwell, "Such, Such Were the Joys," *A Collection of Essays* (San Diego: Harcourt Brace, 1981), p. 5.
19 Many useful suggestions can be found in Marilyn Watson, *Learning to Trust* (San Francisco: Jossey-Bass, 2003).
20 See Martin Buber, *I and Thou*, trans. Walter Kaufmann (New York: Charles Scribner's Sons).
21 Nel Noddings, *Educating Moral People: A Caring Alternative to Character Education* (New York: Teachers College Press, 2002), p. 21.
22 See Torberg's comments in Simon Wiesenthal, *The Sunflower* (New York: Schocken Books, 1976), p. 208.
23 See my discussion in Nel Noddings, *Women and Evil* (Berkeley: University of California Press, 1989).
24 Adolf Hitler, *Mein Kampf* (New York: Reynal & Hitchcock, 1925/1939), p. 408.

CHAPTER 6: THE COMMON CORE STANDARDS

1 See the account in Diane Ravitch, *National Standards in American Education* (Washington, DC: Brookings Institution Press, 1995).
2 See the discussion in Ibid.
3 See National Governors Association Center for Best Practices and Council of Chief State School Officers, *Common Core State Standards for Mathematics* (Washington, DC: Author, 2010).

4 Frederick M. Hess, *The Same Thing Over and Over* (Cambridge, MA: Harvard University Press, 2010), p. 18.

5 See "The National Education Goals," in Ravitch, *National Standards*, appendix.

6 See again the account in Herbert Kliebard, *The Struggle for the American Curriculum 1893–1958* (New York: Routledge, 1995), especially the objections of G. Stanley Hall, p. 12.

7 On the fear and loathing of mathematics, see Reuben Hersh and Vera John-Steiner, *Loving and Hating Mathematics* (Princeton: Princeton University Press, 2011).

8 See National Governors Association Center for Best Practices and Council of Chief State School Officers, *Common Core State Standards for English, Language Arts and Literacy/Social Studies, Science, and Technical Subjects* (Washington, DC: Author, 2010).

9 Ibid., p. 40.

10 William A. Brownell, "The Place of Meaning in the Teaching of Arithmetic," in *Classics in Mathematics Education*, ed. Thomas Carpenter, John A. Dossey, and Julie L. Koehler (Weston, VA: National Council of Teachers of Mathematics, 2004), p. 13. The original article appeared in *The Elementary School Journal* (47), 1947: 256–265.

11 See again, W. Norton Grubb, ed., *Education through Occupations in American High Schools*, vols. 1 and 2 (New York: Teachers College Press, 1995).

12 Virginia Woolf, *Three Guineas* (New York: Harcourt Brace, 1938/1966), p. 143.

13 Ibid., pp. 108–109.

14 Ibid., p. 109.

15 Voltaire, Candide in *The Portable Voltaire*, ed. Ben Ray Redman (New York: Penguin Books, 1977), pp. 324–325.

16 Simone Weil, *Simone Weil Reader*, ed. George A. Panichas (Mt. Kisco, NY: Moyer Bell Limited, 1977), p. 290.

17 The quote appeared in Ashley Parker, "Reclaiming the Words That Smear," *New York Times*, Sunday Review, April 13, 2014: p. 5.

18 See the account in Bridget Stegman, "Inquiry, New Literacies, and the Common Core," *Kappa Delta Pi Record*, January–March 2014: 31–36.

19 On the misleading discussions on testing and rankings, see David C. Berliner, Gene V. Glass, et al., *50 Myths and Lies That Threaten America's Public Schools* (New York: Teachers College Press, 2014).

20 Diane Ravitch, *The Death and Life of the Great American School System* (New York: Perseus Books, 2010), p. 1.

21 Nel Noddings, "Responsibility," *LEARNing Landscapes*, 2(2), 2009: 17–22.

22 Nicholas Kristof, "Job Crushing or Lifesaving?," *New York Times*, May 1, 2014: p. A25.

23 Stephen Sawchuk, "Vision, Reality Collide in Common Tests," *Education Week*, April 23, 2014: pp. S8–S12.

CHAPTER 7: CRITICAL THINKING

1 For a fuller discussion of this debate, see Noddings, *Philosophy of Education* (Boulder, CO: Westview Press, 2012), chapter 5.

2 William A. Brownell, "The Place of Meaning in the Teaching of Arithmetic," in *Classics in Mathematics Education*, ed. Thomas Carpenter, John A. Dossey, and Julie L. Koehler (Weston, VA: National Council of Teachers of Mathematics, 2004), p. 13.

3 Martin Gardner, *The Annotated Alice* (Lewis Carroll) (New York: World Publishing, 1963).

4 Diane Ravitch, *The Life and Death of the Great American School System* (New York: Basic Books, 2010), p. 18.

5 Ibid., p. 234.

6 John Dewey, *Democracy and Education* (New York: Macmillan, 1916), p. 87.

7 Jane Addams in Ellen Condliffe Lagemann, ed., *Jane Addams on Education* (New York: Teachers College Press, 1985), p. 214.

8 Kevin Tierney, *Darrow: A Biography* (New York: Thomas Y. Crowell, 1979), p. 84.

9 Gradgrind appears in Charles Dickens, *Hard Times* (Harmondsworth, England: Penguin Books, 1982). The professor's quote is from Samuel Butler, *Erewhon* (London: Penguin Books, 1872/1985), p. 189.

10 See, for example, William Galston, *Liberal Purposes: Goods, Virtues and Diversity in the Liberal State* (Cambridge: Cambridge University Press, 1991).

11 Eamonn Callan, *Creating Citizens: Political Education and Liberal Democracy* (Oxford: Oxford University Press, 1997).

12 On participatory democracy, see Amy Gutmann, *Democratic Education* (Princeton: Princeton University Press, 1987).

13 Callan, *Creating Citizens*, p. 215.

14 D. C. Phillips, "Dealing 'Competently with the Serious Issues of the Day': How Dewey (and Popper) Failed," *Educational Theory*, 62 (2), 2012: 125–142.

15 See the fascinating account of Darwin's religious views in Janet Browne, *Charles Darwin: The Power of Place* (New York: Alfred A. Knopf, 2002).

16 See the arguments explained by Mark Lilla, *The Stillborn God* (New York: Alfred A. Knopf, 2007).

17 Jane Roland Martin, "Critical Thinking for a Humane World," in Stephen P. Norris, ed., *The Generalizability of Critical Thinking* (New York: Teachers College Press, 1992), p. 164.

18 David Hume, *An Enquiry Concerning the Principles of Morals* (Indianapolis: Hackett, 1751/1983), p. 15.

19 Quoted in Manley Thompson, *The Pragmatic Philosophy of C. S. Peirce* (Chicago: University of Chicago Press, 1963), p. 194.

20 See David Fromkin, *A Peace to End All Peace* (New York: Henry Holt & Company, 1989).

21 See Lizbeth Cohen, *A Consumers' Republic* (New York: Vintage Books, 2003).

CHAPTER 8: COLLEGIALITY, CARING, AND CONTINUITY

1 Andrew Delbanco, *College: What It Was, Is, and Should Be* (Princeton: Princeton University Press, 2012), p. 30.

2 See Elizabeth G. Cohen, *Designing Groupwork* (New York: Teachers College Press, 1986).

3 Alfie Kohn, *The Homework Myth* (Cambridge, MA: Perseus Books, 2006).
4 Edward O. Wilson, *The Creation: An Appeal to Save Life on Earth* (New York: W. W. Norton, 2006), p. 136.
5 Ibid., p. 136.
6 Ibid., p. 5.
7 Ibid., p. 36.
8 See Nel Noddings, *Caring: A Relational Approach to Ethics and Moral Education* (Berkeley: University of California Press, 2013); also *The Challenge to Care in Schools* (New York: Teachers College Press, 2005); and *Starting at Home: Caring and Social Policy* (Berkeley: University of California Press, 2002).
9 Martin Buber, *Between Man and Man* (New York: Macmillan, 1965), p. 98.
10 Ibid., p. 98.
11 Ibid., p. 100.
12 Scott Nearing, *The Making of a Radical: A Political Autobiography* (White River Junction, VT: Chelsea Green, 2000), p. 21.
13 Ibid., p. 22.
14 Ibid., p. 60.
15 Mark Edmundson, *Why Teach? In Defense of a Real Education* (New York: Bloomsbury USA, 2013), p. 46.
16 See again Andrea Elliott, "Invisible Child," *New York Times*, five parts, December 9–13, 2013.
17 See my discussion of friendship in *The Challenge to Care in Schools*.
18 See Benjamin S. Bloom, *All Our Children Learning* (New York: McGraw-Hill, 1981).
19 See the discussion in Herbert Kliebard, *The Struggle for the American Curriculum 1893–1958* (New York: Routledge, 1995).
20 For more on the richer plan for junior high (middle school) education, see John H. Lounsbury and Gordon F. Vars, *A Curriculum for the Middle School Years* (New York: Harper & Row, 1978).

CHAPTER 9: THE CURRICULUM AND ITS SETTING

1 Barry Mazur, *Imagining Numbers* (New York: Picador, 2004), p. 76.
2 Quoted Ibid., p. 33. See Virginia Woolf, *To the Lighthouse* (New York: Harcourt Brace Jovanovich, 1927), p. 34.
3 See the accounts in Herbert Kliebard, *The Struggle for the American Curriculum 1893–1958* (New York: Routledge, 1995); George F. Kneller, ed., *Foundations of Education* (New York: John Wiley and Sons, 1963); and David Tyack, *Seeking Common Ground: Public Schools in a Diverse Society* (Cambridge: Harvard University Press, 2003).
4 See Stephen Thornton, *Teaching Social Studies That Matters: Curriculum for Active Learning* (New York: Teachers College Press, 2005).
5 Neil Postman, *The End of Education* (New York: Vintage Books, 1995), p. 131.
6 Ibid., p. 131.
7 See, for example, Robert Graves, *Goodbye to All That* (London: Folio Society, 1929/1981); Gabriel Chevalier, *Fear*, trans. Malcolm Imrie (London: Serpent's Tail, 1930/2012).

8 Thornton, *Teaching Social Studies That Matters*.
9 See my discussion in Noddings, *Education and Democracy in the 21st Century* (New York: Teachers College Press, 2013).
10 Quoted in Kliebard, *Struggle for the American Curriculum*, p. 197.
11 Ibid., p. 198.
12 See the exchange between H. L. Mencken, "Shall We Abolish School Frills? Yes," appendix 2 in John Dewey, Essays, Reviews, Miscellany, and *A Common Faith*, vol. 9: 1933–1934, ed. Jo Ann Boydston (Carbondale and Edwardsville: Southern Illinois Press, 1989), pp. 406–411, and John Dewey, "Shall We Abolish School Frills? No," in the same volume, pp. 141–146.
13 Dewey, Ibid., p. 141.
14 Mencken, "Shall We Abolish School 'Frills'? Yes," p. 410.
15 Ibid., p. 410.
16 Rena Upitis, *Raising a School: Foundations for School Architecture* (Ontario: Wintergreen Studios Press, 2010), p. ix.
17 Ibid., p. 27.
18 See Karsten Harries, *The Ethical Function of Architecture* (Cambridge: MIT Press, 1998).
19 Ted Steinberg, *Down to Earth* (Oxford: Oxford University Press, 2002), p. 247.
20 Larry R. Ford, *The Spaces between Buildings* (Baltimore: Johns Hopkins University Press, 2000), p. 208.
21 Wendell Berry, *The Unsettling of America* (San Francisco: Sierra Club, 1977/1996), p. xi.
22 Sara Stein, *Noah's Garden: Restoring the Ecology of Our Own Back Yards* (Boston: Houghton Mifflin, 1993), pp. 175–176.
23 David W. Orr, *The Nature of Design: Ecology, Culture, and Human Intention* (Oxford: Oxford University Press, 2002), p. 181.
24 See again Upitis, *Raising a School*. Each of these important topics of conversation is given a full chapter.
25 Eric Grissell, *Insects and Gardens: In Pursuit of a Garden Ecology* (Portland, OR: Timber Press, 2001), p. 214.

CHAPTER 10: PLANNING, ENACTING, EVALUATING

1 See the account in Jean Bethke Elshtain, *Jane Addams and the Dream of American Democracy* (New York: Basic Books, 2002).
2 See the chapter on Kronecker in E. T. Bell, *Men of Mathematics* (New York: Simon and Schuster, 1965).
3 Lee Cronbach, "The Logic of Experiments on Discovery," in *Learning by Discovery*, ed. Lee S. Shulman and Evan R. Keislar (Chicago: Rand McNally, 1966), p. 77.
4 David Hawkins, "How to Plan for Spontaneity," in *The Open Classroom Reader*, ed. Charles E. Silberman (New York: Vintage Books, 1973), p. 496.
5 Ibid., p. 496.
6 See Benjamin S. Bloom, *All Our Children Learning* (New York: McGraw-Hill, 1981).
7 See Derek Stolp, *Mathematics Miseducation: The Case against a Tired Tradition* (Lanham, MD: Scarecrow Education, 2005).

CHAPTER 11: THE PROFESSIONAL PREPARATION
OF TEACHERS

1 For the history of normal schools, see David Tyack and Elizabeth Hansot, *Managers of Virtue: Public School Leadership in America, 1820–1980* (New York: Basic Books, 1982); L. Dean Webb, Arlene Metha, and K. Forbis Jordan, *Foundations of American Education* (Upper Saddle River, NJ: Prentice-Hall, 2000); and Linda Darling-Hammond and John Bransford, eds., *Preparing Teachers for a Changing World* (San Francisco: Jossey-Bass, 2005).

2 See Darling-Hammond and Bransford, *Preparing Teachers for a Changing World.*

3 See Nel Noddings, "The Professional Life of Mathematics Teachers," in *Handbook of Research on Mathematics Teaching and Learning*, ed. Douglas A. Grouws (New York: Macmillan, 1992), pp. 197–208.

4 See Holmes Group, *Tomorrow's Teachers* (East Lansing: Author, 1986); also Holmes Group, *Tomorrow's Schools of Education* (East Lansing: Author, 1995).

5 Noddings, "Professional Life," p. 206.

6 Gerald Grant and Christine E. Murray, *Teaching in America: The Slow Revolution* (Cambridge: Harvard University Press, 1999), p. 57.

7 Simon Conway Morris, *Life's Solution: Inevitable Humans in a Lonely Universe* (Cambridge: Cambridge University Press, 2003), p. xv.

8 Ibid., p. 112. See also Michael Ruse, *The Evolution–Creation Struggle* (Cambridge: Harvard University Press, 2005), pp. 223–224.

9 See Darling-Hammond and Bransford, *Preparing Teachers for a Changing World.*

10 Joseph Kahne, *Reframing Educational Policy: Democracy, Community, and the Individual* (New York: Teachers College Press, 1996).

11 Ibid., p. 140.

12 Contrary to popular belief, the New Math and like curricula were not prompted by *Sputnik*, but it did accelerate the process. See Frank J. Swetz, "Culture and the Development of Mathematics," in *Culturally Responsive Mathematics Education*, ed. Brian Greer, Swapna Mukhopadhyay, Arthur B. Powell, and Sharon Nelson-Barber (New York: Routledge, 2009), pp. 11–41.

13 See Robert W. Heath, ed., *New Curricula* (New York: Harper & Row, 1964).

14 See Jerome Bruner, *The Process of Education* (Cambridge: Harvard University Press, 1960).

15 See the story of this attack in Jerome Bruner, *In Search of Mind: Essays in Autobiography* (New York: Harper Colophon Books, 1983).

16 For an account of the strong opposition to government sponsorship of curricula, see Jon Schaffarzick and Gary Sykes, eds., *Value Conflicts and Curriculum Issues* (Berkeley: McCutchan, 1979).

17 See Arthur G. Powell, Eleanor Farrar, and David K. Cohen, *Shopping Mall High School: Winners and Losers in the Educational Marketplace* (Boston: Houghton Mifflin, 1985). For a substantial list of books and articles criticizing the proliferation of courses, see David Tyack, *Seeking Common Ground: Public Schools in a Diverse Society* (Cambridge: Harvard University Press, 2003).

18 See Jeannie Oakes, *Multiplying Inequalities: The Effects of Race, Social Class and Tracking on Students' Opportunities to Learn Mathematics and Science* (Santa Monica: Rand, 1990); also Jeannie Oakes, *Keeping Track: How Schools Structure Inequality* (New Haven: Yale University Press, 2005); and Jeannie Oakes and John Rogers, *Learning Power: Organizing for Education and Justice* (New York: Teachers College Press, 2006).

19 The problem appeared in *Education Week*, September 24, 2014: 12.

20 Grant and Murray, *Teaching in America*, p. 57.

21 John Dewey, *Democracy and Education* (New York: Macmillan, 1916), p. 83.

CHAPTER 12: REFLECTING ON THE BRIGHTER VISION

1 John W. Gardner, *Excellence* (New York: W. W. Norton, 1984), p. 128.

2 Gaston Bachelard, *The Poetics of Space*, trans. Maria Jolas (New York: Orion Press, 1964), p. 6.

Bibliography

Achtenhagen, Frank, and Grubb, W. Norton. "Vocational and Occupational Education: Pedagogical Complexity, Institutional Diversity." In *Handbook of Research on Teaching*, ed. Virginia Richardson. Washington, DC: American Educational Research Association, 2001, pp. 604–639.

Angus, David L., and Mirel, Jeffrey E. *The Failed Promise of the American High School: 1890–1995.* New York: Teachers College Press, 1999.

Aries, Phillipe. *Centuries of Childhood*, trans. Robert Baldick. New York: Vintage Books, 1962.

Arum, Richard, and Roksa, Josipa. *Academically Adrift: Limited Learning on College Campuses.* Chicago: University of Chicago Press, 2011.

Bachelard, Gaston. *The Poetics of Space*, trans. Maria Jolas. New York: Orion Press, 1964.

Bartkowski, Frances. *Feminist Utopias.* Lincoln: University of Nebraska Press, 1989.

Baugh, John. "Linguistic Considerations Pertaining to *Brown v. Board*: Exposing Racial Fallacies in the New Millennium." In *With More Deliberate Speed, 105th NSSE Yearbook*, ed. Arnetha Ball. Malden, MA: Blackwell, 2006, pp. 90–103.

Baumrind, Diana. *Child Maltreatment and Optimal Caregiving in Social Contexts.* New York: Garland, 1995.

Beck, Clive, and Kosnik, Clare. *Growing as a Teacher: Goals and Pathways of Ongoing Teacher Learning.* Rotterdam: Sense Publishers, 2013.

Bell, E. T. *Men of Mathematics.* New York: Simon and Schuster, 1937/1965.

Bellamy, Edward. *Looking Backward.* New York: New American Library, 1897/1960.

Berlin, Isaiah. *Four Essays on Liberty.* Oxford: Oxford University Press, 1969.

Berliner, David C., Glass, Gene V., et al. *50 Myths + Lies That Threaten America's Public Schools.* New York: Teachers College Press, 2014.

Berry, Wendell. *The Unsettling of America.* San Francisco: Sierra Club, 1996.

Bestor, Arthur, Jr. *Educational Wastelands: The Retreat from Learning in Our Public Schools.* Urbana: University of Illinois Press, 1953.

Bettelheim, Bruno. *The Uses of Enchantment: The Meaning and Importance of Fairy Tales.* New York: Alfred A. Knopf, 1976.

Bloom, Benjamin S. *All Our Children Learning*. New York: McGraw-Hill, 1981.

Bloom, Paul. "The Baby in the Well." *New Yorker*, May 20, 2013: 118–121.

Bok, Sissela. *Lying: Moral Choice in Public and Private Life*. New York: Vintage Books, 1979.

Browne, Janet. *Charles Darwin: The Power of Place*. New York: Alfred A. Knopf, 2002.

Brownell, William A. "The Place of Meaning in the Teaching of Arithmetic." *Elementary School Journal* 47, 1947: 256–265.

Bruner, Jerome. *The Process of Education*. Cambridge: Harvard University Press, 1960.

In Search of Mind: Essays in Autobiography. New York: Colophon Books, 1983.

Buber, Martin. *Between Man and Man*. New York: Macmillan, 1965.

I and Thou. Trans. Walter Kaufmann. New York: Charles Scribner's Sons, 1970.

Buck, Pearl S. *The Exile*. New York: Triangle, 1936.

Butler, Samuel. *Erewhon*. London: Penguin Books, 1872/1985.

Callan, Eamonn. *Creating Citizens: Political Education and Liberal Democracy*. Oxford: Oxford University Press, 1997.

Chevallier, Gabriel. *Fear*. Trans. Malcolm Imrie. London: Serpent's Tail, 1930/2012.

Chmielewski, Ann K., Dumont, Hanna, and Trautwein, Ulrich. "Tracking Effects Depend on Tracking Type: An International Comparison of Students' Mathematics Self-Concept." *AERA Journal* 50 (5), 2013: 925–957.

Cohen, Elizabeth G. *Designing Groupwork*. New York: Teachers College Press, 1986.

Cohen, Lizabeth. *A Consumers' Republic*. New York: Vintage Books, 2003.

Collins, Gail. *America's Women: 400 Years of Dolls, Drudges, Helpmates, and Heroines*. New York: Harper Collins, 2003.

Comer, James P. *Leave No Child Behind*. New Haven: Yale University Press, 2004.

Commission on the Reorganization of Secondary Education. *Cardinal Principles of Secondary Education*. Bureau of Education Bulletin No. 35. Washington, DC: GPO, 1918.

Conway Morris, Simon. *Life's Solution: Inevitable Humans in a Lonely Universe*. Cambridge: Cambridge University Press, 2003.

Counts, George S. *Dare the School Build a New Social Order?* Carbondale and Edwardsville: Southern Illinois University Press, 1932/1978.

Crawford, Matthew B. *Shop Class as Soulcraft*. New York: Penguin Press, 2009.

Cronbach, Lee J. "The Logic of Experiments on Discovery." In *Learning by Discovery*, ed. Lee S. Shulman and Evan R. Keislar. Chicago: Rand McNally, 1966, pp. 76–92.

Crowe, Norman. *Nature and the Idea of a Man-Made World*. Cambridge: MIT Press, 1997.

Darling-Hammond, Linda, and Bransford, John, eds. *Preparing Teachers for a Changing World*. San Francisco: Jossey-Bass, 2005.

Davidson, Matthew, Lickona, Thomas, and Khmelkov, Vladimir. "Smart and Good Schools: A New Paradigm for High School Character Education." In *Handbook of Moral and Character Education*, ed. Larry Nucci and Darcia Narvaez. New York: Routledge, 2008, pp. 370–390.

Dawkins, Richard. *The God Delusion.* Boston: Houghton Mifflin, 2006.

Day, Dorothy. *The Long Loneliness.* San Francisco: Harper & Row, 1952.

Decety, Jean, ed. *Empathy: From Bench to Bedside.* Cambridge: MIT Press, 2012.

Delbanco, Andrew. *The Death of Satan: How Americans Have Lost the Sense of Evil.* New York: Farrar, Straus and Giroux, 1995.

College: What It Was, Is, and Should Be. Princeton: Princeton University Press, 2012.

Desimone, Laura M., Bartlett, Pilar, Gitomer, Madeline, Mohsin, Yasmin, Pottinger, Danielle, and Wallace, Jonathan D. "What They Wish They Had Learned." *Phi Delta Kappan,* April 2013: 62–65.

Dewey, John. *Democracy and Education.* New York: Macmillan, 1916.

Dickens, Charles. *Hard Times.* Harmondsworth, England: Penguin Books, 1854/ 1982.

Edmundson, Mark. *Why Teach? In Defense of a Real Education.* New York: Bloomsbury, USA, 2013.

Eisner, Elliot. *The Educational Imagination: On the Design and Evaluation of School Programs.* New York: Macmillan, 1979.

Eliot, Charles W. "Industrial Education as an Essential Factor in Our National Prosperity." In *National Society for the Promotion of Industrial Education Bulletin No. 2.* New York: The Society, 1908, pp. 12–13.

Elliot, Andrea. "Invisible Child." *New York Times,* five part series, December 9–13, 2013.

Elshtain, Jean Bethke. *Jane Addams and the Dream of American Democracy.* New York: Basic Books, 2002.

Ford, Larry R. *The Spaces between Buildings.* Baltimore: Johns Hopkins University Press, 2000.

Forster, E. M. *Howards End.* New York: Barnes & Noble, 1910/1993.

Frank, Thomas. *What's the Matter with Kansas?* New York: Henry Holt, 2004.

Fromkin, David. *A Peace to End All Peace.* New York: Henry Holt & Company, 1989.

Galston, William. *Liberal Purposes: Goods, Virtues and Diversity in the Liberal State.* Cambridge: Cambridge University Press, 1991.

Gardner, John W. *Excellence.* New York: W. W. Norton, 1984.

Gardner, Martin. *The Annotated Alice (Lewis Carroll).* New York: World Publishing, 1963.

Gilman, Charlotte Perkins. *Herland.* New York: Pantheon, 1915/1979.

Goldstein Dana. "... And Don't Help Your Kids with Their Homework." *The Atlantic,* April 2014: 84–85.

Grant, Gerald, and Murray, Christine E. *Teaching in America: The Slow Revolution.* Cambridge: Harvard University Press, 1999.

Graves, Robert. *Goodbye to All That.* London: Folio Society, 1929/1981.

Grissell, Eric. *Insects and Gardens: In Pursuit of a Garden Ecology.* Portland, OR: Timber Press, 2001.

Grubb, W. Norton, ed. *Education through Occupations in American High Schools.* Vols. 1 and 2. New York: Teachers College Press, 1995.

Gutmann, Amy. *Democratic Education.* Princeton: Princeton University Press, 1987.

Hacker, Andrew, and Dreifus, Claudia. *Higher Education?* New York: Times Books, 2010.

Hadamard, Jacques. *The Psychology of Invention in the Mathematical Field.* New York: Dover, 1954.

Haroutunian-Gordon, Sophie. *Interpretive Discussion: Engaging Students in Text-Based Conversations.* Cambridge: Harvard Education Press, 2014.

Harries, Karsten. *The Ethical Function of Architecture.* Cambridge: MIT Press, 1998.

Hawkins, David. "How to Plan for Spontaneity." In *The Open Classroom Reader,* ed. Charles E. Silberman. New York: Vintage Books, 1973, pp. 486–503.

Heath, Robert W., ed. *New Curricula.* New York: Harper & Row, 1964.

Heath, Shirley Brice. *Ways with Words.* New York: Cambridge University Press, 1983.

Hersh, Reuben. *What Is Mathematics Really?* Oxford: Oxford University Press, 1997.

Hersh, Reuben, and John-Steiner, Vera. *Loving and Hating Mathematics.* Princeton: Princeton University Press, 2011.

Hess, Frederick M. *The Same Thing Over and Over.* Cambridge: Harvard University Press, 2010.

Hitler, Adolf. *Mein Kampf.* New York: Reynal & Hitchcock, 1925/1939.

Hoffer, Eric. *The True Believer.* New York: Harper & Row, 1951.

Hoffman, Martin. *Empathy and Moral Development: Implications for Caring and Justice.* New York: Cambridge University Press, 2000.

Holmes Group. *Tomorrow's Teachers.* East Lansing, MI: Author, 1986.

Tomorrow's Schools of Education. East Lansing, MI: Author, 1995.

Howe, Kenneth. *Understanding Equal Educational Opportunity.* New York: Teachers College Press, 1997.

Hume, David. *An Enquiry Concerning the Principles of Morals.* Indianapolis: Hackett, 1751/1983.

Hutchins, Robert Maynard. *The Higher Learning in America.* New Haven: Yale University Press, 1936/1999.

Kahne, Joseph. *Reframing Educational Policy: Democracy, Community, and the Individual.* New York: Teachers College Press, 1996.

Kliebard, Herbert. *The Struggle for the American Curriculum 1893–1958.* New York: Routledge, 1995.

Kneller, George F., ed. *Foundations of Education.* New York: John Wiley and Sons, 1963.

Kohn, Alfie. *The Homework Myth.* Cambridge: Perseus Books. 2006.

Koziol, Ken, and Grubb, W. Norton. "Paths Not Taken." In *Education through Occupations in American High Schools,* vol. 2, ed. W. Norton Grubb. New York: Teachers College Press, 1995, pp. 115–140.

Kristof, Nicholas. "Job Crushing or Lifesaving?" *New York Times,* May 1, 2014: A25.

Lagemann, Ellen Condliffe, ed. *Jane Addams on Education.* New York: Teachers College Press, 1985.

Lewis, C. S. *The Problem of Pain.* New York: Macmillan, 1962.

Lilla, Mark. *The Stillborn God.* New York: Alfred A. Knopf, 2007.

Lounsbury, John H., and Vars, Gordon F. *A Curriculum for the Middle School Years.* New York: Harper & Row, 1978.

Martin, Jane Roland. "Critical Thinking for a Humane World." In *The Generalization of Critical Thinking,* ed. Stephen P. Norris. New York: Teachers College Press, 1992, pp. 163–180.

Mazur, Barry. *Imagining Numbers.* New York: Picador, 2004.

Miller, John P. *Whole Child Education.* Toronto: University of Toronto Press, 2010.

Miyazawa, Kenji. *Once and Forever.* Trans. John Bester. Tokyo: Kodansha International, 1993.

Murdoch, Iris. *The Sovereignty of Good.* London: Routledge and Kegan Paul, 1970.

Murray, Charles. *Real Education.* New York: Random House, 2008.

National Council of Teachers of Mathematics. *Classics in Mathematics Education Research,* ed. Thomas Carpenter, John A. Dossey, and Julie L. Koehler. Weston, VA: NCTM, 2004.

National Governors Association Center for Best Practices and Council of Chief School Officers. *Common Core State Standards for Mathematics.* Washington, DC: Author, 2010.

National Governors Association Center for Best Practices and Council of Chief School Officers. *Common Core State Standards for English, Language Arts and Literacy/Social Studies, Science, and Technical Subjects.* Washington, DC: Author, 2010.

Nearing, Scott. *The Making of a Radical: A Political Autobiography.* White River Junction, VT: Chelsea Green, 2000.

Newman, James R., ed. *The World of Mathematics.* 4 vols. New York: Simon and Schuster, 1956.

Nieto, Sonia. *The Light in Their Eyes: Creating Multicultural Learning Communities.* New York: Teachers College Press, 1999.

Noble, David F. *A World without Women.* Oxford: Oxford University Press, 1993.

Noddings, Nel. *Caring: A Relational Approach to Ethics and Moral Education.* Berkeley: University of California Press, 1984/2013.

Women and Evil. Berkeley: University of California Press, 1989.

The Challenge to Care in Schools. New York: Teachers College Press, 1992.

"The Professional Life of Mathematics Teachers." In *Handbook of Research on Mathematics Teaching and Learning,* ed. Douglas A. Grouws. New York: Macmillan, 1992, pp.197–208.

Educating for Intelligent Belief or Unbelief. New York: Teachers College Press, 1993.

"On Community." *Educational Theory,* 46 (3), 1996: 245–267.

Educating Moral People. New York: Teachers College Press, 2002.

Happiness and Education. Cambridge: Cambridge University Press, 2003.

Critical Lessons: What Our Schools Should Teach. Cambridge: Cambridge University Press, 2006.

"Responsibility." *LEARNing Landscapes,* 2(2), 2009: 17–22.

Education and Democracy in the 21st Century. New York: Teachers College Press, 2012.

Peace Education: How We Come To Love and Hate War. Cambridge: Cambridge University Press, 2012.

Philosophy of Education. Boulder, CO: Westview Press, 2012.

Education and Democracy in the 21st Century. New York: Teachers College Press, 2013.

Nucci, Larry, and Narvaez, Darcia, eds. *Handbook of Moral and Character Education.* New York: Routledge, 2008.

Oakes, Jeannie. *Multiplying Inequalities: The Effects of Race, Social Class and Tracking on Students' Opportunities to Learn Mathematics and Science.* Santa Monica: Rand, 1990.

Keeping Track: How Schools Structure Inequality. New Haven: Yale University Press, 2005.

Oakes, Jeannie, and Rogers, John. *Learning Power: Organizing for Education and Justice.* New York: Teachers College Press, 2006.

Orme, Nicholas. *Medieval Children.* New Haven: Yale University Press, 2001.

Orr, David W. *The Nature of Design: Ecology, Culture, and Human Intention.* Oxford: Oxford University Press, 2002.

Orwell, George. *A Collection of Essays.* San Diego: Harcourt Brace, 1946/1981.

Parker, Ashley. "Reclaiming the Words That Smear." *New York Times,* Sunday Review, April 13, 2014.

Payne, Ruby K. *A Framework for Understanding Poverty.* Highlands, TX: Aha! Press, 1998.

Phillips, D. C. "Dealing 'Competently with the Serious Issues of the Day': How Dewey (and Popper) Failed." *Educational Theory,* 62(2), 2012: 125–142.

Postman, Neil. *The End of Education.* New York: Vintage Books, 1995.

Powell, Arthur G., Farrar, Eleanor, and Cohen, David K. *Shopping Mall High School: Winners and Losers in the Educational Marketplace.* Boston: Houghton Mifflin, 1985.

Power, F. Clark, and Higgins-D'Alessandro, Ann. "The Just Community Approach to Moral Education and the Moral Atmosphere of the School." In *Handbook of Moral and Character Education,* ed. Larry P. Nucci and Darcia Narvaez. New York: Routledge, 2008, pp. 230–247.

Ravitch, Diane. *National Standards in American Education.* Washington, DC: Brookings Institution Press, 1995.

The Death and Life of the Great American School System. New York: Perseus Books, 2010.

Rendell, Ruth. *No Man's Nightingale.* New York: Scribner, 2013.

Rifkin, Jeremy. *The Empathic Civilization.* New York: Jeremy P. Tarcher, 2009.

Ronfeldt, Matthew, Loeb, Susanna, and Wycoff, James. "How Teacher Turnover Harms Student Achievement." *American Educational Research Journal,* 50(1), 2013: 4–36.

Rose, Mike. *The Mind at Work: Valuing the Intelligence of the American Worker.* New York: Penguin, 2004.

Rosin, Hanna. "Hey! Parents Leave Those Kids Alone." *The Atlantic,* April 2014: 75–86.

Ruddick, Sara. *Maternal Thinking: Toward a Politics of Peace.* Boston: Beacon Press, 1989.

Ruse, Michael. *The Evolution-Creation Struggle.* Cambridge: Harvard University Press, 2005.

Rybczynski, Witold. *Home: A Short History of an Idea.* New York: Viking, 1986.

Sawchuk, Stephen. "Vision, Reality Collide in Common Tests." *Education Week,* April 23, 2014: S8–S12.

Schaffarzick, Jon, and Sykes, Gary, eds. *Value Conflicts and Curriculum Issues.* Berkeley: McCutchan, 1979.

Schmidt, B. June, Finch, Curtis R., and Faulkner, Susan L. "The Roles of Teachers." In *Education through Occupations in American High Schools,* vol. 2, ed. W. Norton Grubb. New York: Teachers College Press, 1995, pp. 82–101.

Shulman, Lee S., and Keislar, Evan R., eds. *Learning by Discovery: A Critical Appraisal.* Chicago: Rand McNally, 1966.

Silberman, Charles E., ed. *The Open Classroom Reader.* New York: Vintage Books, 1973.

Silver, Brenda R. "Mothers, Daughters, Mrs. Ramsay: Reflections." *WSQ: Women's Studies Quarterly,* 37 (3–4), 2009: 259–274.

Smith, Alexander McCall. *The Minor Adjustment Beauty Salon.* New York: Pantheon Books, 2013.

Stegman, Bridget. "Inquiry, New Literacies, and the Common Core." *Kappa Delta Pi Record,* Jan.–March 2014: 31–36.

Stein, Sara. *Noah's Garden: Restoring the Ecology of Our Own Back Yards.* Boston: Houghton Mifflin, 1993.

Steinberg, Ted. *Down to Earth.* Oxford: Oxford University Press, 2002.

Stolp, Derek. *Mathematics Miseducation: The Case against a Tired Tradition.* Lanham, MD: Scarecrow Education, 2005.

Stone, Merlin. *When God Was a Woman.* New York: Dial Press, 1976.

Swetz, Frank J. "Culture and the Development of Mathematics." In *Culturally Responsive Mathematics Education,* ed. Brian Greer, Swapna Mukhopadhyay, Arthur B. Powell, and Sharon Nelson-Barber. New York: Routledge, 2009, pp. 11–41.

Tannahill, Reay. *Food in History.* New York: Stein and Day, 1973.

Thompson, Manley. *The Pragmatic Philosophy of C. S. Peirce.* Chicago: University of Chicago Press, 1963.

Thompson, Patricia J. *The Accidental Theorist.* New York: Peter Lang, 2002.

In Bed with Procrustes. New York: Peter Lang, 2003.

Fatal Abstractions. New York: Peter Lang, 2004.

Thornton, Stephen. *Teaching Social Studies That Matters.* New York: Teachers College Press, 2005.

Tierney, Kevin. *Darrow: A Biography.* New York: Thomas Y. Crowell, 1979.

Tillich, Paul. *The Courage to Be.* New Haven: Yale University Press, 1952.

Tyack, David. *Seeking Common Ground: Public Schools in a Diverse Society.* Cambridge: Harvard University Press, 2003.

Upitis, Rena. *Raising a School: Foundations for School Architecture.* Ontario: Wintergreen Studios Press, 2010.

"Vision, Reality Collides in Common Tests." *Education Week,* April 24, 2014: S8–S12.

Voltaire. *Candide.* In *The Portable Voltaire,* ed. Ben Ray Redman. New York: Penguin Books, 1977, pp. 229–328.

Walker, Vanessa Siddle, and Snarey, John R., eds. *Race-ing Moral Formation: African American Perspectives on Care and Justice.* New York: Teachers College Press, 2004.

Ward, Geoffrey C., and Burns, Ken. *Not for Ourselves Alone: The Story of Elizabeth Cady Stanton and Susan B. Anthony.* New York: Alfred A. Knopf, 1999.

Watson, Marilyn. *Learning to Trust.* San Francisco: Jossey-Bass, 2003.

Webb, L. Dean, Metha, Arlene, and Jordan, K. Forbis. *Foundations of American Education.* Upper Saddle River, NJ: Prentice-Hall, 2000.

Weil, Simone. *Simone Weil Reader,* ed. George A. Panichas. Mt. Kisco, NY: Moyer Bell Limited, 1977.

White, James Terry. *Character Lessons in American Biography.* New York: The Character Development League, 1909.

White, Jerry, and White, Cathy. Letter to the *New York Times,* Sept. 19, 2013: A30.

White, Leslie A. "The Locus of Mathematical Reality: An Anthropological Footnote." In *The World of Mathematics,* vol. 4, ed. James R. Newman. New York: Simon and Schuster, 1956, pp. 2348–2364.

Wiesenthal, Simon. *The Sunflower.* New York: Schocken Books, 1976.

Wilson, Edward O. *The Creation: An Appeal to Save Life on Earth.* New York: W. W. Norton, 2006.

Woolf, Virginia. *To the Lighthouse.* New York: Harcourt Brace/Harvest, 1927/1955. *A Room of One's Own.* New York: Harcourt Brace, 1929. *Three Guineas.* New York: Harcourt Brace, 1938/1966.

Index